Spontaneous Play in the Language Classroom

David Hann

Spontaneous Play in the Language Classroom

Creating a Community

David Hann
Faculty of Wellbeing, Education
and Language Studies
Open University
Milton Keynes, UK

ISBN 978-3-030-26303-4   ISBN 978-3-030-26304-1   (eBook)
https://doi.org/10.1007/978-3-030-26304-1

© The Editor(s) (if applicable) and The Author(s) 2020
This work is subject to copyright. All rights are solely and exclusively licensed by the Publisher, whether the whole or part of the material is concerned, specifically the rights of translation, reprinting, reuse of illustrations, recitation, broadcasting, reproduction on microfilms or in any other physical way, and transmission or information storage and retrieval, electronic adaptation, computer software, or by similar or dissimilar methodology now known or hereafter developed.
The use of general descriptive names, registered names, trademarks, service marks, etc. in this publication does not imply, even in the absence of a specific statement, that such names are exempt from the relevant protective laws and regulations and therefore free for general use.
The publisher, the authors and the editors are safe to assume that the advice and information in this book are believed to be true and accurate at the date of publication. Neither the publisher nor the authors or the editors give a warranty, expressed or implied, with respect to the material contained herein or for any errors or omissions that may have been made. The publisher remains neutral with regard to jurisdictional claims in published maps and institutional affiliations.

This Palgrave Macmillan imprint is published by the registered company Springer Nature Switzerland AG
The registered company address is: Gewerbestrasse 11, 6330 Cham, Switzerland

Contents

1 Introduction   1
  1.1   The Trigger for My Research   3
  1.2   The Structure of This Book   5
  References   11

2 The Underexplored Role of Humorous Play in the Second Language Classroom   13
  2.1   The Traditional Neglect of the Language Classroom as an Arena for Social Interaction   14
  2.2   Language Learners Have Identities Too   15
  2.3   Individual and Collective Identities   17
  2.4   The Nature of Humorous Play   19
    2.4.1   Play as Stepping Outside the Norm   20
    2.4.2   Play and Humour: Overlapping Concepts   24
    2.4.3   Language and Its Relationship to Play and Humour   26
    2.4.4   Humorous Language Play and Its Subversive Nature   30

v

vi   Contents

	2.4.5 Defining Humorous Language Play for the Purposes of This Book	31
2.5	Humorous Language Play and the Second Language Learner	32
	2.5.1 The Challenges of HLP for the Second Language Learner	32
	2.5.2 The Advantages of Play for the Second Language Learner	35
2.6	HLP in the Second Language Classroom: Pedagogical and Research Perspectives	37
	2.6.1 HLP: A Neglected Dimension in Classroom Interaction	37
	2.6.2 HLP Is More Than a Barometer of Language Proficiency	39
	2.6.3 HLP Is More Than a Single Event	41
2.7	Conclusion	42
References		43

3 The Language Classroom: A Hothouse Where Play Can Germinate   49

3.1	The Research Setting: The BizLang Organisation	50
	3.1.1 The BizLang English for Business Course	51
	3.1.2 The BizLang Classroom Setting	52
	3.1.3 The Typical Profile of BizLang EfB Course Participants	53
	3.1.4 Situating BizLang's Pedagogical Approach	55
	3.1.5 The Training Rooms and Equipment	59
	3.1.6 The Research Advantages of the BizLang Classroom Setting	60
3.2	Methodology	60
	3.2.1 My Position as Researcher	62
	3.2.2 De-limiting the Context	64
	3.2.3 The Practicalities of Data Collection	68
	3.2.4 Obtaining Other Perspectives	69

Contents vii

3.2.5	Transcription Conventions	70
3.2.6	Relevant Information on the Research Participants	71
3.2.7	Conclusion	73
References		74

4 Exploiting Frames for Fun 79
4.1 Goffman's Frame 80
    4.1.1 Frames in the Adult Language Learning Classroom 81
    4.1.2 The Challenges That Classroom Frameworks Present to Learners 82
    4.1.3 Frames, Scripts and Schemata 83
4.2 Blending Frames for Comic Effect 84
    4.2.1 Subverting the Established Order 92
    4.2.2 Asserting the Established Order 95
    4.2.3 Releasing Tension When the Frame Dissolves 96
4.3 Conclusion 97
References 98

5 Evoking Frames Through Associated Language 101
5.1 Theoretical Perspectives on Language, Context, Play and Learning 102
    5.1.1 The Relationship Between Language and Its Context of Use 102
    5.1.2 The Relationship Between Language, the Speaker and the Social Group 104
    5.1.3 Recontextualisation in a Bakhtinian Conceptualisation of Language 105
    5.1.4 Recontextualisation and Humour 108
    5.1.5 Recontextualisation, Language Learning and Language Play 110
5.2 Evidence of Recontextualisation for Playful Purposes 112

viii Contents

	5.2.1	Taking Ownership of Learnt Language and Evoking Shared Experience	112
	5.2.2	Subverting Learnt Language for the Speaker's Own Intentions	117
	5.2.3	Using Language Associated with the Trainer	121
	5.2.4	Evoking Assumed Shared Knowledge Through Associated Language	125
5.3		Playing with the Semantic Properties of Language	127
5.4		Conclusion	129
References			130

6 A Case Study: Overcoming Failure in the Search for Common Ground 133

6.1		Rationale for Recording a Group Over a Continuous Period	133
6.2		Background to the Case Study	135
6.3		The Obstacles to Play as Revealed by the Data	137
	6.3.1	Lack of Mastery of the Structures and Phonology of the TL	137
	6.3.2	Searching for Common Cultural Ground	140
	6.3.3	Overcoming Obstacles to Play: Body Language and Other Resources	144
	6.3.4	Playing with Structure and Sound	151
6.4		Conclusion	157
References			158

7 Prior Talk: A Key Resource for Play 161

7.1	A Thread of Play Woven Together to Create a Cultural Reference Point	162
7.2	Playing with Errors, Playing with Identities	172
7.3	Recontextualising Learnt Language	178
7.4	Conclusion	185
References		187

Contents ix

8 Humorous Play and Its Implications for Classroom Practice 191

8.1 The Literature on the Language Teacher's Role in Play 193
8.2 The Timing and Rhythm of Play Episodes 195
8.3 Observations About the Rhythm and Pattern of Play 196
8.4 The Roles Teachers Might Assume in Play Episodes 202
    8.4.1 The Teacher as Scaffolder for Play 202
    8.4.2 The Teacher as Role-Shifter 205
    8.4.3 The Teacher as Teaser 206
    8.4.4 The Teacher as Fellow Outsider 208
    8.4.5 The Teacher as Primer for Play 211
8.5 Conclusion 213
References 215

9 Humorous Language Play: Lessons from the Second Language Classroom 219

9.1 What the Findings Tell Us About the Nature of Play in the Language Classroom 219
    9.1.1 Putting Right a Research Oversight: Play's Part in Building a Classroom Community 220
    9.1.2 Limitations Can Be Strengths: Playing with What's Available 223
9.2 The Limitations of the Research: Avenues for Further Investigation 226
    9.2.1 HLP and the Acquisition Process 227
    9.2.2 HLP and the Teacher's Role 228
    9.2.3 HLP and Different Learner Profiles 230
    9.2.4 HLP Beyond the Classroom 232
9.3 Conclusion 233
References 234

Appendix 237

Bibliography 239

Index 251

List of Episodes

Episode 1	Do you want a glass of champagne?	85
Episode 2	More champagne?	87
Episode 3	Here's our big gift	89
Episode 4	Viktor died	90
Episode 5	Our society director	93
Episode 6	You director	93
Episode 7	You are a little bit late	95
Episode 8	Hands up!	97
Episode 9	Yesterday pubs	113
Episode 10	You want compare a Volvo with a Ferrari?	114
Episode 11	Good question	115
Episode 12	Let's sum up	117
Episode 13	Sorry, may I stop you for a moment?	118
Episode 14	Yesterday you miss	119
Episode 15	Repeat!	122
Episode 16	Take one and pass them on	123
Episode 17	You should	124
Episode 18	Same procedure	126
Episode 19	I'm on the left of you	127
Episode 20	Without	128
Episode 21	Losers	138

xii   List of Episodes

Episode 22	I would have gone back to Spain	139, 203, 206
Episode 23	I remember a PC game	141
Episode 24	Do you remember Falcon Crest?	142
Episode 25	Minority Report	143
Episode 26	Or you present a quiz	145, 205
Episode 27	Are you married?	146
Episode 28	Square	147
Episode 29	And this is for Barcelona supporters	149
Episode 30	Woodwork	152
Episode 31	Woodwork 2	153
Episode 32	You can forget	153
Episode 33	I negotiate with	154
Episode 34	With only five years?	155, 204
Episode 35	When the doctor need to operate you	156
Episode 36	This a form of anaesthetic	157
Episode 37	It's not my problem	163, 212
Episode 38	Mmm-hmm	164
Episode 39	But before you died	165
Episode 40	The call exercise was very fun	166
Episode 41	Tomorrow Juan is going with Harry	167
Episode 42	Oooh… OK	169
Episode 43	And for us OK	170
Episode 44	Be careful with the OK	171
Episode 45	I would like to speak to Jens	173
Episode 46	I'm Helmut	174
Episode 47	I can't change my identity	175
Episode 48	My name is	176
Episode 49	No Jens no Harry	177
Episode 50	Who's that?	178
Episode 51	Are you married?	179
Episode 52	Ahead to the schedule	180
Episode 53	We are ahead the programme	180
Episode 54	These things happen	181
Episode 55	These things happen 2	182
Episode 56	These things happen 3	183
Episode 57	These things happen 4	184
Episode 58	We're on a Roll	207
Episode 59	Try and say that after a pint	208
Episode 60	Comfort station	209

1

Introduction

Three men are sitting in a language classroom—a British man, a Spaniard and a Czech. One of them, David, has just discussed his confusion when first visiting the USA on encountering the sign "comfort station", meaning public toilets. This triggers an anecdote from the Czech Marek:

("@" represents one syllable of laughter. See Appendix for full transcription conventions)

1 Marek: in Poland you have (.) two marks (.)
2 David: yeah yeah (5)
3 Marek: ((*draws a triangle and circle in his notebook and shows the others*)) I always confuse (2)
4 David: and that is for (.) toilet? (.)
5 Marek: that is for woman and for for man (.) ((*points to the symbols*))
6 David: oh really? (2)
7 Marek: I didn't- I didn't- (.) I can't <@ I can't (.) remember what is what > =
8 All: = @@@ =

© The Author(s) 2020
D. Hann, *Spontaneous Play in the Language Classroom*,
https://doi.org/10.1007/978-3-030-26304-1_1

2   D. Hann

9 Marek: = <@ and I waited for (.) I waited for someone who will =
10 David: = OK =
11 Marek: = who will (.) (come) in > =
12 All: @@@[@@*
13 David: [serious Marek (.) serious* (3)
14 Juan: ((*leans across and draws a square in Marek's notebook*)) and
            this is for Barcelona supporters =
15 All: = @@@@@@

You are doubtless puzzled by the final remark by the Spaniard Juan and the laughter it produces within the group. There seems to be nothing funny about it except perhaps in the sense of strange rather than amusing. It could not be retold as a joke to other people (despite being framed as such in the opening sentence of this introduction). It might be argued that you had to be there to appreciate what was happening but, in truth, that only tells half the story. In fact, you would have to have been there for some time in order to understand the exchanges and savour the wit in Juan's utterance because his punchline only works with reference to exchanges which the group had had earlier in the day.

The interaction above actually forms part of an investigation which is at the centre of this book, so you will need to read on if you want to find out why Juan's remark was so appreciated by his conversational participants. This data, and others like it, only makes sense in the context of a group's shared history. It is only when seen through the prism of that shared history that Juan's wit becomes evident. Had it not been recorded, this brief and unremarkable interaction would doubtless soon have been forgotten. Indeed, it occurred on the very last day of this particular group's time together. Yet I hope that the content of this book makes clear that the significance of this episode and others like it lies beyond the fleeting pleasure it gave to those present at the time. I argue that it provides a vital insight into the language classroom as a dynamic cultural entity and reveals that humorous play is often a very important part of that dynamism.

1.1 The Trigger for My Research

The seed of an idea which eventually germinated and became the research project on which this volume is based was sown while I was working as an English language teacher. For a long time, I was employed by an organisation which, for the purposes of my research, I will call BizLang. It was based in London and offered English language and communication skills training to business executives. As part of my job, I often oversaw the short intensive courses which the company ran. It was my responsibility to ensure that participants were allocated to suitable groups, to monitor their progress and welfare and to provide pedagogical support to the teaching team when needed. I came to realise that when I heard the sound of laughter emanating from a classroom, I felt reassured that all was going well behind its closed door. This realisation got me thinking about the related but not identical phenomena of laughter, humour and play, and their place in the language classroom setting. This heightened awareness planted questions in my head, especially when I was teaching groups myself. Why, for example, did I find that when I took over a group from another teacher, I was often puzzled by things that the group members said which would make them laugh but leave me initially perplexed? Why was it that the presence of humour, play and laughter seemed to be such a useful barometer of a group's well-being? How did learners, especially those at the lower end of the proficiency spectrum, manage to have fun in a language over which, on the face of it, they had little mastery?

These questions set me on a path to find out more about the nature of humour and play. My initial exploration of the literature made me realise that play among L1 speakers[1] of English—people who had spoken the language since childhood—seems to involve competences that

---

[1] I use the terms 'L1 speaker', 'L1 user' or 'native speaker' in the book to refer to someone who had spoken a language for communicative purposes since childhood, and 'L2 speaker' or 'non-native speaker' for "..somebody who has an L1, or L1s other than English" (Seidlhofer 2011: 6). I often use the term "learner" or "learners", especially when differentiating L2 speakers from their teacher. None of these terms are uncontroversial but this is a debate that would side track my focus, so I will simply acknowledge it here.

the course participants I was focussing on do not generally possess when operating in English. Play among L1 speakers often depends on mutually understood cultural references, prowess at manipulating the forms of the language, or indeed both (Carter 2004; Chiaro 1992; Cook 2000; Crystal 1998; Holmes 2007; Norrick 2007). Yet the learners who are the focus of the research featured in this book have acknowledged limitations when communicating in English (otherwise, they would have no need to enrol on a language course) and, given that they are put into mixed nationality groups, seem to have few shared cultural reference points on which to draw. Furthermore, the BizLang course participants are strangers when they first meet and part company after only three, five or at most ten days together. This is significant because, although the use of humour can accrue significant social benefits, it also carries high social risks if it backfires, which is one reason why it tends to occur more frequently in intimate or informal settings (Carter 2004; Straehle 1993). Furthermore, the course participants work together in a pressurised, hothouse atmosphere where measurable progress in their English communication skills can subsequently have a direct impact on their career prospects. All these factors suggest a context which would militate against the use of humorous play. Yet experience suggested to me that this setting is actually one where humour and laughter can, and often do, thrive.

The research I undertook as a result of my ruminations about humorous play in the language classroom forms the basis for this book. By its nature, my investigative focus is a narrow one. However, I believe that the findings set out in the course of this volume have implications beyond the limited confines of my research setting. They will be of interest to academics studying and working in the fields of applied linguistics, second language acquisition (SLA) and humour studies who want to learn more about humorous play's role in individual agency, identity, group dynamics and the building of cultures and communities. The research focus chimes well with a growing realisation of the importance of humour and storytelling as social tools. Furthermore, the content is relevant to classroom practitioners, especially those working in ELT and ESOL, who are eager to find out more about the extent to which accommodating to, encouraging or, indeed, instigating play in the language classroom can benefit a group of learners socially and, indeed, in terms of their language acquisition.

1.2 The Structure of This Book

The book is divided into nine chapters, including this introduction. Below is an outline of the areas covered in the rest of the chapters.

Chapter 2: The underexplored role of humorous play in the second language classroom
Chapter 2 investigates the second language classroom as a social and cultural entity, the nature of humorous language play and the need to take a longitudinal research perspective when looking at the relationship between language play, the language learner and the second language classroom setting, something which has hitherto not been attempted.

There has been an increasing recognition in recent years that people's cultural identities are not merely defined in terms of tribe or nation and that, in their daily lives and the various stages of those lives, they participate and move between various cultures, such as that of their family, their workplace and their leisure pursuits. This realisation that culture can be small-scale, multidimensional and fluid has helped reframe the ways in which various locales of human activity can be understood. One of these locales is the second language classroom. The chapter argues that, for too long, the language classroom as a cultural entity has largely been ignored, and its members seen merely as acquirers of language rather than as social actors in their own right. Even as this social dimension has belatedly been recognised, its emergent nature remains to be investigated.

The chapter goes on to discuss the nature of humorous language play, something which can be seen paradoxically as an integral part of our everyday behaviour and a break from its norms. It is argued that play is an important feature of the officially driven agenda of nearly all language classrooms, both in play-as-rehearsal where hypothetical scenarios can extend language practice and in the systematic manipulation of forms in language drilling. However, although play in these senses is

6   D. Hann

important for this study, the investigative focus is primarily on behaviour where play and humour come together to form something which is often destabilising, subversive, ambiguous and incongruous. The chapter teases out the differences and commonalities between play and humour, and it establishes a working definition of the term "humorous language play" (HLP) as used in the book. The latter's essentially subversive and "off-task" nature may possibly be one reason why it has previously been overlooked in the classroom setting and viewed as peripheral or even inimical to language acquisition. In fact, as the chapter makes clear, engaging in HLP potentially presents learners with both social and language-acquisitional benefits as well as risks and challenges.

Previously, the relationship between humorous play and the second language learner has tended to be seen in rather narrow terms where evidence of the former has generally been regarded as indicative of language proficiency in the latter. However, this does not chime with my own teaching experience, and one of the aims of the study is to discover how learners at the lower end of the proficiency spectrum are able to have fun in the target language despite the evident linguistic challenges that this poses.

Chapter 3: The language classroom: A hothouse where humorous play can germinate

Chapter 3 talks about the setting for this investigation: short, intensive English courses for people who use English as a second language in their business lives. It highlights how the setting's enclosed nature is ideal for investigating humorous play's role in the development of a culture and sense of individual and collective identity among newly assembled groups of learners and their teachers. It also discusses how the multilingual and multicultural make-up of the groups under investigation means that learners are unable to rely on shared first languages or cultural reference points in order to generate humorous play. The fact that there is no reliable pre-existing framework of references on which a group can weave together a shared fabric of humorous play sets the research context apart from most other investigations in this field.

The chapter also notes that the learners in the project represent people at the forefront of globalisation whose use of English as a lingua franca (ELF) in their professional encounters is indicative of the commercial, scientific and academic communications which take place daily around the world. This vital and growing sector of the English language learning community is underrepresented in the literature.

The chapter goes on to discuss the research approach taken in the study which is ethnographic in nature and also draws upon Conversation Analysis.

Chapter 4: Exploiting frames for fun

This chapter is the first of five which engages with the empirical findings from the project. Chapter 4 draws on recorded data gathered from three small classes of low-proficiency learners (each consisting of between three and five participants) and their teachers while undertaking various classroom activities. The notion of the interpretative frame (Goffman 1974) is central to the chapter and is an important concept in understanding play. The frame tells interlocutors what is going on at any given moment. In the language classroom context, the play-as-rehearsal frame is often a part of the official schedule. The data shows how learners are able by various means to turn such scenarios into play-as-fun frames which they variously use either to subvert or to reinforce classroom norms.

Chapter 5: Evoking frames through associated language

This chapter looks at the same three groups that feature in Chapter 4. As well as exploited play-as-rehearsal frames, the second major resource that learners use to have fun is language associated with particular situations which their group has experienced together. A striking feature of the collected data which the chapter highlights is that learners often generate humour by recontextualising and re-accenting language they have encountered collectively which had originally encoded different intentions and meanings. As such, the language of play is often used to metonymically refer to prior events experienced together by the group members and, in the process, helps to build up a pool of significant common reference points which symbolise their shared history. This allows the learners to take ownership of the language by infusing it with their own communicative intentions.

8   D. Hann

Chapters 6, 7 and 8: A case study: The brief cultural history of a group

Having identified salient patterns of HLP in Chapters 4 and 5, noting that the incremental evocation of shared language and experience is central to play, Chapters 6, 7 and 8 are dedicated to a case study of a pair of learners and their teacher which allows the nature and development of the playful interactions between them to be traced over two of the three days in which they worked together. In so doing, it explores how such play is central to establishing identities and relationships within the group.

Chapter 6: A case study: Overcoming failure in the search for common ground

Chapter 6 looks in detail at how the challenges and risks of playing in the target language are manifest in the case study data, and at the resources the learners use in order to overcome some of the obstacles they face. Failure when attempting to play, although less easy to identify than success, provides telling insights into the challenges which learners face in trying to generate humorous play through a language other than their own. The data demonstrates that these challenges are both linguistic and cultural.

The data also reveals the importance of non-linguistic elements such as body language which the learners draw on in order to overcome the obstacles to play that they face. Another, perhaps more surprising finding, is the degree to which the structures and sounds of the target language provide a resource for pleasurable play, a phenomenon which has parallels with the playground chants and rhymes that children enjoy as they learn to take ownership of their first language. The chapter goes on to argue that learners in the comparatively early stages of acquisition of the target language are, in one way, at an advantage over their more advanced peers in that they are not yet inured to its properties and thus are more readily able to see its potential as a plaything.

Chapter 7: Prior talk: A key resource for play

As the data in Chapter 4 indicates, shared exchanges and experiences are a central resource which speakers exploit for playful purposes. The case study allows the use of allusions to common experience to be traced from their beginnings. They show that it is often moments where the learners' shortcomings in linguistic competence are revealed which provide the inspiration for play. Thus, failure, with its potential for face threat and humiliation, can be transformed into something celebratory and act as an affirming social glue within the group. A number of threads are explored from the moment they were first seeded and are shown to develop and flower through repeated reference to them. Thus, significant cultural reference points are woven into the fabric of communication within the group. The development of these shared reference points also throws light on two phenomena which have long been regarded as important ingredients in the development of cultural identity—ritual and myth. The chapter shows how the beginnings of both can be seen in the way in which an oft-recycled piece of language takes on its own stylised intonational contours with each repetition, and how the group develops its own stories which, although not historically accurate, become part of a shared mythology.

Chapter 8: Humorous play and its implications for classroom practice
Chapter 8 explores the role of the language teacher in spontaneous play, an area which has not been systematically investigated previously in the literature. It also looks at the relationship between play and the classroom activities around which it occurs and the pedagogical implications of this.

The rhythm and patterning of play over the two days of recording of the case study group is analysed. It is noted how play tends to cluster at the beginnings and ends of official activities. Also, it seems to occur during periods of revision and reflection. This suggests that the opportunity for reflection is not just important in the process of language acquisition, something widely acknowledged, but can also act as an important period of relationship-building within a group, a process that often involves play.

The chapter also explores the ways in which the teacher in the case study allows or fosters play. Despite the clear role differences that the classroom context allots to teachers and learners, the data shows how the teacher, consciously or not, positions himself in such a way as to identify with the learners. The different roles that the teacher takes up throw light on how he navigates play's potentially subversive and disruptive nature.

Chapter 9: Humorous language play: Lessons from the second language classroom

The final chapter looks at the study's findings and their implications both in terms of further research and pedagogical practice.

In the light of the study's findings, the chapter argues for the importance of the longitudinal dimension when investigating the social significance of interaction. This is true not only of studies which have a particular interest in the second language classroom, but also in humour studies in general and, indeed, communication more broadly. The chapter therefore urges future research to take account of the accumulated and very particular meanings that words and phrases take on in specific groups and communities.

This study suggests a number of possible avenues for future research in the specific area of HLP in the second language classroom, such as investigating variables including gender and learner motivation (the participants in this study were, ostensibly at least, instrumental learners of English).

Although acquisition was not the primary focus of the study and no definitive claims are made about the direct benefits of humorous play for learning, the data points to potential benefits: the way in which play allows learners to take ownership of the language, the recycling and repetition of words and phrases, how play enables learners to assume different roles, and the heightened affective sense that accompanies play episodes. The chapter therefore encourages future research that takes a systematic approach to the exploration of the relationship between acquisition and play.

The teacher's relationship to HLP in the classroom has received scant research attention to date, and although this study has sought to begin to attend to this neglect, much more work is needed on the degree to which teacher behaviour affects group dynamic and the generation of humour in particular.

Finally, in relation to the second language classroom, the featured study encourages a fresh approach to failure in the classroom context, by both the researcher and the practitioner. The study shows how failure in use of the target language can itself trigger play and learning, allowing a source of potential face threat and embarrassment to be alchemised into something positive. Furthermore, the exploration of how the research participants use humour to their own ends reveals the learner, regardless of proficiency level, as an agent and creator of their own learning environment.

The chapter finally encourages more research into the role of humorous language play in the world beyond the classroom where English is being used as a lingua franca daily across the world in a myriad of social, commercial, political and other settings.

References

Carter, R. (2004). *Language and creativity: The art of common talk*. Abingdon: Routledge.

Chiaro, D. (1992). *The language of jokes: Analysing verbal play*. London: Routledge.

Cook, G. (2000). *Language play, language learning*. Oxford: Oxford University Press.

Crystal, D. (1998). *Language play*. London: Penguin Books.

Goffman, E. (1974). *Frame analysis*. Boston: Northeastern University Press.

Holmes, J. (2007). Making humour work: Creativity on the job. *Applied Linguistics, 28*(4), 518–537. https://doi.org/10.1093/applin/amm048.

Norrick, N. R. (2007). Interdiscourse humor: Contrast, merging, accommodation. *Humor, 20*(4), 389–413. https://doi.org/10.1515/HUMOR.2007.019.

Seidlhofer, B. (2011). *Understanding English as a Lingua Franca*. Oxford: Oxford University Press.

Straehle, C. (1993). "Samuel?" "Yes, dear?" Teasing and conversational rapport. In D. Tannen (Ed.), *Framing in discourse* (pp. 210–230). New York: Oxford University Press.

2

The Underexplored Role of Humorous Play in the Second Language Classroom

Any teacher will tell you that the experience of teaching one group of learners can vary greatly from that of teaching another. Factors such as age, cultural background, gender mix, aptitude and prior knowledge of the subject being taught are evidently important in helping to shape what and how to approach teaching a particular group. However, all groups of learners, even those which seem superficially homogenous, develop their own distinctive collective identities and behaviours. The result is that even the same lesson plan delivered by the same teacher to two different classes can be realised in very different ways with each of them. Therefore, in order to understand what happens in a classroom, consideration needs to be given to the particular group dynamics that prevail in that setting. This holds true for the second language classroom as it does for any other.

This chapter discusses the importance of examining the classroom as a cultural and social entity, something which is often ignored in SLA literature. It considers the language classroom as a Community of Practice (Lave and Wenger 1991) with its own emergent cultural norms. In this regard, humorous play has an important role in forging a group's cultural identity and the chapter also looks at humour's potential in the

© The Author(s) 2020

D. Hann, *Spontaneous Play in the Language Classroom*,

https://doi.org/10.1007/978-3-030-26304-1_2

process of learning a second language. It explores the sometimes uneasy relationship between humorous play and the classroom setting, something which may explain why it is a phenomenon which has generally been overlooked in the literature. When looking at play's role in the building of culture, the important longitudinal dimension is also largely neglected in the existing literature. In the course of the chapter, I move towards a definition of humorous language play as it is understood in this book.

2.1 The Traditional Neglect of the Language Classroom as an Arena for Social Interaction

In SLA research, language learning has largely been seen in terms of the ability of learners to acquire and master particular features of the target language (TL). The social dimension that is inevitably involved in this process has been somewhat overlooked. Given that a language classroom exists for one main purpose—to improve its members' performance in a particular TL—it is perhaps unsurprising that researchers have tended to concentrate on how successfully that objective is met. The easiest means of measuring progress in acquiring a TL is to investigate learners' acquisition of lexis or mastery of grammatical structure. This preoccupation with the end product as exemplified by the immediate objective of acquiring the question form or filling in the information gap has meant the social dimension of the classroom has largely gone unremarked (Rampton 2007: 588).

The reason for the neglect of the social dimension may lie in part with ideas from advocates of certain pedagogical approaches, such as task-based teaching (e.g. Samuda and Bygate 2008), which tend to see language as salient only in so far as it relates to and prepares the learner for the real world beyond the classroom itself. Even basic terminology seems to encourage this view. After all, embedded in the meaning of the word "acquisition" seems to be the idea that something has to be obtained before it is put to use, a notion which perpetuates the fiction that language is a closed system that is not subject to its users (Bell and Pomerantz 2014). As Cook (2000: 170–173) points out, what constitutes real language and interaction goes far beyond the narrow conceptualisation that such an outlook allows. After all, what happens in the classroom has real social consequences. It is a place where friendships are made, alliances formed and identities negotiated.

2.2 Language Learners Have Identities Too

The traditional focus on language acquisition in SLA research has tended to reduce the language learner to an acquirer—a receptacle—of the lexical, grammatical or phonological features of the TL. This has been especially true of research in the classroom, where its members are often reduced to an undifferentiated mass. This previous oversight in the field of linguistics has led to a need to catch up with developments in other social sciences (Block 2007: 2). After all, it is over half a century since Goffman (1959) highlighted how much of our interactional energy is taken up with constructing and preserving our social selves and it is much longer still since the establishment of disciplines such as psychiatry and psychology put identity and personality at the heart of our understanding of human behaviour and interaction.

In fact, the classroom can be of particular interest in relation to the social identity of learners, especially one made up of people who find themselves away from their familiar surroundings of family and friends. Of course, a sense of self is very important at all times but, as Block (2007: 21) recognises, when people cross geographical and sociocultural borders, "..individuals often find that any feelings they have of a stable self are upset and that they enter a period of struggle to reach a balance". Similarly, Pellegrino's (2005: 9) remarks, although relating specifically to the experiences of university students on exchange programmes, can equally be applied to all those who find themselves in a different country, using another's language:

Stripped of the comfortable mastery of their first language and culture and societal adroitness, learners in an immersion environment, such as

16   D. Hann

study abroad, often report feeling as if those around them may perceive them to be unintelligent, lacking personality or humor, or as having the intellectual development of a small child.

This chimes with my own teaching experience at BizLang, where some course participants, especially at the lower end of the proficiency spectrum, feel a loss of status: from being important people in their work organisation, they are, in their own eyes at least, reduced to the state of helpless children who are sometimes unable to communicate basic needs and thoughts. It is noteworthy, in terms of this book's concerns, that Pellegrino mentions the importance of humour in retaining a sense of self. For some people at least, being able to demonstrate humour in another language may be crucial in validating their identity in that language.

Since the late 1990s, there has been a belated awakening of interest in the notion that second language learners have individual identities which find expression in what they say and how they behave in their learning environments. This is perhaps exemplified by the arrival in 2002 of a journal specifically dedicated to issues around language and identity—*The Journal of Language, Identity and Education*. The foci of its articles reflect where research interests in this field lie at present. It is illuminating to look at these in relation to the research concerns of this book.

It is perhaps to be expected that contributions to the journal often investigate bilinguals (Kanno 2003; Li 2007) or immigrants (DaSilva Iddings and McCafferty 2007; Liang 2006). For bilinguals, their attitude to and usage of their two languages seem, on the face of it, crucial to their sense of self, especially as, in most cases, their cognitive development has coincided with the acquisition of their language codes. In the case of immigrants, their relationship with the language(s) of their new community seems vital in successfully adapting to their new surroundings.

In Gardner and Lambert's (1972) influential account of the importance of motivation in second language acquisition, immigrants would seem to have a primarily integrative motivation for acquiring the TL. At first sight, there appears to be far less at stake for what Gardner and

Lambert call instrumental learners of a TL, that is those whose reasons for improving their English are largely practical in nature. This is the category into which most of the research participants in the featured study fall. They need their English in order to carry out their work more efficiently, and even then, only when dealing with the international or cross-border dimensions of their jobs. The TL appears to have far less of a bearing on the speaker's identity as its context of use is narrower than that of many immigrants, and its acquisition, unlike that of most bilinguals, usually comes at a stage when the speaker has already forged a sense of self. However, one need only consider the still growing importance of English in our global transactions, politically and commercially (Crystal 2003; Jenkins 2007; Seargeant 2012; Seidlhofer 2011), to see that work encounters in English form an ever-increasing part of the identities of second language—L2—learners of the language. Nowadays, some argue that English is not so much colonising the world as being colonised and shaped by it (Jenkins 2007). A strong case could be made that speakers of English such as those that feature in this book seem to have at least some say in the development and destiny of the language.

2.3 Individual and Collective Identities

Traditionally, people's cultural and social identities have been largely defined in terms of relatively static and broad groupings such as those to do with gender, nationality and class. Although the concept of the collective national identity is still seen as important—see, for example, the titles of papers which I have cited in this section (Kanno 2003; Li 2007)—there is a growing recognition that such classifications are more fluid than traditionally thought and that, in any case, they do not in themselves do justice to the complexities of people's social networks or sense of self. Individuals' identities, especially in today's increasingly interconnected world, are multi-layered and ever-changing. People move between different groupings—professional, familial, social—on a daily basis and adapt their behaviours accordingly.

The classroom can be regarded as one such grouping, albeit an often ephemeral one. It is useful in terms of my research context and concerns to regard it as what Holliday (1999) would call a "small culture". In contrast to the "large" cultures from which the learners come and by which they are defined through their nationalities, "[t]he dynamic aspect of small culture is central to its nature, having the capacity to exist, form and change as required" (Holliday 1999: 248). People may, by dint of their place of birth and other factors, belong to particular large cultures. On the other hand, they have a greater say in shaping the numerous small cultures of which they are a part. The small culture cuts across the large cultures of nationality and is emergent and negotiable in nature. This conceptualisation of culture makes the small culture's members creators of their own sociocultural community. As such, culture can be regarded as a verb rather than a noun (Street 1993), an idea which dovetails with my research interest in the degree to which humorous play contributes to the developing culture of a group.

Another useful way of conceptualising the language classroom as a social entity is as a Community of Practice. Eckert and McConnell-Ginet's definition of the term, itself influenced by Lave and Wenger's (1991) conceptualisation, seems closely to describe what such a group is for:

> A community of practice is an aggregate of people who come together around mutual engagement in an endeavour. Ways of doing things, ways of talking, beliefs, values, power relations - in short - practices - emerge in the course of this mutual endeavour. (Eckert and McConnell-Ginet 1992: 464)

This is a definition which foregrounds the shared aim of the group. In my own research setting, without having in common a perceived need to improve their English, the members of the BizLang group would not come together in the first place. Secondly, the emphasis on the emergent nature of the norms which help define a community of practice is particularly apt given that a BizLang group has to start from scratch in forging a cohesive working relationship and culture (see Chapter 3). True, there is already an established institutional culture that frames the development of the group, but the group's particular practices are, to a large extent, established by its members. I would include a group's teacher as well as its learners in the community of practice. After all, the former shares the latter's main aim, although, of course, the role designated to her or him in the achievement of that aim is rather different. At BizLang, the teacher is also usually a constant for the duration of a group's existence.

Centre stage in both the notions of small culture and community of practice is their emergent nature. Of course, even groupings of the broadest kind are not static: the culture of a particular society or nation can change noticeably over time as it is being continuously shaped by social factors. However, at the level of people's everyday social networks, individuals have a greater leverage in shaping the groupings of which they are members. As a result, their nature and culture can be ever changing. Therefore, a true understanding of the specific social nature and dynamic within a particular group requires an appreciation, not only of the group's norms and practices at any particular moment, but also of the forces which have forged those norms and practices over time. As will be seen (Sect. 2.6), research has tended to overlook the longitudinal dimension in relation to the language classroom, an oversight which is of particular significance in the exploration of humorous play.

2.4 The Nature of Humorous Play

This section explores the commonalities and contrasts between "play" and "humour" and, in so doing, works towards a definition of "humorous language play" as it is used in this book.

Play is a ubiquitous phenomenon in human societies. The impulse to play is a universal one among people of all cultures. Johan Huizinga (1970, first published 1944), the Dutch philosopher, coined the term *Homo Ludens* to encapsulate this essential element in our nature. Indeed, the pervasive importance of play has been highlighted in recent times through corpus analysis which shows its presence in our everyday communications (e.g. Carter 2004). However, despite or maybe because of its ubiquity, attempting to define play, and specifically its manifestations in our oral communications, has proved difficult. This is not surprising, given its multifunctional and multifaceted nature. Furthermore, as will become clear in the course of this chapter, play is inherently ambiguous, making any attempt to pinpoint its nature ultimately elusive. Swann and Maybin (2007: 492) observe that researchers have been lax in their interchangeable uses of terms such as "play", "humour" and "creativity". Other linked and overlapping concepts such as "wordplay" and "joking" could as easily be added to this list. Nevertheless, it is worth de-limiting the concept from the outset. I am particularly interested in play that is conducted primarily through language. It is playing through language which, ostensibly, the low intermediate learners of English who feature in this book are at the greatest disadvantage in relation to L1 speakers (see Sect. 3.1.3 for a precise definition of the proficiency levels of the learners in the study). After all, play is a means of showing prowess in a language (Sect. 2.6). Furthermore, it is the play that arises in the to and fro of interaction rather than anything pre-planned or pre-scripted such as "canned jokes" (Chiaro 1992; Norrick 1993), which is the concern of this book. The challenges that learners face when attempting to take part in spontaneous play are both productive and receptive in nature. Learners not only have to be able to actively produce playful language but also be able to react in kind when others do so.

Given the complexity of human behaviour, attempting a neat and watertight definition of play would be a vain undertaking. However, there are useful characteristics of the phenomenon that can help in its identification.

2.4.1 Play as Stepping Outside the Norm

The higher animals, as Cook (2000: 102) points out, share a proclivity for play. Anyone who has ever had a dog knows that it spends much of its time satisfying this impulse both in its interactions with other dogs but also, across species, with its owners. Although wild animals often have to channel their energies into activities more central to their

2 The Underexplored Role of Humorous Play ...

survival such as searching for food or ensuring that they themselves do not become food, play is still an important feature of their lives (e.g. Beckoff and Byers 1998; Henig 2008).

When playing, animals pattern their behaviour on primary activities such as fighting or hunting. It is important, therefore, that they are able to differentiate between play and the behaviours on which they are based; otherwise, they could suffer physical harm. In this regard, it is worth drawing upon the ideas of twentieth-century sociologist Erving Goffman, himself influenced by the work of anthropologist Gregory Bateson's (1972) study of the play behaviour in animals. One of the many important concepts that Goffman uses to explain human interaction is that of the frame—a framework of interpretation—that allows us, at any given moment, to answer the question "what is going on here?" (Goffman 1974: 8). His notion of frame is conceptualised in terms of the individual's experience rather than in terms of society's wider structures (1974: 13). It is, therefore, a psychological construct in which context is not "out there" but exists in relation to the individual's experience of it and is something which can also be created and shaped by the individual, much as a dog signals a play frame when it wags its tail as it pretend-fights. Furthermore, frames are a means by which we, as social actors, attempt to understand each other's actions and intentions. For the most part, this interpretation process is subconscious:

> ..observers actively project their frames of reference into the world immediately around them, and one fails to see their so doing only because events ordinarily confirm these projections, causing the assumptions to disappear into the smooth flow of activity. (Goffman 1974: 39)

It is noteworthy that Goffman does not regard play as an activity within one of our primary frame works for understanding the world around us. Rather, he sees it as something based on but different from such an activity (1974: 43–44). As such, it becomes a conscious happening, both for the play instigator who has to signal that he or she is in a "play frame" at a given moment, and for the audience, for whom the ordinary flow of events is somehow disrupted. This echoes Huizinga's assertion that play is not ordinary: "It is rather a stepping out of 'real' life into a temporary sphere of activity with a disposition all of its own" (Huizinga 1970: 26). When the play frame is opened up by, for example, a joke or humorous remark, it gives others the licence to follow it up with wordplay or thematically linked stories or jokes of their own. This is why much of the data collected on such linguistic behaviour shows that it clusters, occurring in play episodes (Carter 2004: 100–101; Coates 2007: 38–43; Holmes 2007: 529–530). Even when playful language is focussed on one speaker, such as in the telling of a humorous story, the participation and response of the audience are vital in ensuring its success (Toolan 2006: 65). Thus, play is a collaborative venture which only succeeds with the participation of at least two parties.

The out-of-the-place nature of play does not mean that it has no consequences in the world beyond the narrative or play frame. The young, human or otherwise, who play-fight may not seriously hurt each other but this does not mean that their play has no effect on the power dynamics within their social group (e.g. Symons 1978). As Gordon (2008: 324) citing Bateson (1972) observes, the play bite is not real but it is also NOT not real. This means that play gives its participants the leeway to do and say things which would not otherwise be allowed, a potential for subversion which will be returned to throughout this book. That play is both integral to and an interlude in our ongoing existence (Huizinga 1970: 27) gives it an ambiguity which, in turn, makes it a particularly powerful social tool, something which becomes evident in the research data to come.

It is worth reflecting on the notion of frame in relation to the language classroom. There is a striking parallel between the speaker who sets up a play frame as a fun diversion from the mainstream flow of interaction and the language teacher who establishes a hypothetical frame in order to practise particular functional or structural features of the TL, such as "giving advice" or "the simple past". In both cases, there are simultaneous frames which are in operation, what Goffman would call the "primary" one (1974: 21ff.), which in the classroom consists of the teacher teaching and the learner learning, and either the simulated or comedic one. In the simulated frame, the student may temporarily be a shopper, a neighbour or whatever the simulation demands in order to practise particular elements of the language. The play frame, as will be seen, can also create a wide spectrum of roles for the participants. A difference between them, of course, is that the simulated frame forms part of the official classroom business of learning and is initiated and managed by the teacher, whereas a play frame is unofficial in that it forms an interlude in the main activity, even though it may be sanctioned by the teacher. In the light of its unofficial nature, triggering a play frame seems like a risky undertaking for a learner. The relationship between the play frame and the simulated frame is an area of interest in this investigation.

As well as role-play, there is another form of play which is officially promoted in many language classrooms, and that is language drilling. This is an activity which came to the fore in language teaching in the middle of the twentieth century with the rise of the audiolingual method (Richards and Rodgers 2001) which itself was heavily influenced by behaviourism. This is an approach which resulted in a mushrooming of language laboratories in schools during the 1960s and 1970s where students would practise manipulating grammatical forms and attempt to imitate the standard pronunciation of a TL. Drilling fell out of favour with some language teaching practitioners in the latter half of the twentieth century. However, it remains prevalent in many institutions and, in the BizLang setting, still constitutes an important element in the organisation's pedagogical approach.

Drilling might more readily be associated with work rather than play. However, the rationale for using it—giving the learner enough mastery of the different forms of the TL to use it effectively in real-life encounters—echoes the widely accepted benefits of play as an important means of helping children and young animals to develop the requisite social and other skills which will prepare them for later life. Furthermore, the sort of manipulations of forms and meanings that occur in language drilling seem to have some affinity with wordplay which is often closely associated with humour. However, my investigations differentiate the role-play and drilling of the classroom from the types of play which I focus on in my research. I have already mentioned that I'm more interested in unofficial classroom play than that which is an official part of the classroom agenda. However, the differences between the two go beyond their official status or otherwise. In this regard, Lantolf

(1997: 4–5) makes a useful distinction between play as fun and play as rehearsal.

In helping to draw a distinction between play as fun and play as rehearsal, humour has a useful role.

2.4.2 Play and Humour: Overlapping Concepts

As mentioned previously, humour and play are often used interchangeably. This is unsurprising as they have overlapping characteristics. It is in this area of overlap where the unofficial and spontaneous type of play which is of interest in this book can be found. Unsurprisingly, researchers who are interested in language play among L1 speakers (Coates 2007: 31; Cook 1997: 227) and among L2 speakers (Bell 2005: 196; Belz and Reinhardt 2004: 328; Cekaite and Aronsson 2005: 174; DaSilva Iddings and McCafferty 2007: 33; Davies 2003: 1363; Sullivan 2000: 122) usually have the notions of "amusement", "humour" or "fun" at the forefront of their definitions.

Humour, like play, is difficult to pin down, and in part, this slipperiness comes from an ambiguity at the heart of both. We have already seen that the play frame permits people to inhabit two worlds at once. The language classroom role-play, for example, lets the learners and their teacher enter the world of the simulation but still exist within the classroom environment. Another common manifestation of play—teasing—is also essentially ambiguous. It can generate both enjoyment and discomfort because it can simultaneously be interpreted both seriously and non-seriously. The fact that teasing can be seen as both playful and humorous indicates that attempting to provide discrete definitions of the two may be a lost cause. However, there are types of play which are humorous and those which are not, and it is the former which is of interest in this book.

So, what constitutes humorous play? A simple answer would be to say that it is play which causes amusement. From this perspective, humorous play can be identified by the behaviours that signal it or react to it rather than by attempting to determine its essential features. It tends to be realised in discrete episodes which need to be signalled and understood clearly in order to be successful. After all, the ambiguity of humorous play means that it can be misinterpreted and the common observation that a recipient of play "took it the wrong way" suggests that this is an ever-present risk. One means of minimising such a risk is to signal that a play frame is in operation. The dog assumes the "play bow" (Henig 2008), and the cat retracts its claws to show their playmates that they mean them no harm. Human beings have their own ways of communicating play frames that Gumperz (1982: 131) calls "contextualisation cues". These recognise that context is not a static setting in which communication takes place but that it is, at least in part, something that both shapes and is shaped by the language and behaviour of those within it. Thus, the line "I'm going to kill you", if accompanied by a broad smile, is rarely an indicator that homicide is on the speaker's mind. Other contextualisation cues for play include prosody (Holmes 2007: 531; Straehle 1993: 214), unusual lexical choices such as neologisms (Broner and Tarone 2001: 371), overlapping speech (Coates 2007: 38–41) and exaggerated gestures (Davies 2003: 1373). In a second language context, these cues may well be that much more crucial because participants cannot rely on each other's linguistic and sociocultural antennae for intended play being particularly fine-tuned.

A further indicator of humorous play is people's reaction to it which often takes the form of laughter. The presence of laughter is a common method used by researchers to identify play episodes (e.g. Pomerantz and Bell 2007: 563; Rogerson-Revell 2007: 12). This does not mean, however, that laughter is merely a reactive phenomenon. It can itself be a signal of playful intent (Glenn 2003: 28). In this sense, as Coates (2007: 44) asserts, it is not only a response to humorous talk but is itself talk. However, it needs to be remembered that as well as signalling amusement, laughter can, among other things, function to cover embarrassment.

Defining humorous play in terms of people's reaction to it begs its own question of why such a reaction is triggered. An answer requires a further exploration of the nature of humour. There are a number of theories of humour but the most enduring and influential encompasses the notion of combining ideas that are incongruous (e.g. Morreall 1987; Raskin 1985): we are amused by that which seems

26   D. Hann

out of place in some way, which surprises us or destabilises our expectations. Although there are many things we laugh at which are not incongruous and, conversely, many things which are incongruous which we do not find amusing, there does indeed seem to be an out-of-place quality, a surprising element, to much that is humorous. And, as the next section shows, language is the natural conduit for incongruity, an incongruity which is often ambiguous in nature.

2.4.3 Language and Its Relationship to Play and Humour

Language is at the forefront of my concerns. It is central to the rationale for investigating humorous play among speakers for whom the language they are operating in is regarded, by themselves as much as anyone else, as not their own. How are they able to generate humour in a language over which they do not have mastery?

The previous section touched upon the incongruous nature of humour. Language is a natural vehicle for allowing the combination of incongruous elements. In part, this is because of its symbolic nature (Saussure 1959, first published 1916) which allows words to be homonymous. This, in turn, means that, through language, we are capable of amalgamating two conflicting frameworks of interpretation in a word or phrase by, for example, punning on different meanings. Victor Raskin sees the combining of different elements as a condition for humour:

> ..any text should be partially or fully compatible with two different scripts and secondly, a special relation of script oppositeness should obtain between the two scripts. (1985: xiii)

What Raskin calls scripts, he defines in the following terms:

> scripts of "common sense" which represent his/her knowledge of certain routines, standard procedures, basic situations etc., for instance, the knowledge of what people do in certain situations, how they do it, in what order, etc. (1985: 81)

2 The Underexplored Role of Humorous Play ...   27

A simple everyday example of the combining of scripts for humorous intent illustrates Raskin's point. As I type these words, I have a coffee mug in front of me with a picture of a woman on the phone. A speech bubble next to her reads: "Can you please hold?...". The next line reveals the joke: "..Incontinence Hotline, can you please hold?". Expectations of a particular script as set up by the use of formulaic telephone language. These are then suddenly subverted by the following lines which activate another script where the verb "hold" takes on a rather different meaning, triggering humour (at least for some). It is worth noting here that instigating such humorous play in spontaneous interaction depends not only on a knowledge of the multiple semantic meanings of particular words, but also the dexterity to draw upon that knowledge at a given moment, a challenging task, especially for someone who is not speaking their L1. In the light of these difficulties, one of the investigative aims of this volume is to explore the degree to which language learners can bring together conflicting scripts without necessarily having access to play based on an extensive semantic knowledge of the TL.

As well as facilitating the bringing together of incongruous elements, language can generate playful ambiguity because of its essentially metaphorical nature. It is significant that Huizinga, in describing language's intrinsically playful nature, refers to metaphor:

> In the making of speech and language, the spirit is continually 'sparking' between matter and mind, as it were, playing with [the] nominative faculty. Behind every abstract expression there lie the boldest of metaphors, and every metaphor is a play upon words. (1970: 23)

The notion of the fundamental metaphorical nature of language finds a parallel in Lakoff and Johnson's (1980) seminal work which sees language as reflecting the metaphorical nature of human thought itself. They assert that we naturally make mappings between conceptual domains which become so embedded in our language that we are usually unaware of the fact that everyday expressions like "falling prices" are, in fact, metaphorical in nature. Although shortcomings have been found in Lakoff and Johnson's framework (e.g. Cameron 2003; Gibbs

1999), it nevertheless strongly suggests that much of our language, before it becomes conventionalised by use, starts life when a comparative link is forged between two conceptual domains. Thus, for instance, an adjective like "tough", a word from the domain of physical properties, is transferred and applied to an abstract concept such as a "problem". The initial transference of such a word to what is now a commonplace application in an abstract domain suggests a figurative dimension to much of our innovative language use, although it would be misleading to suggest that all metaphorical language is playful. However, the fact that, at its birth, a metaphor forges novel conceptual connections may be one reason why research into language play among native speakers of English (e.g. Carter 2004; Coates 2007) shows that figurative language is a prominent feature of the data and, indeed, that play between the literal and metaphorical meanings of words is a common everyday means of generating humour. Again, this reinforces the idea that ambiguity is often the nexus between language, humour and play.

The fact that language attracts play through its figurative nature can also be seen in another way. It is important, when considering its potential for playfulness, to remember that language does not exist in a vacuum. It both shapes and is shaped by its use in our interactions. Mikhail Bakhtin (1981, first published 1935) roots language firmly in its sociocultural milieu. He sees it as heteroglossic—many voiced—in nature, its meanings forged and altered by usage, so that words carry within them previous intentions, connotations and contextual flavours.

The idea of words evoking previous usages and settings is an important one and takes us back to the figurative nature of language alluded to previously. In play among native speakers at least, it is not only language's metaphorical nature which is important with regard to play, but also its metonymic dimension. To quote Chandler (2002: 130):

> While metaphor is based on apparent unrelatedness, metonymy is a function which involves using one signified to stand for another signified which is *directly related* to it or *closely associated* with it in some way. (author's italics)

2 The Underexplored Role of Humorous Play ...   29

To illustrate this, Chandler gives various examples including "Number 10" where the place stands for the person, that is, the place where the British Prime Minister officially resides is used to refer to the Prime Minister him or herself. When playing, people, usually in their friendship groups, often evoke an episode or scenario from their shared history with a word or phrase which is associated with that moment and which comes to stand for it. Although it may not usually be thought of as such, I would maintain that such usage is metonymic and, therefore, figurative in nature. The language used comes to mean something beyond its mere denotation but represents the whole of which it was originally just a part. An example illustrates the point. Below is a snippet from a long-running and popular BBC radio programme *Just a Minute* where contestants have to speak on a subject allocated to them for a minute without hesitation or deviation. In the following extract, Nicholas Parsons, the host of the show, is about to read out the points totals to his guests who include the comedian Paul Merton:

Nicholas Parsons: What a fair result!
Paul Merton: What did Will get?

(Audience laughter and applause)
(BBC R4 *Just a Minute*, first broadcast 22 November 2010)

On the face of it, there is nothing funny about Merton's line at all. In fact, it makes no sense to someone tuning into the programme at that moment. In order to understand the significance of what Merton has said, you would need to listen to the broadcast from the beginning. In fact, the thread which he exploits had started early in the game with an unsolicited intervention from a member of the audience (Will). This is then referred to and played with by members of the game panel on various occasions throughout the show. By the end, the name of Will not only refers to a member of the audience but also metonymically stands for a collective experience. The pleasure and humour here seem to come from two characteristics of the exchanges. Firstly, the references are shared and inclusive. This means that, once established, not all the elements of a humorous thread subsequently need not be explicitly spelt out, and there is pleasure to be derived from such unsaid mutual understanding. In this regard, it is worth bearing in mind that commonly understood and shared cultural reference points can act as shortcuts to such implicit understanding. Secondly, there is an incongruity that lies in the fact that an unsanctioned intervention is treated as an official contribution to the game. It is noteworthy here that the humour builds incrementally over the course of the programme. The incremental, inclusive and incongruous dimensions to humorous play are revisited in the analysis of the research data. Although, in this case, the particular significance of Will's name is fleeting and dies with the end of the radio broadcast, such play can provide an important social glue which contributes to the building of an in-group culture and can be related to Bakhtin's notion of the dialogical nature of language: utterances both respond to and are infused with previous meanings, as well as anticipating responses to come. In his own words: "[t]he living utterance [...] can not fail to brush up against thousands of living dialogic threads" (1981: 276–277).

2.4.4 Humorous Language Play and Its Subversive Nature

Section 2.4 has been exploring the nature of play and humour. The way in which play can be regarded as stepping outside the norm, or at least the normal flow of interaction, has been discussed, as has its ambiguous nature. To differentiate it from the officially sanctioned play of classroom drilling and simulation, its humorous element is important, a facility to amuse which seems to be triggered by an incongruity at humorous play's heart. This incongruity is facilitated by language's figurative and dialogical nature. The fact that it can destabilise our expectations, that it is often ambiguous and that it can be seen as operating outside the norm hints at a common characteristic of much humorous play—its subversive tendencies.

On the one hand, it could be argued that humorous play is often benign in nature. According to Brown and Levinson's Politeness Theory (1987: 102), humour can be a means of claiming common ground, a useful tool in ensuring the smooth flow of our everyday interactions. Brown and Levinson build upon Goffman's (1959) notion of face, a preferred self-image which speakers present to the world and which, ordinarily, they and their interlocutors seek to protect. Brown and Levinson view humour as a means of protecting the speaker's and hearer's "positive face"—this requires that the individual's "wants be desirable to at least some others" (1987: 62). It also protects an interlocutor's "negative face"—the need that "his actions be unimpeded by others" (1987: 62) by diluting the threat inherent in such acts as directives and criticisms. However, Brown and Levinson's mention of humour (a concept which they do not define) does not take into consideration the fact that it can be an astringent as well as a balm.

That humorous language play can be the natural means of expressing a less benign side of our human impulses can be seen by looking again at its ambiguity. Teasing an interlocutor, for example, can simultaneously demonstrate both antagonism and affection. Such language use is deniable—"I was only joking". In other words, it has a characteristic of humour which Attardo (1994) calls "decommitment", making an utterance easily retractable. This allows speakers to operate at the edge of acceptable norms in order to assert or subvert those norms.

2.4.5 Defining Humorous Language Play for the Purposes of This Book

As has been noted in this chapter, language play, humour, wit and other associated concepts have not been consistently defined in the literature. Humorous language play is often associated with the clever manipulation of the structural and semantic properties of a language. However, the previous discussion points to the rather narrow conceptualisation of play that this suggests. I would like to differentiate such play—let's call it "wordplay"—from humorous language play (HLP) which is a broader term, encompassing but not restricted to wordplay. HLP is a situated, incremental, ambiguous, collaborative and often subversive phenomenon which has an important role in the social dimension of communication. The investigations to follow will allow for this

32 D. Hann

definition to be built upon and developed. Given the characteristics of HLP which have been identified, the questions of why the L2 learner might be drawn to participating in it, the challenges and risks such participation would present, and the potential benefits that would accrue are all very pertinent to the concerns of this book, especially in relation to the classroom context.

2.5 Humorous Language Play and the Second Language Learner

Having the ability to indulge in humorous play is a distinct social advantage. Adjectives such as "witty" and "humorous" to describe someone are highly complimentary. By exploiting such features as homonyms, homophones and synonyms (e.g. Norrick 1993), a speaker can show their command of the language code itself. Such language use can have a competitive edge, as can be seen and heard in settings as diverse as parliamentary debates and rapping contests. From an evolutionary perspective, as Cook (2000: 68) points out, such a demonstrable mastery of language may attract mates: like a lyre-bird's tail display, it symbolises the ability to defend and provide. This theory seems to be validated by the fact that the desirability of having such an attribute in potential mates has been distilled in the acronym GSOH—good sense of humour—on dating sites. So, being able to play in a language is a distinct advantage but, for the L2 speaker, it presents particular challenges.

2.5.1 The Challenges of HLP for the Second Language Learner

Of course, the particular type of play alluded to above seems to refer specifically to what I call wordplay (Sect. 2.4.5). Given the linguistic and cultural dexterity needed for such play, it is something which would seem to disadvantage the second language learner. It is unsurprising therefore that sources which investigate this type of play tend to concentrate on L1 speakers (Carter 2004; Chiaro 1992; Crystal 1998; Norrick 1993). Of course, for the second language learner, such display presents particular problems because he or she has only a partial command of the language (although whether anyone has a full command of it is a moot point). For instance, the kind of mastery of the TL's semantic properties needed for the simultaneous evocation of two or more of Raskin's scripts (1985: 111) would be beyond many language learners. Indeed, it is significant that Raskin himself frames the notion of wit in terms of a speaker's productive and receptive competence (1985: 51). It is not surprising, therefore, that much of the research into play among language learners seems to analyse it in terms of the extent to which it provides evidence of acquisition of the TL. For example, Bell (2005: 212), in her research into the language play of three non-native speakers of English living in the USA, found that the most proficient of her participants was able to draw on a greater variety of linguistic resources than her fellow participants, and she concludes that ".. the ability to engage in humorous language play is linked to proficiency". In a similar vein, Belz and Rheinhardt (2004) demonstrate how a learner of German was able to use language play to demonstrate his mastery and awareness of the multi-functionality of the language (albeit in computer-mediated communication rather than face-to-face interaction). Invaluable though these investigations are, they risk promoting a deficit model of language play among L2 learners where their ability to indulge in play is dependent on the degree to which they can achieve a native-like competence in the TL. Such a notion runs contrary to my own teaching experiences, where play is as likely to occur among speakers at the lower end of the proficiency spectrum as among speakers at its higher end.

HLP as I have defined it goes beyond wordplay, but even in a broader understanding of the phenomenon, there are challenges for the L2 speaker, not least because of its collaborative nature. Generating humorous play is a joint enterprise. To participate in it, an L2 speaker has to be able to both produce and recognise the conversational cues that signal play frames. In addition, once instigated, building upon such a frame in a humorous play episode is particularly demanding because of the need to stay within the form or theme constraints introduced by the previous contribution. Furthermore, an utterance that attempts humour, even if it does not demand a contribution in kind, does require a reaction, if only of laughter. It could be argued that this is true of any conversational turn. However, the stakes are so much higher for both speaker and listener in humorous exchanges because the danger of failure and a resultant social embarrassment are ever present. As has already been alluded to (Sect. 2.4.3), humour often involves an implicit understanding where the listener fills in the gaps of what remains unsaid. For example, if there is any fun to be had from innuendo, it is that the listener identifies the lewd dimension of meaning while the speaker can act the innocent. Therefore, the addressee's reaction to play is integral to the meaning-making process. Clearly, given the implicit mutual understandings that play can entail, the cultural dimension is an important one in determining the success or otherwise of humorous play. In this regard, the importance of mutually understood reference points in native-speaker play has already been mentioned (see Sect. 1.1).

As well as having to overcome limitations to both their linguistic and cultural knowledge in order to play, L2 speakers face another problem which they can do little about—how they are perceived by dint of the fact that they are not native speakers of a language. Harder (1980: 268) memorably coins the concept of the second language learner's "reduced personality" where "…a foreigner is not permitted to go beyond a certain limited repertoire". As a result, any attempt at wit may be discounted. Prodromou (2007: 21), following up Widdowson's (1998) observations about the perceived authenticity of utterances in relation to their speakers, puts it this way:

> What is considered creative in the mouth of the L1-user is often seen as deviation in the mouth of even the most advanced successful bilingual user of the language.

This suggests that, however dexterous the second language speaker in the TL, he or she will never attain the status of native privilege which allows for language play.

So, participating in play can be both challenging and risky, especially for someone who is operating in a second language. However, as the

2.5.2 The Advantages of Play for the Second Language Learner

Given that humorous play is often a joint enterprise, it is hardly surprising that it can help to create social bonds. Even at the more aggressive end of the spectrum, something like teasing is as much a sign of bonding as it is of competition (Bongartz and Schneider 2003; Carter 2004; Holmes 2007; Straehle 1993). In addition, as previously mentioned, there is social kudos to be accrued from the ability to play and it seems to have an important role in the validation of identity, especially where that identity needs to be established and ratified, such as for the learner away from home in a second language classroom. Indeed, humour's importance is occasionally glimpsed in research papers that explore the ways in which individuals try to project and maintain identities in another language and country. For example, Schmidt's (1983: 160) classic study of how Wes, a Japanese man living in Hawaii, successfully conducts himself in everyday encounters despite a limited command of English, highlights how his sense of humour helps make up for shortcomings at the grammatical level in his social interactions. Similarly, Karol, another migrant living in America with limited linguistic skills, nurtures friendships through his telling of witty stories (Teutsch-Dwyer 2002: 190).

Language play may well be one means by which adult language learners assert a sense of control in a cultural and linguistic environment where they must often feel its lack. A learner's use of humour to help shape the context in which language is learnt, used, and recast is part of what Kramsch (2006) calls a speaker's "symbolic competence", which includes their ability to shape the conditions of their own social survival. Pomerantz and Bell (2007) seem to find evidence of just such activity in the Spanish conversation classes that they investigate. However, their research participants share a common L1 and a common culture, and much of the undermining of the prevailing

36   D. Hann

official discourse is carried out with the aid of that shared first language. Learners from a variety of cultural and linguistic backgrounds, such as those in my research setting, are denied a shared common first language as a resource for play.

As well as social benefits, Cook (2000: 141–144) posits that play is a means of developing and expanding people's cognitive abilities, whether they are second language learners or not. He finds an analogy between language play and random changes that occur to genes: mutations allow us the potential to conceptualise the world in novel ways. Language play, where form, meaning and function are often in dynamic communion, is one way in which such mutations can occur. Humour often arises from a sense of the incongruous, and this may trigger new ways of thinking.

In the field of SLA, it is interesting to reflect on whether an L2 speaker's comparatively fresh perspective on the language code can be a trigger to play and a source of innovative thought. In this regard, it is noteworthy that children play with the properties of language as they acquire it: witness the ways in which children play with sounds and meanings in such routines as "knock knock" jokes, nursery rhymes and playground chants (Cook 2000: 13–31). This is not to deny the clear differences between the acquisition of a first language among children who are in the process of cognitive development and that of a second language among socialised and mature adults.

As well as its general cognitive benefits, play may help in the language acquisition process itself. Apart from the obvious advantages of hearing and using wordplay in getting to understand and appreciate the semantic and phonological properties of the TL, it could be posited that the heightened affective sense that humorous interactions can trigger may, in turn, influence the depth at which particular language items are processed. Furthermore, given the fact that much language play is cumulative and incremental (Carter 2004), it may be that the repetition of particular items or phrases helps in their assimilation (Tarone 2002). Evidence from Bell's (2005) study suggests that at least one of her participants remembered the various meanings of a particular vocabulary item through the play that it had originally generated.

As well as the potential social and cognitive benefits of play for the second language learner, it could be posited that the language learning role lends itself to play. For instance, the area of identity is one where a perceived difficulty could also be regarded as a strength. Appel (2007) alludes to the "in-between" identities that learners often feel that they have when operating in another language. Hall (1995) touches upon a similar fragmentation of self, maintaining that becoming competent in a second language involves "ventriloquating" i.e. developing a range of voices. Might this otherness that the learner status promotes also be a licence to experiment? Rather like the masked reveller at carnival, a second language may allow a speaker to take risks that their first language cannot afford them. In this regard, it is worth remembering that an intensive language course such as that on which my research participants enrolled is a place where the short-term nature of the experience may bestow a sense of liberation. After all, it is probable that the participants will never encounter each other again.

The above points do not underestimate the difficulties that a learner faces in attempting not only to speak a TL but also play and have fun with it. However, they do suggest that such play may be less off-limits to the learner, even one at the lower end of the proficiency scale, than might at first appear to be the case.

2.6 HLP in the Second Language Classroom: Pedagogical and Research Perspectives

In exploring HLP's relationship with the second language learner, it is important to consider the setting in which such learning takes place—the language classroom. In looking at this particular context, both previous research and prevailing pedagogical practices need to be taken into consideration as the two inform each other.

2.6.1 HLP: A Neglected Dimension in Classroom Interaction

The nature of play as discussed so far in this chapter provides some clues as to why it has been under-researched in the language classroom setting. It has already been noted that play can have a subversive side

(Sect. 2.4.4) and that ambiguity lies at its heart (Sect. 2.4.2). Many people remember from their schooldays that if they heard laughter issuing forth from a classroom, it could indicate one of two things: the students were having a good time or the teacher was losing control (of course, the two were not necessarily mutually exclusive!). Given that researchers and practitioners in the field of SLA have, for the most part, been interested in the classroom as an arena for language acquisition, they may well dismiss laughter and humorous play as irrelevant or even detrimental to their research or pedagogical focus. The stepping-outside-the-norm nature of play may be regarded as a disruption, an aside from the prevailing business of learning the TL. Furthermore, the sometimes subversive and abrasive nature of play would seem to go against the grain of much SLA literature which, either implicitly or explicitly, advocates a non-combative, stress-free atmosphere as optimal for learning. Krashen (1982), for instance, argues for an anxiety-free learning environment, while even Tarone (2000), an advocate of play as facilitative of SLA, couches her support in terms of the way in which it lowers affective barriers. Yet, although play can be a means of relieving stress (as indeed evidenced later in my own data), this does not take account of the fact that it has more than one face and is not totally innocent and threat-free.

The neglect of play because of what could be viewed as its disruptive off-task nature may, in part, be due to contextual, function-based approaches to language learning which have often focussed on the transactional rather than the interpersonal dimension of communication: language use is the means to an end, a tool that is put to work in the execution of a task. The net result of the focus on the transactional is the promotion of a rather safe and restricted notion of pedagogical practice and the types of communication that need to be practised and mastered by the second language learner:

> A good deal of contemporary language teaching, then, deliberately turns its attention away from language play, and focuses more or less exclusively upon simulation of discourse of the 'bulge' - in which students go about their daily business, motivated by external pressures, doing the things they will have to do in the language, and interacting with people they have to negotiate their needs with along the way. This is of course what many of them are learning language for. (Cook 2000: 158)

Cook's description of the types of learners and communicative needs that contemporary classroom practices restrictively cater for seems, on the face of it, to apply rather neatly to my own research participants. They seem to operate in "the bulge", a term coined by Nessa Wolfson (1988) to describe that non-intimate social framework where participants are, ostensibly at least, on an equal footing and where identities, relations and meaning have to be negotiated with great care. Their motivations for improving their English come from the external pressures of their jobs and the need to go about their daily business in the language. On the face of it, these characteristics militate against the use of play, thus making its occurrence that much more significant.

Some might argue that my description of the worlds of language theory and pedagogical practice as sober and humourless is unfair. After all, open a typical course book for the teaching and learning of a language and you are likely to find games and fun activities among the explanations of particular structures and lexical groupings. However, such content should not be confused with the type of play which is the focus of this study. English language teaching publications, which are sold throughout the world, tend to avoid any hint of culturally sensitive controversy or subversion (e.g. Meddings 2006). Rinvolucri (1999: 14) talks of a bland EFL—English as a Foreign Language—subculture and "..the soft, fudgey, sub-journalistic, woman magaziney world of EFLese course materials". In such a world, there seems to be no room for the types of play which have ambiguity and subversion at their heart.

2.6.2 HLP Is More Than a Barometer of Language Proficiency

Since the turn of the twenty-first century, the place of humorous play in the language acquisition process, whether in the classroom or outside it, has belatedly been recognised by the research community (e.g. Cook 2000; Reddington and Waring 2015; Van Dam and Bannink 2017). Some now regard play as an excellent means by which learners can marry form and function through the natural child-like impulse to play with sounds, to revel in nonsense words and to indulge in make-believe (e.g. Cook 2000). However, although the research community has discovered the potential to be found in investigating humorous play among learners, it has done so rather narrowly in terms of its manifestations and its contexts of use. For one thing, research to date has tended to continue the SLA field's traditional focus on acquisition and evidence thereof. Thus, humorous language play has been analysed in terms of the extent to which it provides evidence of competence in the TL (Bell et al. 2014; Belz 2002; Cekaite and Aronsson 2005). This focus has, perhaps unsurprisingly, led researchers into analysing those elements of communication that are measurable in terms of acquisition, i.e. the formal features of the language (see my previous comment on this). In the area of language play, this means conceptualising the phenomenon as the native-like exploitation of the forms, meanings and sounds of words for humorous effect. This narrow understanding of what constitutes language play, especially if measured by native-speaker standards, is, as has already been discussed, one that seems to present particular problems for the learner. Indeed, seeing play primarily as evidence of proficiency highlights the product rather than the social process that brings it into being.

My own experience of the classroom suggests to me that this notion of play as a barometer of language competence does not tell the whole story. Although it could reasonably be hypothesised that there is a greater chance of encountering punning or other forms of wordplay among speakers with a high level of proficiency, this does not mean that the generation of humour in and through the language increases in relation to learners' mastery of it. Its manifestations may change as learners go up the proficiency scale, but what is missing from the literature is an exploration of the means speakers at the lower end of the proficiency scale use to find their way around their linguistic limitations in order to play. Indeed, although manifestations of play may take rather different forms among less competent speakers than their more proficient fellow learners or, indeed, native speakers, the nature of such play may not be so different in either its origins or its functions. It was this interest in how learners overcome their own linguistic limitations in order to play which led me to focus my research on learners at the lower end of the competence spectrum. Indeed, I wanted to find out whether play could be a means of overcoming, or at least coping with some of those very limitations.

2.6.3 HLP Is More Than a Single Event

One other limitation to the investigations to date on play in the language classroom relates to the fact that the classroom is itself a cultural entity (see Sect. 2.3). As such, its nature is fluid and ever-evolving. Therefore, the researcher cannot claim to understand it simply by observing it at any given moment. Similarly, the incremental nature of humorous play cannot be appreciated by documenting and analysing any given token of its usage. There are various studies in the literature on both L1 and L2 speakers which hint at the importance of this incrementality. In research into the language play of native speakers, Carter (2004: 100–108) identifies the importance of what he calls "pattern-forming" and "pattern-reforming" choices, the former building on previous contributions to the interaction and the latter breaking with them, but both helping in the collaborative activity of weaving an often-humorous conversational tapestry. However, Carter's findings are constrained by the fact that he draws on corpus data and, thus, the conversations he looks at appear as discrete episodes, lacking the perspective to look beyond the immediate conversation to how humorous language and references might have developed over time. Coates (2007) focuses on the importance of humour derived from shared knowledge and in-group norms within all-female social networks, norms which are established, in part, through the stories the women tell each other. Norrick (1993) too notes the importance of humorous personal anecdotes and in-group mocking in maintaining and developing relationships, where particular stories and ritualised behaviour become part of a group's culture, while Tannen (2006) shows how past arguments can be referred to and framed humorously to defuse tension.

Although there are a number of longitudinal studies of language play phenomena in SLA research such as Bell's two-year study of three research participants in the USA which documents the learners' growing sociocultural knowledge of their host country (Bell 2005: 202–203), the data provide snapshots of language play rather than revealing an incremental dimension to it. In other SLA studies, the focus is on play's possible role in the cognitive and linguistic development of the research participants, not its part in any development of an in-group cultural identity (Bongartz and Schneider 2003; DaSilva Iddings and McCafferty 2007; Davies 2003). Possibly because of this, the data tends to be presented in separate episodes which are not related in terms of the language items used by speakers. However, there are glimpses of the incremental nature of language play in some investigations. For example, in Pomerantz and Bell (2007), one of the students tries out new and playful meanings for the Spanish word *pues* as evidenced in various pieces of the data. In Cekaite and Aronsson's paper (2005), it is interesting to note how learners pick up and develop each other's funny contributions in a Swedish immersion class for young immigrant and refugee children. Victoria (2011) noted how particular words and phrases become significant for a group of immigrants on an Employment Preparation Programme in Canada, being used to trigger amusement and pleasure by evoking their shared experiences. However, even in this case, the development of such phrases as in-group identity markers is not traced in detail. Thus, their growing social significance is not plotted nor are any changes in the phrases themselves as they are reused in play episodes.

Finally, in considering the relationship between play and the classroom setting, it is worth considering the fact that the language classroom has the potential to offer its own unique opportunities for play. It is, after all, a frame-rich environment where simulation allows the learner to take on many different roles and try out many different voices. There can, therefore, more than one reality "at play" at any given moment. Furthermore, there can sometimes be a bit of give—or, dare I say it, play—between the different realities which may allow learners and their teacher humorously exploit these realities for their own ends.

2.7 Conclusion

The language classroom is a living, cultural entity which is made up of learners and their teacher who are themselves social actors. In the past, research in the field of SLA has tended to overlook this fact, concentrating on the end product of language acquisition rather than the social processes which facilitate (or inhibit) such acquisition. In recent years, that neglect has started to be rectified, with a growing interest in the classroom as a social arena. Given play's important role in people's social lives, it is perhaps inevitable that a focus on the social dimension to the language classroom should also lead to a growing interest in play in that context. However, research into play in the language classroom still largely concentrates on its occurrence as a means of measuring the acquisition of phonological and semantic knowledge of the TL rather than as a social phenomenon in its own right. As such, the focus has tended to be on wordplay rather than the broader phenomenon of HLP, the incremental, dialogical, often subversive play that is an everyday part of people's social lives. The importance of such play in the building of social relationships and group identities needs to be more systematically investigated in the classroom setting.

The nature of the language classroom and the role of the language learner, even one at the lower end of the proficiency spectrum, suggest that play can flourish in classroom interactions despite the clear challenges that learners face in participating in it. The next chapter looks at the particular research setting that features in this book, detailing how BizLang's pedagogical approach shapes not only the interactions within its classrooms but also the physical layout and equipment of those classrooms. In the course of this explanation, the significance and advantages of these features in relation to the research focus of HLP are commented on. In addition, the methodology is discussed together with its strengths and limitations, along with any measures that were taken in order to minimise or counter the latter.

References

Appel, J. (2007). Language teaching in performance. *International Journal of Applied Linguistics, 17*(3), 277–293.

Attardo, S. (1994). *Linguistic theories of humour.* Berlin: Mouton de Gruyter.

Bakhtin, M. M. (1981). *The dialogic imagination.* Austin: University of Texas Press.

Bateson, G. (1972). *Steps to an ecology of mind.* New York: Ballantine.

Beckoff, B., & Byers, J. A. (1998). *Animal play: Evolutionary, comparative and ecological perspectives.* Cambridge: Cambridge University Press.

Bell, N. D. (2005). Exploring L2 language play as an aid to SLL: A case study of humour in NS-NNS interaction. *Applied Linguistics, 26*(2), 192–218. https://doi.org/10.1093/applin/amh043.

Bell, N. D., & Pomerantz, A. (2014). Reconsidering language teaching through a focus on humor. *EuroAmerican Journal of Applied Linguistics and Languages, 1*(1), 31–47.

Bell, N. D., Skalicky, S., & Salsbury, T. (2014). Multicompetence in L2 language play: A longitudinal case study. *Language Learning, 64*(1), 72–102. https://doi.org/10.1111/lang.12030.

Belz, J. (2002). Second language play as representation of the multicompetent self in foreign language study. *Journal of Language, Identity and Education, 1*(1), 13–39.

Belz, J., & Reinhardt, J. (2004). Aspects of advanced foreign language proficiency: Internet-mediated German language play. *International Journal of Applied Linguistics, 14*, 324–362.

Block, D. (2007). *Second language identities*. London: Continuum.

Bongartz, C., & Schneider, M. L. (2003). Linguistic development in social contexts: A study of two brothers learning German. *The Modern Language Journal, 87*, 13–37. https://doi.org/10.1111/1540-4781.00176.

Broner, M., & Tarone, E. (2001). Is it fun? Language play in a fifth-grade Spanish immersion classroom. *Canadian Modern Language Review, 58*(4), 493–525. https://doi.org/10.3138/cmlr.58.4.493.

Brown, P., & Levinson, S. (1987). *Politeness*. Cambridge: Cambridge University Press.

Cameron, L. (2003). *Metaphor in educational discourse*. London: Continuum.

Carter, R. (2004). *Language and creativity: The art of common talk*. Abingdon: Routledge.

Cekaite, A., & Aronsson, K. (2005). Language play, a collaborative resource in children's L2 learning. *Applied Linguistics, 26*(2), 169–191. https://doi.org/10.1093/applin/amh042.

Chandler, D. (2002). *Semiotics: The basics*. London: Routledge. https://doi.org/10.1519/JSC.0b013e3181e7ff75.

Chiaro, D. (1992). *The language of jokes: Analysing verbal play*. London: Routledge.

Coates, J. (2007). Talk in a play frame: More on laughter and intimacy. *Journal of Pragmatics, 39*(1), 29–49. https://doi.org/10.1016/j.pragma.2006.05.003.

Cook, G. (1997). Language play, language learning. *ELT Journal, 51*(3), 224–231. https://doi.org/10.1093/elt/51.3.224.

Cook, G. (2000). *Language play, language learning.* Oxford: Oxford University Press.

Crystal, D. (1998). *Language play.* London: Penguin Books.

Crystal, D. (2003). *English as a global language.* Cambridge: Cambridge University Press.

DaSilva Iddings, A. C., & McCafferty, S. G. (2007). Carnival in a mainstream kindergarten classroom: A Bakhtinian analysis of second language learners' off-task behaviors. *Modern Language Journal, 91*(1), 31–44. https://doi.org/10.1111/j.1540-4781.2007.00508.x.

Davies, C. E. (2003). How English-learners joke with native speakers: An interactional sociolinguistic perspective on humor as collaborative discourse across cultures. *Journal of Pragmatics, 35*(9), 1361–1385. https://doi.org/10.1016/S0378-2166(02)00181-9.

Eckert, P., & McConnell-Ginet, S. (1992). Think practically and look locally: Language and gender as community-based practice. *Annual Review of Anthropology, 21*(1), 461–490. https://doi.org/10.1146/annurev.anthro.21.1.461.

Gardner, R. C., & Lambert, W. E. (1972). *Attitudes and motivation in second language learning.* Rowley, MA: Newbury House.

Gibbs, R. W. (1999). Taking metaphor out of our heads and putting it into the cultural world. In R. W. Gibbs & G. Steen (Eds.), *Metaphor in cognitive linguistics.* Amsterdam: John Benjamins.

Glenn, P. (2003). *Laughter in interaction.* Cambridge: Cambridge University Press.

Goffman, E. (1959). *The presentation of self in everyday life.* London: Penguin Books.

Goffman, E. (1974). *Frame analysis.* Boston: Northeastern University Press.

Gordon, C. (2008). A(p)parent play: Blending frames and reframing in family talk. *Language in Society, 37*(3), 319–349. https://doi.org/10.1017/S0047404508080536.

Gumperz, J. J. (1982). *Discourse strategies.* Cambridge: Cambridge University Press.

Hall, J. K. (1995). (Re)creating our worlds with words: A sociohistorical perspective of face-to-face interaction. *Applied Linguistics, 16*(2), 206–232. https://doi.org/10.1093/applin/16.2.206.

Harder, P. (1980). Discourse as self-expression—On the reduced personality of the second-language learner. *Applied Linguistics, 1,* 262–270.

Henig, R. M. (2008, February). Taking play seriously. *New York Times Magazine*. Retrieved from http://www.nytimes.com/2008/02/17/magazine/17play.html.

Holliday, A. (1999). Small cultures. *Applied Linguistics, 20*(2), 237–264.

Holmes, J. (2007). Making humour work: Creativity on the job. *Applied Linguistics, 28*(4), 518–537. https://doi.org/10.1093/applin/amm048.

Huizinga, J. (1970). *Homo Ludens*. London: Paladin.

Jenkins, J. (2007). *English as a Lingua Franca: Attitude and identity*. Oxford: Oxford University Press.

Kanno, Y. (2003). Imagined communities, school visions and the education of bilingual students in Japan. *Journal of Language, Identity and Education, 2,* 285–300.

Kramsch, C. (2006). From communicative competence to symbolic competence. *The Modern Language Journal, 90*(2), 249–252.

Krashen, S. D. (1982). *Principles and practice in second language acquisition*. Oxford: Pergamon.

Lakoff, G., & Johnson, M. (1980). *Metaphors we live by*. Chicago: University of Chicago Press.

Lantolf, J. (1997). The function of language play in the acquisition of L2 Spanish. In W. R. Glass & A. T. Perez-Leroux (Eds.), *Contemporary perspectives on the acquisition of Spanish* (pp. 3–24). Somerville, MA: Cascadilla Press.

Lave, J., & Wenger, E. (1991). *Situated learning: Legitimate peripheral participation*. Cambridge: Cambridge University Press.

Li, X. (2007). Souls in exile: Identities of bilingual writers. *Journal of Language, Identity and Education, 6,* 259–275.

Liang, X. (2006). Identity and language functions: High school Chinese immigrant students' code-switching dilemmas in ESL classrooms. *Journal of Language, Identity and Education, 5,* 143–167.

Meddings, L. (2006, January 20). Embrace the parsnip. *The Guardian*. Retrieved from https://www.theguardian.com/education/2006/jan/20/tefl4.

Morreall, J. (1987). *The philosophy of laughter and humour*. New York: State University of New York.

Norrick, N. R. (1993). *Conversational joking: Humour in everyday talk*. Bloomington: Indiana University Press.

Pellegrino, V. (2005). *Study abroad and second language use: Constructing the self*. Cambridge: Cambridge University Press.

Pomerantz, A., & Bell, N. D. (2007). Learning to play, playing to learn: FL learners as multicompetent language users. *Applied Linguistics, 28*(4), 556–578. https://doi.org/10.1093/applin/amm044.

Prodromou, L. (2007). Bumping into creative idiomaticity. *English Today, 23*(1), 14. https://doi.org/10.1017/S0266078407001046.

Rampton, B. (2007). Neo-Hymesian linguistic ethnography. *Journal of Sociolinguistics, 11*(5), 584–607.

Raskin, V. (1985). *Semantic mechanisms of humor.* Dordrecht, Holland: D. Reidel.

Reddington, E., & Waring, H. Z. (2015). Understanding the sequential resources for doing humor in the language classroom. *Humor— International Journal of Humor Research, 28*(1), 1–23.

Richards, J. C., & Rodgers, T. S. (2001). *Approaches and methods in language teaching.* Cambridge: Cambridge University Press.

Rinvolucri, A. (1999). The UK, ELFese sub-culture and dialect. *Folio, 5,* 12–40.

Rogerson-Revell, P. (2007). Humour in business: A double-edged sword: A study of humour and style shifting in intercultural business meetings. *Journal of Pragmatics, 39*(1), 4–28. https://doi.org/10.1016/j.pragma.2006.09.005.

Samuda, V., & Bygate, M. (2008). *Tasks in second language learning.* Basingstoke: Palgrave Macmillan.

Saussure, F. de. (1959). *Course in general linguistics.* London: Peter Owen.

Schmidt, R. (1983). Interaction, acculturation, the acquisition of communicative competence. In N. Wolfson & E. Judd (Eds.), *Sociolinguistics and TESOL.* Rowley, MA: Newbury House.

Seargeant, P. (2012). English in the world today. In *English in the world: History, diversity, change* (pp. 5–35). Abingdon: Routledge.

Seidlhofer, B. (2011). *Understanding English as a Lingua Franca.* Oxford: Oxford University Press.

Straehle, C. (1993). "Samuel?" "Yes, dear?" Teasing and conversational rapport. In D. Tannen (Ed.), *Framing in discourse* (pp. 210–230). New York: Oxford University Press.

Street, B. (1993). Culture is a verb: Anthropological aspects of language and cultural process. In D. Graddol, L. Thompson, & M. Byram (Eds.), *Language and culture: British studies in applied linguistics, 7.* Clevedon: Multilingual Matters.

Sullivan, P. (2000). Playfulness as mediation in communicative language teaching in a Vietnamese classroom. In J. P. Lantolf (Ed.), *Sociocultural theory and second language learning* (pp. 115–131). Oxford: Oxford University Press.

Swann, J., & Maybin, J. (2007). Introduction: Language creativity in everyday contexts. *Applied Linguistics, 28*(4), 491–496. https://doi.org/10.1093/applin/amm047.

Symons, D. (1978). The question of function: Dominance and play. In E. O. Smith (Ed.), *Social play in primates* (pp. 193–230). New York: Academic Press.

Tannen, D. (2006). Intertextuality in interaction: Reframing family arguments in public and private. *Text and Talk, 26*(4–5), 597–617. https://doi.org/10.1515/TEXT.2006.024.

Tarone, E. (2000). Getting serious about language play: Language play, interlanguage variation and second language acquisition. In B. Swierzbin, F. Morris, M. E. Anderson, C. Klee, & E. Tarone (Eds.), *Second language acquisition: Selected proceedings of the 1999 second language research forum* (pp. 31–54). Somerville, MA: Cascadilla Press.

Tarone, E. (2002). Frequency effects, noticing, and creativity. *Studies in Second Language Acquisition, 24*(2), 287–296. https://doi.org/10.1017/S0272263102002139.

Teutsch-Dwyer, M. (2002). [Re]constructing masculinity in a new linguistic reality. In A. Pavlenko, A. Blackledge, I. Piller, & M. Teutsch-Dwyer (Eds.), *Multingualism, second language acquisition and gender* (pp. 175–198). New York: Mouton de Gruyter.

Toolan, M. (2006). Telling stories. In J. Maybin & J. Swann (Eds.), *The art of English: Everyday creativity* (pp. 54–102). Basingstoke: Palgrave Macmillan.

Van Dam, J., & Bannink, A. (2017). The first English (EFL) lesson: Initial settings or the emergence of a playful classroom culture. In N. Bell (Ed.), *Multiple perspectives on language play* (pp. 245–280). Berlin: Walter de Guyter.

Victoria, M. (2011). *Building common ground in intercultural encounters: A study of classroom interaction in an employment preparation programme for Canadian immigrants*. The Open University.

Widdowson, H. G. (1998). The theory and practice of critical discourse analysis. *Applied Linguistics, 19*(1), 136–151. https://doi.org/10.1093/applin/19.1.136.

Wolfson, N. (1988). The bulge: A theory of speech behaviour and social distance. In J. Fine (Ed.), *Second language discourse: A textbook of current research*. Norwood, NJ: Ablex.

3

The Language Classroom: A Hothouse Where Play Can Germinate

We have seen in the last chapter how play among second language learners is a neglected area of research. Firstly, the social role of play in forging relationships and building a sense of community among such learners has received scant attention. How it manifests itself among speakers with low proficiency in the language is in particular need of investigation.

This chapter contextualises the research setting. Firstly, it provides an outline of the BizLang institution and its pedagogical approach and then links this information to my particular investigative aims, identifying the advantages that the setting affords these aims. The chapter moves on to the research approach taken. This approach draws, in part, on the traditions of ethnography and Conversation Analysis in that it recognises the fluid nature of context and the way in which it shapes and is shaped by talk. The analytical frameworks used here, as with any other, carry inherent risks and limitations as well as strengths, and these are identified and acknowledged in the course of the chapter.

© The Author(s) 2020
D. Hann, *Spontaneous Play in the Language Classroom*,
https://doi.org/10.1007/978-3-030-26304-1_3

3.1 The Research Setting: The BizLang Organisation

BizLang is a staff-owned private language school founded in 1965. From its beginnings, it has specialised in English language training for business people and employs teachers—or "trainers" in BizLang parlance—with a wide range of ages and experience.

The core activity of the company is EfB training. However, since the 1980s, more general communication skills courses have steadily grown and now make up about half of the organisation's revenue. This side of the organisation's activities encompasses skills for business including presentations, writing and negotiations, cross-cultural training and team working. Nowadays, many of BizLang's clients are native speakers of English who attend courses, for instance, to learn how to adapt their language to international contexts. Trainers are expected to be able to teach in these two main business areas (English-for-Business and communication skills) which means that the pedagogical approaches in one of the two areas influence and inform those in the other. At any one time, half the training is being delivered in the London offices and the rest in the premises of client companies around the world.

BizLang's in-house jargon reflects how it sees itself. Teachers are referred to as trainers for the same reasons that the classroom is the "training room" and BizLang dropped "school" from its title in the 1980s. It regards and sells itself as more of a service provider and consultancy firm than an educational institution. Its recruitment and training of staff is also indicative of this outlook. It does not demand formal teaching qualifications from the TEFL world or elsewhere as a prerequisite for joining, insisting rather on experience of and a feel for the business world. It runs its own five-week induction programme for new trainers and develops all its own training materials.

From the research point of view, private language organisations such as BizLang have tended to be overlooked in the research field and so the types of places where many learners worldwide study and acquire a second language are underinvestigated. The humour and play literature among L2 speakers is no exception in this regard. Researchers in

3 The Language Classroom: A Hothouse Where Play Can Germinate 51

this area have either explored the phenomenon beyond the classroom (e.g. Bell 2005) or in kindergarten (e.g. DaSilva Iddings and McCafferty 2007), school (e.g. Van Praag et al. 2017) or university (e.g. Petraki and Pham Nguyen 2016). This means that the focus has tended to be on children, teenagers and young adults rather than the over-25s that make up the majority of BizLang's intake. The average age of the 14 participating learners in the study for this book, for example, was 36.

3.1.1 The BizLang English for Business Course

The featured research took place in BizLang's "English-for-Business" (EfB) course which is open to participants from all sectors and nationalities. Course participants are sorted roughly by proficiency level into groups of no more than six—in practice, the group size tends to average out at about four. Although choosing to put together people of roughly equal proficiency in the language remains the most important criterion for constituting the course groups, there are other significant considerations. Among these, a good nationality mix is regarded as salient to the eventual success of a group. When practical, people of the same nationality are put into different groups, as are colleagues from the same company who may have booked together. The fact that the great majority of people in the course groups are strangers to each other and that they are not of the same nationality dovetails nicely with my research interests. It means that the group members who feature in this book had to establish their relationships from scratch exclusively in English and that they could not rely on obvious cultural common ground as a means for doing so. This is a fruitful backdrop for studying how play in a language other than the speakers' own is used to build relationships and forge group identity.

The duration of EfB open courses is also favourable from the research perspective. To a large extent, their length is dictated by the time which participants can dedicate to training away from their jobs—usually not very long at all. As a result, a typical group course is for five days. They can be as short as three days and the maximum length is two weeks (ten training days). In practical research terms, this allowed me the chance to investigate a group for the duration of its existence. Furthermore, the members of a group on an EfB course have long contact hours relative to their total stay. They are in class from 9 a.m. until 5.30 p.m. and are rarely out of each other's company. Of course, they interact in various contexts beyond the classroom—over lunch, in the lounge during coffee break, in the pub with their fellow learners, at the hotel or host family breakfast table, etc. However, given the long training hours, the classroom is where the group members spend the major slice of their time together. Thus, the research setting was a relatively enclosed one where the interactions between a group's members could be captured from the group's birth to its demise. As a result, its shared history could be recorded, and the extent to which that history was used to create reference points for play and the building of a common culture could be investigated.

3.1.2 The BizLang Classroom Setting

BizLang's EfB courses take place in training rooms which are designed for the purposes of teaching and learning and have, at most, six learners and one trainer. Unless participants are moved to another group at the beginning of the course, they remain together throughout. Also, if their course lasts for one week or less, they are usually allocated only one trainer for the duration of their stay. Furthermore, the physical environment, unlike the settings of most other classroom research, does not allow for what Maybin calls "unofficial spaces" (2006: 13)—those spaces where words are spoken or actions taken which the teacher may not notice. In the BizLang classroom, very little can be said that is not overheard by the trainer. This means that any language play takes place in a sanctioned arena. This makes it distinct from some of the other research into play in the language classroom which often occurs away from the gaze of authority (Broner and Tarone 2001; Cekaite and Aronsson 2005; DaSilva Iddings and McCafferty 2007; Pomerantz and Bell 2007). In the BizLang setting, power dynamics are particularly pertinent. While it is true that the interactional dynamics of an all-adult classroom such as that found in BizLang are typically rather different to those found among, say, a class full of inner-city teenagers (Rampton 2006), the issue of who has authority and how that is exercised is a real one in the all-adult context too, as any teacher of adults will verify. Although it might be expected that there are more overt and frequent challenges to authority in an urban school classroom than a training room peopled by motivated adults whose learning is often inextricably connected with their professional advancement, this does not mean that challenges do not occur in the latter context. With this in mind, how the subversive dimension of language play finds voice was of interest in my research. The power dimension in the context of my study was complicated by the fact that the learners, or at least their employers, are also paying customers. The intricate dynamics of these interactions and the role that subversive play has within them becomes particularly significant when they are acted out in front of the teacher as an officially recognised representative of the larger institution.

On the face of it, a disadvantage of such an intensive, hot-housing environment such as the BizLang classroom from my research viewpoint is that it does not seem to be naturally conducive to play, something which would be expected to be more likely to occur in more informal, relaxed settings (Carter 2004: 165). It is, after all, the place where the work of improving the learners' English takes place. The world of work is conventionally contrasted with that of play, yet Holmes' investigations (2000, 2007) among native speakers seem to suggest that this sharp divide may be misleading. Her research indicates that humorous play can relieve tension and energise discussion, suggesting that the two are perhaps not as mutually exclusive as some might think and, indeed, as Cook posits (2000: 150), may overlap. So, the occurrence of play in the type of environment that BizLang provides is informative in terms of the work/play dimension.

3.1.3 The Typical Profile of BizLang EfB Course Participants

From the outset, BizLang sought to establish its own niche in the market by offering English language courses exclusively for business people. This was useful for my investigative purposes because the research

54   D. Hann

community has tended to overlook those learners with what Gardner and Lambert (1972) would call an "instrumental" motivation, such as business people, who need English for their international interactions and transactions. This is a puzzling neglect given the fact that function-based approaches to language learning tend to view communication in transactional terms (see Sect. 2.6). It is also a significant omission considering that English is used so often and by so many in international meetings, conferences and telecommunications in the fields of commerce, politics, science and academia. Indeed, business people, politicians, scientists and academics frequently speak English together without a native speaker participating. It is claimed that only one in four users of English can now be classified as a native speaker (Crystal 2003). Some assert (e.g. Jenkins 2007: 4) that if we accept that language is shaped by its contexts of use (Bakhtin 1981), then it follows that the development of English is, in part, in the hands of its L2 speakers. The SLA community, therefore, needs to investigate those contexts, virtual and physical, where international communication through English as a Lingua Franca (ELF) takes place. In this regard, BizLang attracts clients from all over the world. Many of them come on courses because they work for multinationals whose company language is English. Others need to talk to suppliers, clients and subcontractors from across the world. As well as speaking the language on their business travels, they also use it through the media of teleconferences, video-conferences and, of course, email. While my study focuses on the research participants using English in a context other than their professional one, it nonetheless provides some insight into interactions between speakers who inhabit that globalised milieu where ELF is the medium of communication.

Because of the nature of the courses on offer, they are not deemed suitable for beginners in English. Those at an advanced level of proficiency tend to opt for BizLang's communication skills courses (which also attract native speakers). As a result, the vast majority of those who enrol on the open EfB courses fall into a category range from high to low intermediate (B+ to D− in BizLang terms). If measured in terms of the widely recognised standard of the European Framework of

Reference for Languages (CEFR),[1] they would fall somewhere between the A2 Basic User who can understand and communicate information on familiar matters and the B1 Independent User who is able to express opinions and ideas on topics with which he or she feels at home. Even for those at the top end of this spectrum, the type of wordplay that indicates a native-like control of the language would prove challenging. For those at the bottom end, it is well-nigh impossible. It is these less proficient course participants who were the focus for my research as they can throw light on how learners play in and through the language without necessarily being able to exploit the structures and potential meanings that are open to the advanced learner or the L1 speaker.

3.1.4 Situating BizLang's Pedagogical Approach

It is important, given that this research is concerned with the ways in which learners play with language, to look at the resources made available to them in their classroom environment which might be used for this purpose. I am not primarily referring to the physical objects and equipment that can be found there (these are mentioned later in this chapter), but to the communicative opportunities that the classroom setting provides. These opportunities, to some extent, are determined by course content and the types of interactions and activities that are either permitted or encouraged within the four walls of the training room. They are inevitably and inextricably linked to the pedagogical approach that is taken on any given course. For this reason, the generalisable elements of this approach and their relevance to my research are discussed.

Partly as a result of the fact that BizLang offers both language and communication skills courses, it sees the two as interlinked, and this is reflected in its teaching methodology and course content. In this sense, BizLang's approach corresponds to a heterogeneous competence model where, according to Ellis (1985: 77) "..the user's knowledge of language rules is interlocked with his knowledge of when, where, and

---

[1]For more information on the Council of Europe's CEFR descriptors, see https://rm.coe.int/cefr-companion-volume-with-new-descriptors-2018/1680787989 (accessed 24.4.19).

56   D. Hann

with whom to use them". Indeed, the BizLang end-of-course report on each participant's progress includes a grade for "communicative competence", the definition of which seems to suggest that it corresponds closely to Hymes's (1971) concept of the same name where competence in a language is primarily about appropriateness rather than grammatical correctness.

The brevity of BizLang's courses has already been mentioned, and the fact that they aim to make a significant difference to their participants' language acquisition in a matter of days, a process that ordinarily can be measured in months and years, means that the institution's course content and pedagogical approach are largely driven by the pragmatic constraints of time. This, to some degree, makes it difficult to categorise BizLang's approach in theoretical terms.

Despite eschewing rigid programmes, BizLang courses reflect a pedagogy with its own viewpoint on language acquisition, however implicit this viewpoint may be. On the rare occasions the organisation has couched its teaching approach in theoretical terms (for example, during its annual retraining programmes), it has sometimes made reference to David Kolb's Learning Cycle (1984). Kolb is an American educational psychologist whose ideas, it is interesting to note, seem to hold more sway in business circles than in the TEFL world,[2] reflecting to some degree BizLang's own hybrid culture that lies somewhere between business training and language teaching.

Kolb believes that concrete experience is vital in the learning process. It is not surprising, therefore, that his own training programmes, e.g. Kolb et al. (1991), have role-play at their centre. In BizLang too, because the aim is to provide clients with the means to be more effective in their jobs within days, practising through role-play the types of situations that they meet in English has always formed a central part of its courses, both in EfB and communications skills. The company's website makes this clear:

---

[2]See, for example, www.businessballs.com/kolblearningstyles.htm (accessed 24.4.19).

3 The Language Classroom: A Hothouse Where Play Can Germinate   57

We constantly simulate the English-speaking environment that you work in, so that you're constantly practising the English you need – not the language of a textbook.

At BizLang, recorded role-play is central to the EfB course and is followed by feedback from the trainer and, subsequently, the learning outcomes from these role-plays may well be tested out in further role-plays with a similar or more challenging dynamic.

In terms of the investigative focus of this book, the predominance of role-play in the typical classroom schedule at BizLang is significant. In Vygotskyian terms (1986), it can be seen as a means to learn through play-as-rehearsal. It has already been noted (Sect. 2.4.1) that play-as-rehearsal and play-as-fun should be differentiated (Lantolf 1997: 4–5). However, this does not mean that they do not come together at all. The fact that play-as-rehearsal is a prominent frame in many language classrooms and particularly the BizLang one makes the relationship between HLP and the frames of reference operative at any given moment a potentially fruitful area for research. Frameworks of interpretation (Goffman 1974) are particularly rich at such moments where, in answer to the question "what's going on here?", the participants could answer that they were participating in an English lesson or negotiating a contract. The extent to which they exploit the give or play between such frameworks is one of the investigative avenues explored in this book. Furthermore, feedback sessions allow the learners to revisit and relive role-plays which afford the opportunity to play upon previous play.

In some ways, the importance of role-play in the BizLang course suggests something akin to the content of a task-based pedagogical approach (Long and Crookes 1992; Skehan 1998). However, in other ways, BizLang's course content has more in common with that of a structural syllabus. A typical teaching programme includes grammar "slots" where the focus is put upon particular aspects of grammatical structure. Language drilling is also regarded as an important part of BizLang EfB courses.[3] Being able to "cue" and drill particular language

---

[3] A British Council inspection in 2012 noted the prominence of language drilling as a particular characteristic of BizLang's approach and further noted the organisation's use of a language laboratory for drilling purposes.

structures is valued as an essential skill among the teaching staff. The language that is drilled often arises from role-plays. The trainers are therefore expected to think on their feet when setting up and practising particular drills. This language is reinforced in the language laboratory which includes a large drilling element. This rather sets BizLang apart from other organisations in the sector where the language laboratory is either defunct or is designed primarily for student-directed self-study using pre-recorded materials. BizLang's approach in this regard puts one in mind of the audiolingual method (Richards and Rodgers 2001). What is interesting pedagogically is that, in contrast to the role-play exercise, pattern and substitution drilling tends to de-contextualise and objectivise the language.

This drilling practice links to my research interest in two ways. Firstly, language play, like drilling, often seems to have an objectivising and distancing effect with regard to the language that it uses. Despite the fact that targeted language is cued in drills, it is largely de-contextualised by the very process of drilling it. It could be argued that this takes semantic meaning out of language and reduces it to its sounds and structures. This decoupling of semantic meaning and form echoes some of the ways in which children play with language as they acquire it (e.g. Cook 2000: 14–17; Ely and McCabe 1994; Inkelas 2006; Kuczaj 1983). It also might encourage learners who in some ways share a child's fresh perspective on the TL (see the discussion of the parallels between the comic and the language learner in Sect. 2.5.2), to play with its sounds and forms. The second reason why drilling links to the focus of this study is that it involves repetition. As research among both children (see the previous references) and adults shows (Carter 2004; Coates 2007; Crystal 1998; Tannen 2007), repetition is often a prominent feature of play.

The nature of interaction in the BizLang class can, like most language classes, be very different depending on the activity which is taking place at any one moment. The structure of talk in what Seedhouse (2004) would call "fluency contexts" is very different from those in "form-and-accuracy contexts". Role-play along with things like general discussion would fall into the former category. Grammar, drilling, listening exercises and, to a degree, feedback from role-play would constitute the latter. In terms of my research, the prominence of play in particular phases of the class is of interest. Does it occur more often in less controlled phases of interaction? Does it occur in those moments where, ostensibly at least, the trainer has a tight rein on the management of talk?

A further area of interest with regard to HLP is a feature which the BizLang training room shares with most language classrooms: it is replete with language which is regarded as erroneous and is subject to repair. Repair carries a risk to the learner's face (Goffman 1959)—the preferred image that they want to present to the world—both for the interlocutor whose utterance is being repaired and for the person repairing it (usually the teacher). Research into play among L2 learners in language classrooms suggests that error and repair can be sources for play (e.g. Cekaite and Aronsson 2005), and this is another rich seam for my investigation.

In sum, it is difficult to categorise BizLang in terms of one recognised pedagogical approach. Like most language teaching institutions, it draws, with varying degrees of conscious intent, on different frameworks and methodologies. However, there are elements of its English for Business course that, at least in combination, other practitioners in the TEFL world would find unusual: the prominence it gives to role-play, its eschewal of mainstream TEFL publications in favour of in-house classroom materials, its insistence on drilling, its long contact hours and, finally, its own pedagogical terminology that expresses a particular training room environment. It is an environment which opens up various potentially interesting areas for investigation with regard to HLP.

3.1.5 The Training Rooms and Equipment

Unsurprisingly, the classroom equipment at BizLang reflects both the expectations of its particular market and the types of activities that take place in the training rooms. As role-play forms such an important part of the courses, each room is fitted with recording equipment. In each, there is a digital video camera as well as the means to make audio recordings. There is also a telephone which can be used to record simulated inter-room calls. All recordings transfer directly onto a computer in every room. Having the classrooms wired up in this way presented me as researcher with obvious logistical advantages. Recording was a routine part of the training programme and learners soon became accustomed to it, thus reducing the effects of "the observer's paradox"—the fact that the observer/researcher by their very presence may alter the behaviour of others (Labov 1972: 209).

3.1.6 The Research Advantages of the BizLang Classroom Setting

The previous discussion shows that BizLang classroom is a fruitful setting for exploring humorous language play. Private language institutions form an important but overlooked sector in the provision of language education. Furthermore, the relatively enclosed nature of the BizLang training room facilitates an investigation into the birth and development of a community of learners, and the role of humorous language play in that process. On the other hand, a number of factors seem to militate against an indulgence in play: the intensive nature of the courses; the multicultural and multilingual make-up of the groups; the fact that course participants are unknown to each other beforehand; nearly all interactions are observable by the teacher; and the course participants who feature in the research have not yet attained a particularly high level of proficiency. However, I maintain that these factors actually make evidence of play much more significant, revealing the strength of the ludic impulse, even in a seemingly unpromising setting.

3.2 Methodology

HLP, with its associated social functions of identity and relationship negotiation, is embedded in the push and pull of everyday interaction. The focus of this book lies in the manifestations and effects of such play in the classroom. It attempts to capture what happens as learners and

3 The Language Classroom: A Hothouse Where Play Can Germinate   61

teachers negotiate the social and linguistic challenges of the second language learning environment. In the light of these considerations, one of the research's main concerns was to ensure a design that did not compromise or unduly interfere with the usual daily occurrences to be found in that setting. It therefore eschewed the option of setting up particular situations (e.g. Davies 2003) or activities (e.g. Belz 2002) as part of its research design.

In its attempt to capture the social universe created through moment-to-moment interactions and its exploration of the small scale in a search for generalisable truths, the research design drew on the tradition of ethnography, itself a rather broad term encompassing a wide range of methodological features (Hammersley 1994: 1). However, many of the elements that Hammersley identifies as ethnographic in nature (1994: 1–2) can be found in the approach that was undertaken in this research:

* it concerns itself with the analysis of empirical data; this data is from the real world context of a language classroom;
* the data is primarily gathered from observation and recording of research participants in the natural course of their learning programme;
* the focus is relatively small scale, involving a small number of classroom groups;
* the analysis of data involves the interpretation of the meanings and functions of a particular aspect of human behaviour (language play) and is qualitative rather than quantitative in nature.

This approach, influenced by the ideas of Grounded Theory (Glaser and Strauss 1967), is, among other things, characterised by a constant movement back and forth between the formulating of ideas and the collecting and analysing of data. Thus, the whole research process is not, as the written layout of this, or any other, academic research publication might indicate, neatly staged and sequential in nature, but involves the continuous modification and alteration of each and every phase of the process throughout the investigation.

However, it should be pointed out that ethnographic approaches often involve the interviewing of participants in order to obtain their perspectives on events (Hammersley and Atkinson 2007: 110–114). For various compelling reasons, interviews with the learners were not carried out in this research, although other means were used to help triangulate my findings (Sect. 3.2.4).

As well as the ethnographic tradition, the research also draws, to a degree, upon Conversation Analysis (CA) (Sacks et al. 1974). CA focuses on the structure of talk and how participants manage their interactions. One of its principles is that interaction is context-shaped and context-renewing. In other words, talk is part of context and cannot be separated from it. In practical terms, CA looks at such aspects as turn-taking and topic management. This is of particular interest to my investigation given that within the language classroom, as mentioned previously, different activities are characterised by very different structures of talk. As HLP is usually something which, by its nature, steps outside the norm and is, thus, potentially disruptive of the usual flow of interaction (see Sect. 2.4.1), CA is a useful means for throwing light on HLP's effect on the structure of talk and how it impacts on social relations.

3.2.1 My Position as Researcher

The BizLang training room is an environment of which I have been a part for about two decades. The wider institutional culture that surrounds it and influences so much of what happens within it is one with which I have been imbued for most of my teaching career. Particularly given that ethnography grew from the impulse to understand and inform the researcher's compatriots about other, exotic societies (Hammersley 1994), this begs the question of how I was able to achieve the requisite researcher's distance that would allow me to look at the context afresh.

There is, of course, always a tension in all such investigations between the need, on the one hand, to be part of the research context in order to understand its social mores and blend in with its culture and, on the other, to retain a certain distance so that a degree of objectivity is possible. Furthermore, as Rampton (2007: 591–592) points out, there are

3 The Language Classroom: A Hothouse Where Play Can Germinate   63

distinct advantages to knowing the context well: it reduces the danger of stereotyping that an outsider's perspective might encourage; it means that time is saved in exploring the rudiments of the social milieu under scrutiny. In addition, researching is itself a distancing process. For example, the acts of watching and listening to recordings and transcribing conversation provide a different perspective on what is happening at any given moment. They are what van Lier (1988: 37) describes as "estrangement devices".

The developmental history of this particular research needs to be mentioned here as my role actually changed in the course of it. With my pilot study (see below), I simply sat in on and observed a group undertaking a simulated negotiation for about an hour. With the next observation session which I undertook, I again assumed the role of observer for one morning (about four hours) of another group's course which encompassed a number of learning activities. In neither my pilot project nor the second observation, did I know the participants prior to sitting in on them. With the third observation which I undertook (again, a morning's observation of a group), I decided that it would be better to have an active role within the class. The BizLang training context is a particularly intimate one where there are never more than seven people in the classroom at any one time (Sect. 3.1.2). Despite the fact that learners on a BizLang course are used to being observed and recorded (Sect. 3.1.5), I felt that the natural flow of events would be least disrupted and the effects of the observer's paradox minimised if I had a designated role within the teaching and learning activities taking place and I was already known to the participants. So, I sat in on a group I had previously taught. Furthermore, I took on the role of "stooge". This is a term used by both trainers and course participants to refer to another member of staff who can take part in a role-play meeting or telephone call to provide the group with the challenge of interacting with someone with native-speaker proficiency other than their trainer. The stooge often helps the trainer in subsequently providing supplementary feedback to the group on their performances during role-play. Finally, in the case study which lies at the heart of my data analysis, I was simultaneously the teacher and researcher for the three days of the group's existence.

So, in the competing needs to be part of the community which I was researching and, at the same time, to retain a distance from it, I surrendered, by stages, the need for distance in favour of integration. For example, taking an active part in the teaching meant that I was, for the most part, unable to take notes to provide supplementary insights into the recorded data. However, I would argue that the most important distancing process in the investigation lay in the analysis of the data which I had collected. Furthermore, being an integral part of the social interactions I witnessed gave me a privileged insight into their significance and brought back to me salient aspects of the interactions when I replayed them soon after.

3.2.2 De-limiting the Context

In acknowledging the importance of context in shaping the actions and utterances of human beings, the researcher is left with a problem: that of attempting to de-limit the seemingly infinite number of contextual factors that could be taken into account, even in the restricted environment of the classroom. In aiming to do this, a useful starting point is to acknowledge the centrality of talk to my research concerns. Indeed, talk is seen here as context-shaping, transforming the setting and the social relations within it (Bauman and Briggs 1990: 68). From such a viewpoint, context becomes a fluid concept, something which it is within the powers of the human agents present to shape and change. Furthermore, the verbal and non-verbal actions which take place are highly complex and interrelated. Attempting to separate them out as component parts may of itself distort them. However, some form of selection must take place to make the data manageable. In doing so, a simple fact should firstly be acknowledged which sometimes goes unmentioned in social research: investigators are themselves experienced social actors. As such, their noticing of certain phenomena in the stream of experience is itself significant. In investigating something like HLP in everyday interactions, the analyst necessarily has to be selective in deciding what is noteworthy. Even when asking participants for their own perspectives on recorded interactions, it is the analyst who,

3 The Language Classroom: A Hothouse Where Play Can Germinate 65

for practical purposes, usually preselects those exchanges which are of significance. This is especially true in the field of HLP where instances of such play may not occur for long stretches of natural interaction. As Holmes (2000: 163) points out in explaining the research methodology she employs in her own research:

> The analyst's identification of instances of humour is a crucial component in the analytical process [...] Instances of humour in this analysis are utterances which are identified by the analyst, on the basis of paralinguistic, prosodic and discoursal clues.

Of course, language is both the medium and subject matter of instruction in the classroom and the main means for accomplishing play, even for those learners who have little proficiency in the TL. One means of identifying relevant data in this investigation is to look for the various surface features of language which seem to occur during language play episodes. Goffman (1974: 42) observes that there is a great deal of repetitiveness in a play frame; Coates (2007: 43) identifies syntactic repetition while Carter (2004: 89–112) notes the use of neologisms and tropes more commonly associated with literary texts. Research in the field of SLA echoes some of the findings from investigations into native speaker interactions. Broner and Tarone (2001: 371) note unusual lexical choices such as neologisms while other researchers (Bell 2005; Belz and Reinhardt 2004) demonstrate how proficient L2 speakers are able to playfully exploit the forms of the language.

However, looking for such surface features would necessarily preclude those learners (probably the majority) who lack the expertise for a native-like exploitation of forms, yet are nevertheless able to play in the TL. The features of utterances do not alone constitute evidence of anything. It could be argued that this is especially true when investigating HLP. Not only does the deniability of much playful language use allow something to be said but not said (North 2007: 553), but "humour often lies in the gap between what is said and what is meant" (Coates 2007: 32). People derive pleasure from understanding each other without having to articulate everything being communicated. Play can only be so classified if the participants in it regard it as such.

This leaves a problem. It means that an "etic" classification of linguistic features, i.e. one based on criteria formulated outside the group, is, on its own, inadequate. However, an "emic" perspective (Cook 2000: 67)—one formulated by the participants themselves—was, in my research context, practically impossible, given the time and other constraints which course participants were under (see Sect. 3.2.4). However, one means of identifying whether the participants regarded particular exchanges as playful was by pinpointing moments of laughter. Indeed, unsurprisingly, this is a method used by a number of researchers in this area to find significant episodes of play (e.g. Bell 2005: 198; Cekaite and Aronsson 2005: 174). Although laughter is a useful pointer to play, it is, of course, by no means foolproof as a detection device as it may, for example, merely signal support or something less benign such as embarrassment or even anger.

Fortunately, it has already been noted (Sect. 2.4.1) that play, being a stepping away from the norm, is usually carefully signalled by its instigator through contextualisation cues (Goffman 1974: 45). Marked or contrasting prosody can be good indicators of such episodes (Bell 2005: 199; Broner and Tarone 2001: 363) as can smiling (Bell 2007: 39). An expansive and exaggerated body language may also indicate that a play frame is operative (DaSilva Iddings and McCafferty 2007: 42). Indeed, intuition suggests that the latter would be a very useful resource for learners needing means other than language to signal play. A further indication of play is that it can affect the structure of talk, disrupting the normative features of a particular type of classroom activity. For instance, the learner may "topicalise" (van Lier 1988: 152)—assume control of the topic of communication—at a moment where, ordinarily, he or she would not have the right to do so. Another aspect which facilitates the identification of play is the fact that it has a tendency, as already mentioned, to occur in clusters (Carter 1999: 199–200; Holmes 2007: 530; Norrick 1993: 42). This seems to arise from an impulse to join in the fun and as a signal of camaraderie. Furthermore, Goffman (1974: 43) posits that, in humans as in animals, the openings and closings of play frames are usually cued

3 The Language Classroom: A Hothouse Where Play Can Germinate   67

clearly in order to avoid misunderstandings. The research cited above indicates the importance of contextualisation cues in signalling when people are entering and then participating in a play frame. Indeed, what research there has been into play in a second language indicates that participants can identify and appreciate such cues, even when the accompanying humour is either not, or only partially, understood (Bell 2007: 377).

In sum, although the researcher has to be wary of the risks in identifying play—contextualisation cues do not necessarily carry the same meanings across cultures (Gumperz 1982) and body language especially is open to a great degree of interpretation (Adolphs and Carter 2007: 136)—there are strong indicators which can help him or her in the task. Play episodes are usually cued by the play instigator. Their initiation and development can be recognised also through the reactions of the others present and evidence of changes in the structure of talk. In addition, play tends to cluster. It is, perhaps, less easy to identify the ending of a play episode, precisely because of the clustering that can take place. However, signals, verbal or otherwise, that indicate a return to the primary activity can usually be discerned. Also the structure of talk may well return to the typical patterns of interaction that were operative before play disrupted them. In other words, normal service can be seen to be resumed.

Another criterion for selecting particular episodes for analysis needs to be mentioned. At the outset of this book, I explained how my interest in investigating HLP among my language learners was triggered in part by noticing their laughter inducing in-group references. The event or exchange from which particular references grow need not necessarily be particularly playful in its origin. Therefore, in tracing the development of incremental play, some exchanges only gain significance with hindsight. Therefore, the selection process was, in part, a retrospective one. In this regard, it should be mentioned that, in the investigative process, certain patterns begin to emerge such that an exchange can become more significant in the light of previous exchanges noted in other groups and at other times.

Group laughter and clustered stretches of joint banter and fun with the language indicate a successful play frame. However, the featured research also finds interest in those moments where an attempt at humour fails. In exploring how learners are able to have fun with language despite a lack of common sociocultural reference points and an incomplete control of the language, it is instructive to investigate failures as well as successes (Bell 2007). Surface features to pinpoint such failures are not always easy to find. However, discordances, asymmetries and arrhythmic exchanges often signal communicative breakdowns of this sort. It has to be acknowledged, however, that by their nature, some failures in humorous play may well go unnoticed.

3.2.3 The Practicalities of Data Collection

In the featured research, given the potential importance of gestures and smiles, video was used to capture relevant interactions. The one exception to this is my pilot study which was audio-recorded but, nonetheless, contains material pertinent to the research. Indeed, there was one particularly important body gesture in that recorded meeting (Sect. 4.2.3) which brought home the importance of using video and convinced me to switch from audio-only to video recording. As already discussed, the BizLang classroom already has video and audio installed in the training rooms.

Despite the advantageous environment for collecting data, this does not, of itself, eradicate the ever-present problem of the observer's paradox. However, even in this regard, the BizLang classroom offers advantages. Firstly, as mentioned previously, recording learners does not impinge significantly on the classroom routine; secondly, the context is one in which they expect to be scrutinised and recorded and indeed they soon get used to it, regardless of whether they are being researched or not. Typically, the BizLang group is observed by people in addition to their trainer and other group members. On the very first day of the course, a member of the teaching team will come and sit in on each class on the course to ascertain whether the group configuration is optimal. The learners are also frequently exposed to a stooge (Sect. 3.2.1). The group's trainer will also take notes when, for example, watching a simulated meeting, the notes forming the basis for

3 The Language Classroom: A Hothouse Where Play Can Germinate   69

the subsequent feedback session. Furthermore, the group is recorded on a daily basis when taking part in role-plays such as meetings or telephone calls.

Not only do the learners become used to being observed and assessed in the normal course of events, but the context also allows the investigator a certain flexibility of role that blurs the already unclear divide between participant and non-participant researchers (Atkinson and Hammersley 1998). All the above allow the classroom to be investigated in its most natural state, although, of course, the very act of investigating a particular context does, in however small a way, change that context.

3.2.4 Obtaining Other Perspectives

Understanding human behaviour always involves interpretation and is thus necessarily subjective. One means of counteracting the inherent dangers of overinterpreting the collected data is through investigator triangulation (Janesick 1998: 46). With this in mind, I recruited one of my BizLang colleagues, Harriet (a pseudonym), at the outset of the research to help in reviewing the raw data. In addition to this, on two occasions, BizLang arranged for a number of my other teaching and non-teaching colleagues to spend a morning looking at preselected extracts of the collected data in order to provide their perspectives on the exchanges they saw and heard. Elements from these have been incorporated into my research findings. Given that there is no absolute truth in any investigative pursuit, especially one involving the inter-subjective world of human relations and interactions, incorporating different perspectives into the findings helps towards what van Lier (van Lier 1988: 46) calls "truth-as-agreement".

Informal interviews with the teachers of the target groups assisted in providing insights into aspects of group dynamics and its emergent culture. These occurred during breaks immediately after the recordings. When, on subsequently viewing the data, I had further questions, I asked the teachers when the opportunity arose.

In terms of the comments I received from my BizLang colleagues, it is worth mentioning that, for the most part, they were only aware of my research topic in the broadest of terms, that is, they knew I was investigating humorous play in the classroom. There was an advantage in hearing comments from other colleagues whose insights were not coloured by my developing research ideas. On the other hand, Harriet was given a greater insight into my developing ideas and was, for example, aware of the importance of the concept of framing to my research.

Despite the importance of the learner participants' perspectives, after some thought, it was decided not to interview them about the data. The reasons for this are primarily practical. Firstly, asking learners to view and comment on recordings of themselves while on course would have been a time-consuming business. Given the tight training schedule, making the space for such interviews was well-nigh impossible. Secondly, even if it had been possible, asking learners to provide metalinguistic and psychological insights in English about the interactions would be beyond the capabilities of those at the lower range of language competency. The option of bringing in interpreters would also have been very difficult in terms of logistics and budget, bearing in mind that the target groups were made up of people with different first languages. In addition, it could be argued that no one is necessarily a privileged commentator on their own behaviour. In the end, the validity of the interpretations found herein resides with the readers of this book, who must decide whether they ring true and resonate with their own experiences (Tannen 2005: 49–50).

Episodes which were identified as significant in terms of HLP were transcribed.

3.2.5 Transcription Conventions

In establishing the transcription conventions (see Appendix), my objective was to make the transcripts reader-friendly, including only those features which were salient in capturing the playful dynamic in the interactions. I do not, for instance, attempt to encapsulate the participants' wide range of pronunciations of English words, especially as these had no bearing on the play which took place. In view of the fact that laughter is an important feature in my selected episodes, after some thought, I decided to follow Du Bois et al. (1993) in using "@" to represent it. The advantages of using this symbol is that, unlike conventions such as "((laughter))", it allows a representation of the syllables and duration of laughter, showing, for example, where it overlaps with talk. Furthermore, "laughing voice", often a cue for play, is easily represented by "<@ text>".

3.2.6 Relevant Information on the Research Participants

As previously mentioned, the main focus of this research is on those learners at the lower end of the proficiency spectrum. Furthermore, a good nationality mix was important so as to ensure that shared cultural norms among a particular class of learners were minimal. These were the main criteria in deciding which open course English for Business learners to observe. Other factors were primarily dictated by practicalities such as my own and other people's availability. The details of the research participants, whose names have all been changed for the purposes of this research, are set out below in the chronological order in which they were recorded:

- Group A consisted of four learners and their teacher, Harriet, who were audio-recorded on their final afternoon of a five-day course. They were classified as D/E in BizLang terms, putting them towards the bottom end of the low intermediate scale. The group, the details of whose jobs and companies I have removed, consisted of:
  - Dieter, a German attending the course privately.
  - Koji, a Japanese sales manager for a pharmaceutical company.
  - Antoine, a French administrator for an engineering company.
  - Mario, an Italian regional sales director for a pharmaceutical company.

- Group B was made up of five learners and was video recorded. They too were classified as D/E and were recorded on the morning of their ninth day of a ten-day course. They were taught by Ray (again, a pseudonym), an experienced BizLang colleague. The group consisted of:

  - Thomas, a German technical manager in a chemical company.
  - Viktor, a Ukrainian regional manager for an agro-sciences company.
  - Takeshi, a Japanese import manager for a pharmaceutical company.
  - Michele, an Italian trainee lawyer.
  - Andrei, a Russian biologist in an agro-sciences company.

- Group C had three members and were video recorded on the final morning of a one-week course. They were deemed to be D level which makes them a shade more proficient than the previous two groups. They had been taught for the first three days by me and then by Harriet. The members were:

  - Joseph, a French/Senegalese test engineer for an engineering company.
  - Sandro, an Italian manager for a family firm with various commercial interests.
  - Bilel, a Tunisian project manager for an engineering company.

- Group D consisted of two learners, video recorded on the second and third days of their three-day group course. I taught the pair at the same time as recording them. They were deemed to be at C/D level. They were:

  - Juan, a Spanish Business Intelligence Unit manager for an IT consultancy firm.
  - Marek, a Czech CEO for an international construction company.

My recordings of the last of these groups (Juan and Marek) form the basis of the case study which features in Chapters 6 and 7.

3 The Language Classroom: A Hothouse Where Play Can Germinate

All the requisite care was taken to ensure that ethical principles were upheld and all the participants were anonymised, and personal information which conceivably identifies the participants was removed.

None of the participants had met before their arrival at BizLang, despite the fact that Viktor and Andrei worked for the same company, as did Joseph and Bilel. This is not unusual given that many course participants work for big multinational companies. It is noteworthy here that all the learners (although not all the teachers) were male. This did not form part of the original research design but was the result of happenchance. As alluded to later in this chapter and discussed at more length in the book's conclusion, this is obviously a factor in ascertaining the generalisability of my findings.

The recordings of the first three groups amount to about eight hours of classroom time. These were used primarily to identify discernible patterns of play behaviour. The recordings of the pair of learners amount to about sixteen hours of classroom time, encompassing all the training that took place on the second and third days of their course. This data was used not only to find commonalities with that of previous recordings, but also to trace the incremental nature of any playful episodes and the role such play had in developing the participants' shared reference points, and their relationship with their trainer and each other (see Chapter 7). The pair of learners form the main focus of the book.

I also talked to the trainers of Groups A, B and C—Harriet and Ray who provided me with pertinent information about the groups. In addition, as mentioned previously, Harriet assisted me with some of my analysis.

As mentioned in Sect. 3.2.4, I showed preselected snippets of my data to BizLang colleagues on two different occasions in order to garner their reactions and these appear in my data analysis where appropriate.

3.2.7 Conclusion

The focus of this investigation is the world of social interaction. Its perspective is one where reality is not "out there" but something which is experienced and created by social actors. The social reality of a given moment encompasses as many perspectives, motivations and preconceptions as there are participants in it. Thus, the actions of others (verbal or otherwise) are open to a multitude of interpretations. As Hammersley and Atkinson (2007: 236) put it:

> The very assumption that there is some single, available world in which we all live is rejected in favour of the idea that there are multiple realities.

Of course, this does not mean that any one interpretation of events is as valid as any other. A researcher's explanation must be credible. In order to be so, it needs to be able to identify patterns and regularities in human actions and, through a process of inter-subjective validation, come to a truth about it. My inter-subjective validation was provided by a colleague who assisted me in analysing the data and other colleagues who gave their own insights into preselected episodes from the data.

As set out above, the raw data were looked at to identify play through features such as laughter and contextualisation cues. Once identified, significant exchanges were transcribed and then analysed by looking at features such as repetition and disruptions in the structure of talk. Given the incremental nature of play (Sect. 2.4.3) and the focus on the development of an in-group culture, evocations of previous play were also identified.

Although there is an inherent recognition in this research design of the uniqueness of every particular context investigated, the aforementioned patterns and regularities that are discernible across different classroom groups and different moments can give an insight into generalisable processes which demonstrate how an in-group culture is established and the role of HLP in such processes.

References

Adolphs, S., & Carter, R. (2007). Beyond the word. *European Journal of English Studies, 11*(2), 133–146. https://doi.org/10.1080/13825570701452698.

Atkinson, P., & Hammersley, M. (1998). Ethnography and participant observation. In N. K. Denzin & Y. S. Lincoln (Eds.), *Strategies of qualitative enquiry* (pp. 110–136). Thousand Oaks, CA: Sage.

3 The Language Classroom: A Hothouse Where Play Can Germinate   75

Bakhtin, M. M. (1981). *The dialogic imagination*. Austin: University of Texas Press.

Bauman, R., & Briggs, C. L. (1990). Poetics and performance as critical perspectives on language. *Annual Review of Anthropology, 19,* 59–88.

Bell, N. D. (2005). Exploring L2 language play as an aid to SLL: A case study of humour in NS-NNS interaction. *Applied Linguistics, 26*(2), 192–218. https://doi.org/10.1093/applin/amh043.

Bell, N. D. (2007). Humor comprehension: Lessons learned from cross-cultural communication. *Humor, 20*(4), 367–387. https://doi.org/10.1515/HUMOR.2007.018.

Belz, J. (2002). Second language play as representation of the multicompetent self in foreign language study. *Journal of Language, Identity and Education, 1*(1), 13–39.

Belz, J., & Reinhardt, J. (2004). Aspects of advanced foreign language proficiency: Internet-mediated German language play. *International Journal of Applied Linguistics, 14,* 324–362.

Broner, M., & Tarone, E. (2001). Is it fun? Language play in a fifth-grade Spanish immersion classroom. *Canadian Modern Language Review, 58*(4), 493–525. https://doi.org/10.3138/cmlr.58.4.493.

Carter, R. (1999). Common language: Corpus, creativity and cognition. *Language and Literature, 8*(3), 195–216. https://doi.org/10.1177/096394709900800301.

Carter, R. (2004). *Language and creativity: The art of common talk.* Abingdon: Routledge.

Cekaite, A., & Aronsson, K. (2005). Language play, a collaborative resource in children's L2 learning. *Applied Linguistics, 26*(2), 169–191. https://doi.org/10.1093/applin/amh042.

Coates, J. (2007). Talk in a play frame: More on laughter and intimacy. *Journal of Pragmatics, 39*(1), 29–49. https://doi.org/10.1016/j.pragma.2006.05.003.

Cook, G. (2000). *Language play, language learning.* Oxford: Oxford University Press.

Crystal, D. (1998). *Language play.* London: Penguin Books.

Crystal, D. (2003). *English as a global language.* Cambridge: Cambridge University Press.

DaSilva Iddings, A. C., & McCafferty, S. G. (2007). Carnival in a mainstream kindergarten classroom: A Bakhtinian analysis of second language learners' off-task behaviors. *Modern Language Journal, 91*(1), 31–44. https://doi.org/10.1111/j.1540-4781.2007.00508.x.

76   D. Hann

Davies, C. E. (2003). How English-learners joke with native speakers: An interactional sociolinguistic perspective on humor as collaborative discourse across cultures. *Journal of Pragmatics, 35*(9), 1361–1385. https://doi.org/10.1016/S0378-2166(02)00181-9.

Du Bois, J. W., Schuetze-Coburn, S., Cumming, S., & Paolino, D. (1993). Outline of discourse transcription. In J. A. Edwards & M. D. Lampert (Eds.), *Talking data* (pp. 45–90). Hillsdale, NJ: Lawrence Erlbaum Associates.

Ellis, R. (1985). *Understanding second language acquisition.* Oxford: Oxford University Press.

Ely, R., & McCabe, A. (1994). The language of kindergarten children. *First Language, 14,* 19–35.

Gardner, R. C., & Lambert, W. E. (1972). *Attitudes and motivation in second language learning.* Rowley, MA: Newbury House.

Glaser, B., & Strauss, A. (1967). *The discovery of grounded theory: Strategies for qualitative research.* Chicago: Aldine.

Goffman, E. (1959). *The presentation of self in everyday life.* London: Penguin Books.

Goffman, E. (1974). *Frame analysis.* Boston: Northeastern University Press.

Gumperz, J. J. (1982). *Discourse strategies.* Cambridge: Cambridge University Press.

Hammersley, M. (1994). Introducing ethnography. In D. Graddol, J. Maybin, & B. Stierer (Eds.), *Researching language and literacy in social context* (pp. 1–17). Clevedon: Multilingual Matters.

Hammersley, M., & Atkinson, P. (2007). *Ethnography: Principles in practice* (3rd ed.). Abingdon: Routledge.

Holmes, J. (2000). Politeness, power and provocation: How humour functions in the workplace. *Discourse Studies, 2*(2), 159–185. https://doi.org/10.1177/1461445600002002002.

Holmes, J. (2007). Making humour work: Creativity on the job. *Applied Linguistics, 28*(4), 518–537. https://doi.org/10.1093/applin/amm048.

Hymes, D. (1971). *On communicative competence.* Philadelphia: University of Pennsylvania Press.

Inkelas, S. (2006). J's rhymes: A longitudinal case study of language play. In J. Maybin & J. Swann (Eds.), *The art of English: Everyday creativity* (pp. 183–189). Basingstoke: Palgrave Macmillan.

Janesick, V. J. (1998). The dance of qualitative research design: Metaphor, methodolatry and method. In N. K. Denzin & Y. S. Lincoln (Eds.), *Strategies of qualitative enquiry* (pp. 35–55). Thousand Oaks, CA: Sage.

3 The Language Classroom: A Hothouse Where Play Can Germinate   77

Jenkins, J. (2007). *English as a Lingua Franca: Attitude and identity.* Oxford: Oxford University Press.

Kolb, D. (1984). *Experiential learning.* Englewood Cliffs, NJ: Prentice Hall.

Kolb, D., Rubin, I., & Olsland, J. M. (1991). *Organizational behavior: An experiential approach.* Englewood Cliffs, NJ: Prentice Hall.

Kuczaj, S. A. (1983). *Crib speech and language play.* New York: Springer-Verlag.

Labov, W. (1972). *Language in the inner city: Studies in the Black English vernacular.* Philadelphia: University of Pennsylvania Press.

Lantolf, J. (1997). The function of language play in the acquisition of L2 Spanish. In W. R. Glass & A. T. Perez-Leroux (Eds.), *Contemporary perspectives on the acquisition of Spanish* (pp. 3–24). Somerville, MA: Cascadilla Press.

Long, M. H., & Crookes, G. (1992). Three approaches to task-based syllabus design. *TESOL Quarterly, 26,* 27–56.

Maybin, J. (2006). *Children's voices: Talk, knowledge and identity.* Basingstoke: Palgrave Macmillan.

Norrick, N. R. (1993). *Conversational joking: Humour in everyday talk.* Bloomington: Indiana University Press.

North, S. (2007). "The voices, the voices": Creativity in online conversation. *Applied Linguistics, 28*(4), 538–555. https://doi.org/10.1093/applin/amm042.

Petraki, E., & Pham Nguyen, H. H. (2016). Do Asian EFL teachers use humor in the classroom? A case study of Vietnamese EFL University teachers. *System, 61.* https://doi.org/10.1016/j.system.2016.08.002.

Pomerantz, A., & Bell, N. D. (2007). Learning to play, playing to learn: FL learners as multicompetent language users. *Applied Linguistics, 28*(4), 556–578. https://doi.org/10.1093/applin/amm044.

Rampton, B. (2006). *Language in late modernity: Interaction in an urban school.* Cambridge: Cambridge University Press.

Rampton, B. (2007). Neo-Hymesian linguistic ethnography. *Journal of Sociolinguistics, 11*(5), 584–607.

Richards, J. C., & Rodgers, T. S. (2001). *Approaches and methods in language teaching.* Cambridge: Cambridge University Press.

Sacks, H., Schegloff, E. A., & Jefferson, G. (1974). A simple systematics for the organization of turn-taking in conversation. *Language, 50,* 696–735.

Seedhouse, P. (2004). *The interactional architecture of the language classroom: A conversation analysis perspective.* Oxford: Blackwell.

Skehan, P. (1998). *A cognitive approach to language learning.* Oxford: Oxford University Press.

Tannen, D. (2005). *Conversational style: Analyzing talk among friends*. Oxford: Oxford University Press.

Tannen, D. (2007). *Talking voices: Repetition, dialogue, and imagery in conversational discourse* (2nd ed.). Cambridge: Cambridge University Press.

van Lier, L. (1988). *The classroom and the language learner: Ethnography and second-language classroom research*. Harlow: Longman.

Van Praag, L., Stevens, P. A. J., & Van Houtte, M. (2017). How humor makes or breaks student–teacher relationships: A classroom ethnography in Belgium. *Teaching and Teacher Education, 66,* 393–401. https://doi.org/10.1016/j.tate.2017.05.008.

Vygotsky, L. S. (1986). *Thought and language*. Cambridge, MA: MIT Press.

4

Exploiting Frames for Fun

This is the first of five chapters which engage with the empirical findings from the research project. It examines how the BizLang course participants exploit a resource which they have in common in order to play—their shared time together. This can take the form of the role-play scenarios they are asked to take part in. More broadly, they share learning experiences, many of which relate to the new language that they are exposed to which they subvert for their own comedic ends. At the forefront of the data analysis in the next two chapters are the concepts of frame (Goffman 1974) and the associated concept of recontextualisation (Linell 1998). These concepts feature prominently in the case study that follows in Chapters 6 and 7.

The frame is central to an understanding of play. It has previously been noted (Sect. 2.4) that play frames are signalled by animals and humans when wanting to play, allowing them and others to do so within the frame that the instigator creates. Another type of frame is the role-play which often has a close relationship to play-as-fun: after all, the compound noun "role-play" has the word "play" as one of its constituent parts. When young mammals frolic together, we can see that their activities incorporate both make-believe and fun as they

© The Author(s) 2020
D. Hann, *Spontaneous Play in the Language Classroom*,
https://doi.org/10.1007/978-3-030-26304-1_4

79

80   D. Hann

create simple scenarios in which they take on the roles of hunter, prey or rival. The training element to such activities is clear as the participants hone their skills for the challenges of their adult lives (Cook 2000: 106–107). Make-believe and fun are also evident in much of the play activity of children as they act out hypothetical scenarios which, it could be argued, help to socialise them and prepare them for the challenges of later life.

One of the prominent features of my data is that the research participants actively bring together role-play and play-as-fun in the classroom. Indeed, such a setting presents particular opportunities to do this as teachers often set up play-as-rehearsal scenarios to allow learners to practise particular communicative functions in the TL. The analysis explores the frame-rich environment that the language classroom offers through these play-as-rehearsal scenarios. It shows how, despite the risks and pitfalls that role-plays represent for the learners, they actively use them as a means of having fun in the TL, blending the frames available to them for their own social ends. In the course of the analysis, themes which run through this book begin to emerge, including the ways in which humour can highlight comparisons and contrasts between things.

This chapter begins with an exploration of the concept of frame in theoretical and general terms. It then analyses how the research participants exploit the frames available to them in the classroom. The data analysis itself is structured into subsections looking at the various social functions that are fulfilled by the learners' playful exploitation of frames.

4.1   Goffman's Frame

As mentioned in Sect. 2.4.1, Goffman (1974: 8) sees the frame as a means by which we interpret what is happening around us. This is particularly important in the language classroom environment where what is going on could be either simulated or real, although the division between the two is not always as neat as it first appears. Goffman's concept of the frame comes from Gregory Bateson's (1972) study of the play behaviour of animals which shows that play is patterned on serious activities such as hunting. In order to play, animals need to signal that they are not, in fact, engaging in the activities that their play mimics; otherwise, the consequences could be serious for them or their fellow participants. The frame then is interactional and local in nature. It is operative when the participants agree that it is so: if one participant does not play the game, there is no play. The data gathered in this research show that human beings play even during the serious business of language learning. Before investigating how they do this, it is worth exploring the nature of the language classroom and the potential for play that such an environment affords.

4.1.1 Frames in the Adult Language Learning Classroom

It is hardly surprising that many experts in the field of SLA see the role-play as an important teaching tool, from Vygotsky's disciples such as Lantolf (1997, 2001) to the advocates of task-based learning (Long and Crookes 1992; Skehan 1998). As already noted (Chapter 3), the staff of BizLang, whose training rooms form the setting for the present research, regard role-play as central to the organisation's pedagogical approach where "the best way to learn is to do" is as near as it comes to a mantra. The context for the present study therefore provides the learners with many play-as-rehearsal scenarios.

In Goffman's terms, a role-play set-up in the language classroom, whether a full-blooded negotiation or a fleetingly created hypothetical situation, is a "keyed" activity (Goffman 1974: 40–82), that is, the actions that typically refer to one activity are actually referring to another. As young mammals' play is already meaningful in terms of a primary framework such as fighting, the language learning opportunity is also recognisable as something else (the negotiation of a contract, for instance). Goffman categorises such role-plays as "a kind of utilitarian make-believe" (1974: 59). In such a situation, the context is multi-layered. It contains a "lamination of frames" (1974: 82) where the outer frame is the English lesson and the inner layer is the simulated exchange or exchanges (Appel 2007: 282). Of course, depending on which of these frames the participants understand themselves to be in at any one moment, the roles that they take up with each other will vary.

For instance, the teacher/learner relationship will operate at the outer layer (what Goffman calls the "rim") of the classroom context while, for example, that of customer/supplier will pertain in the inner layer of the simulation. It could be argued that there is a framework even beyond that of the teacher/learner in the BizLang language class: that of the client as embodied by the learner, and the provider as represented by the teacher. It is clear that the dynamic between participants is different in each frame. Goffman uses the term "footing" to help explain this, something he describes as:

> the alignment we take up to ourselves and others present as expressed in the way we manage the production and reception of an utterance. A change in our footing is another way of talking about a change in our frame of events. (Goffman 1981: 128)

The notion of footing then carries within it the potential for the speaker to shift and blend frames for their own social and communicative ends.

4.1.2 The Challenges That Classroom Frameworks Present to Learners

In the classroom, it is teachers who have the responsibility for setting up play-as-rehearsal frames. However, attempting to create a play-as-fun frame is another matter as it represents an unofficial stepping out of the norm. When animals play, they usually signal the play frame by various means. Humans often use conversational cues such as exaggerated prosody, formulaic expressions and particular lexical and syntactic choices (Gumperz 1982: 131). Such signals are not easy for language learners to master, especially those with a low proficiency level, and any attempt to shift to a play-as-fun frame is, therefore, open to misunderstanding, not only because of potentially faulty signalling, but also because of potentially faulty reception. Of course, potential difficulties may lie, in part, in cultural differences in how play signals are given and interpreted.

With regard to the play-as-rehearsal frame, although it might be said that part of its usefulness lies in the fact that it does not carry long-term

4 Exploiting Frames for Fun 83

consequences (the frolicking puppy will not be eaten, the contract will not be lost), it does have its own particular pitfalls for the language learner. As Appel (2007) points out, participating in a role-play puts the act of speaking on display, not only to the teacher but also to fellow learners. This means that it carries the potential for real social consequences in terms of the relationships within the classroom: a humiliation in role may still be a humiliation. Furthermore, it could be felt all the more acutely for those who, in their business lives, feel in control, but suddenly find themselves, in their own eyes at least, in the role of less-than-competent pupil. Thus, the danger of the reduced personality (see the discussion in Sect. 2.5.1) is an ever-present one.

Yet despite the potential minefield of the role-play, especially in terms of exploiting it for fun, the data to follow illustrates how learners often decide to navigate its dangers in order to generate humour and to meet their own social objectives.

4.1.3 Frames, Scripts and Schemata

Before moving on to an analysis of the ways in which the research participants exploit the available classroom frames, it is worth differentiating the notion of "frame" from that of the related but distinct concepts of "script" and "schema".

Goffman's (1974) frame which we use to help us decide what is happening at any one moment has a close affinity with Raskin's (1985) script, which is a person's knowledge of prototypical routines and situations. The term script is itself closely related to schema (Cook 2000: 75), the expectations we bring to any situation in order to make sense of it. Distinctions have been made between script and schema where the latter is seen as a broader concept that encompasses the former (O'Halloran 2006) but, for the purposes of this book, these distinctions are not explored. The term schema was given currency in the field of psychology by Bartlett (1932) who saw memory as constructive in nature rather than being a mere passive receptacle. We do not come to an experience with a blank slate but make sense of events through our expectations of them. Language play can be a means of disrupting these

84 D. Hann

conditioned expectations. This, in turn, may lead to changes in them, something which Cook (1994) calls "schema refreshment".

The concepts of schema and frame need differentiating as both will feature in the course of my analysis. I make a distinction along the lines of that in Tannen and Wallat (1993: 59–61) where schemata (plural of "schema") are to do with our general expectations about people, places, events and things which help us make sense of the world, whereas frames are to do with our interpretation of what is going on at any particular moment. As will be seen, it is within the power of interactants to shift and play with frames during their communicative exchanges, manipulating their interlocutor's schemata as they do so. To take an everyday example, a child may have a particular schema or script for a visit to the dentist, either based on their own experiences or on what they have gleaned from others. These expectations may include sitting helplessly in a chair while a masked man or woman probes between his or her teeth with a pain-causing implement of some sort. For the child's sake, the dentist may frame this potentially unpleasant experience as a hunt for hidden treasure and, when examining or repairing the child's teeth, address the child as a fellow adventurer in the quest. This frame or scenario conjures up very different schemata which may (or may not) alleviate the patient's anxieties.

4.2 Blending Frames for Comic Effect

Language's ambiguous nature makes it a natural conduit for play. According to Raskin (1985: 21), this is why, although children laugh and smile from early in life ".. verbal humour is inaccessible to them till they begin to discern ambiguity in language", something that typically happens from about the age of six. As with the child learning its first language, semantic ambiguity is not as readily accessible to the language learner at an early stage of acquisition as it is to someone with a more extensive command of the TL. However, the learner in the classroom has another resource at their disposal—the classroom's lamination of frames. So, much as the humorist in Raskin's framework can evoke two or more meanings in a particular word or phrase, so the language

4 Exploiting Frames for Fun   85

learner can evoke the real and simulated frames that role-play scenarios allow them for comic effect. Hoyle (1993) shows how children as young as eight can blend frames to generate humour. Her research participants are two boys who comment on real-world happenings through the fantasy sportscaster personae that they adopt when playing computer games. Blending frames allows them to comment on the real world while in role, something which is also a feature of my data.

The first episode to show evidence of participants playing with frames is taken from the pilot study which consisted of the audio-recording of Group A comprising Koji, Dieter, Mario and Antoine, along with their trainer, Harriet (Sect. 3.1.3). They were recorded on the last day of their course together, during their final activity, which was a half-hour simulated negotiation.

By the end of a lively meeting where a contract is renegotiated, a compromise is reached between the suppliers (Antoine and Mario) and their customers (Koji and Dieter) and a price of £180 per unit is agreed. Dieter sums up:

EPISODE 1: DO YOU WANT A GLASS OF CHAMPAGNE?

(@ represents one syllable of laughter. See Appendix for full transcription conventions)
Dieter: one (.) eight zero (2) yes that's what we want (.) it's [OK*
Mario: [(xxx)*=
Dieter: =we have to find a compromise (.) that's fine ((*claps hands*))(.)
           do you want a glass of champagne? =
All: =@@@@@

What Dieter says seems fairly unremarkable but his offer of a glass of champagne is met with a seemingly inordinate amount of laughter. In fact, the humour of the moment lies in his evocation of two frames simultaneously. Firstly, his utterance is perfectly apt for the simulation where people's schema for the successful completion of a negotiation may well include a drink to seal the deal. At the same time, the offer is also relevant to the real-world context of the language classroom. The course is drawing to a close, and the participants have already been informed that there is a glass of champagne awaiting them in the BizLang lounge before they leave London.

So, much as the evocation of two or more semantic meanings in a word or phrase triggers humour in Raskin's framework, Dieter provokes laughter through his ability to use one phrase to refer to two frameworks simultaneously. Why we find such episodes amusing is in part due to the movement between or the unexpected combination of interpretative frameworks, as Brkinjac (2009: 20) notes. The sense of incongruity that this induces is a characteristic of humour which will be revisited later in this chapter.

So, despite his limitations in terms of his knowledge of the TL, something which is clearly evident in the negotiation, Dieter is still able to play through the language by drawing on the frames of reference available to him at that given moment. The example is noteworthy for two other reasons. Firstly, Dieter's utterance comes at the end of the simulated negotiation. Indeed, it not only signals the end of the role-play, but also, more or less, the end of the learners' course. Holmes (2000), in her investigation into workplace humour, finds that play episodes seem to cluster at the beginnings and endings of meetings. The extent to which play among my research participants signals the end of an activity or the transition to another activity is one which is returned to in Chapter 8 where the timing of occurrences of play in the training schedule is explored, thus allowing patterns of play behaviour to be identified in relation to the activities in which they occur. In this regard, it is worth bearing in mind that how learners react is influenced by factors such as time of day or stage of the course.

Secondly, it is interesting that, in the simulation, Dieter's footing (Goffman 1981: 128) gives him an alignment to his interlocutors whereby he has the right, as host, to offer champagne. Yet, in the classroom framework, he is a guest and is not invested with such power. Whether the utterance is an attempt, consciously or not, to claim power in a situation where, as learner, he ostensibly has little, is impossible to ascertain from Dieter's words alone. However, the degree to which play is used as a means to lay claim to power is an area which is returned to throughout the course of the analysis in this book.

4 Exploiting Frames for Fun   87

A second notable episode where the blending of frames occurs is taken from a class of learners in their second week of their two-week course. Group B is made up of Michele (Italian), Andrei (Russian), Thomas (German), Takeshi (Japanese) and Viktor (Ukrainian). By the time of the recording, they had already established their own in-group culture. Nonetheless, the interactions provide an insight into how that culture has been established. On the morning of the recording, the group prepares for and takes part in a simulated meeting. As part of the background to the meeting, the teacher, Ray, plays a recording of a dialogue. He takes the opportunity to use the recording to ask the students to repeat particular phrases in order to practise intonation and pronunciation. Coincidentally, as with EPISODE 1, champagne is mentioned:

EPISODE 2: MORE CHAMPAGNE?

Ray:	Stephen? =
Viktor:	= Stephen your glass is (.) is empty (.)
Ray:	yes (1)
TAPE:	*your glass is empty (1) more champagne?(.)*
Viktor:	more champagne? (1)
TAPE	oh yes. thank [you*
VIktor:	[oh* yes thank [you*
Mich:	[here* you are =
Thom:	= plea[se*
Andrei:	[@*@
Viktor:	((*holds out paper cup*))
Ray:	<@ this is a- this is a (xxxxx[x*)>
Viktor:	[typ*ical (.) typical =
Ray:	= typical [typical evening*
Mich:	[here you are* (1) here [you are*
Ray:	[sorry?* (1)
Andrei:	every [day*
Ray:	[every* day yeah (.)
Viktor:	no every day no

In this episode, the outer frame is the listening exercise where the students are repeating the recorded dialogue. The inner frame is the party

88   D. Hann

that is happening in the recording itself. In Goffman's (1981) terms, in repeating the dialogue, the students are being asked to fulfil the role of "animator"—taking the words of another and bringing them to life. Goffman's ideas about the different potential alignments that speakers take up to the words they utter are relevant to this example and elsewhere in the data. He regarded the animator as "…the talking machine, a body engaged in acoustic activity" (1981: 144). Thus, someone reading from the bible at a church service, for example, takes on the role of animator. Similarly, learners are often asked to fulfil this constrained role in the language classroom in activities like drilling or the acting out of modelled dialogues (Rampton 2006: 180–182). However, Viktor breaks through this frame into the fictional world of the party, making himself appear to be what Goffman would call both the "principal" and the "author" of the words he repeats as animator. For Goffman, the principal is "…someone who is committed to what the words say" while the author is "..someone who has selected the sentiments that are being expressed and the words in which they are encoded" (Goffman 1981: 144). Through breaking into the party frame, Viktor manages to create a further frame that evokes evenings when the group has been out together. Both Ray and Andrei take this up, and the footing of the group changes to one of fellow revellers. Within the exchange can be seen an important element of group bonding. During the morning, the group makes various references to things that they have done together, of which drinking was an integral part. Here, Andrei wants to perpetuate the notion that this is something that the group does every day although, interestingly, Viktor resists the temptation to do so.—"no every day no".

In terms of the organisational structure of the exchanges in this episode, it is noteworthy that the play that Viktor instigates disrupts the turn-taking pattern (Sacks et al. 1974) of the BizLang listening exercise. In this phase of the activity, the learners are being asked to repeat from a recorded dialogue. The turns are rigidly structured: typically, a section of the recording is played and a student chosen by the trainer is asked to repeat the word or words which they hear. So, in terms of Sinclair and Coulthard's (1975) influential model of the prototypical structure of classroom talk—Initiation, Response, Feedback (IRF)—the Initiation is

4 Exploiting Frames for Fun   89

triggered through the taped dialogue by the trainer, the learner responds and, occasionally, the trainer provides feedback as follow-up. This pattern is operative when Viktor decides to disrupt it. The laughter following his initial gesture allows him to topicalise (van Lier 1988: 152) through his utterance "typical". In other words, the disruption lets him introduce the group's drinking as a topic of the exchanges. This one-word allusion to drinking together is immediately taken up by Ray and Andrei, as noted above. So, the play, however, briefly restructures the classroom talk.

It is noteworthy, given the potential communicative hazards mentioned earlier in signalling changing frames, that the contextualisation cue that Viktor employs is physical as well as linguistic. His lifting of the paper cup is clear and unambiguous. Furthermore, the fact that he uses such a modest receptacle to represent a champagne glass adds to the comedy of the moment.

This contrast between the simulated frame and the props employed in the outer frame to represent them is seen most clearly at the end of a role-play involving a group on the last day of their one-week course. Group C is made up of Bilel (Tunisian), Joseph (French, of Senegalese descent) and Sandro (Italian). At the time of the recording, they were being taught by Harriet, although their trainer for the first three days was David[1] (the main researcher).

They are enacting a simulation where, in the role of consultants, they have put forward a proposal to their client as played by David, the stooge. At the end of the meeting, Bilel offers the client a parting present:

EPISODE 3: HERE'S OUR BIG GIFT

David: thank you very [much*
Sandro: [thank* [you*
Joseph: [thank* you (.)
Bilel: ((*proffers cheap biro*)) here's er our big er gift from our [company*

---

[1] I use the name "David" to refer to myself when I feature in the research data.

90   D. Hann

All: [@@*@@@@
David: ((*holding biro, speaking over laughter*)) very impressive (2) very
          impressive

The double consciousness of being in role, and yet being aware that it is a role, is brought to the fore in drawing attention to the gap between features of the physical environment and what they stand for in the simulated frame. The degree to which disbelief has been suspended during the role-play is deliberately highlighted by Bilel choosing to make a humble biro represent something akin to a gold-plated Mont Blanc. This incongruity generates laughter. Maybe this is because, as William Hazlitt from a lecture in 1818 (cited in Morreall 1987: 56) puts it when reflecting on the nature of comedy, humans are "…the only animal that is struck with the difference between what things are and what they ought to be". On viewing this episode, a BizLang trainer, Geraint, commented, "they find sort of universally funny, things like contrasts. So, over the top introduction of a really crap present is just funny".

Contrast is an important element of the play to be found throughout the data. The incongruity of blending frames is also clearly seen in an exchange between members of Group B as they prepare for the simulated meeting mentioned earlier. This meeting revolves around the problem of dividing the estate of a hotel owner who has recently passed away. Thomas is trying to explain the situation to Takeshi by using a hypothetical scenario of his own:

EPISODE 4: VIKTOR DIED

Thom: ((*pointing to Viktor*)) Viktor (2) Viktor had a house (1) [he has*=
Mich: [Viktor died*
Thom: =[two children*
Andrei: [@@* =
Viktor: = (x) (1) not yet =
Thom: = he have two children (2) Viktor died (2)

((*Viktor puts his head on his hands as if asleep*))

Thom: and then the two children [share their* house fifty fifty (x)(.)

Mich:	((*smiles*))	[I and Andrei*
Tak:	normally it's a (.) fifty fifty is un-normal (2) almost =	
Ray:	= it's not normal =	
Tak:	= It's not normal (1) almost first children get (.)	
Andrei:	last children =	
Ray:	= oldest [oldest*	
Tak:	[last* children no =	
Ray:	= oldest =	
Tak:	= oldest children =	
Andrei:	= (xxx) (1)	
Thom:	It's not fair (.)	
Tak:	no no no no =	
Ray:	= life's not fair (.)	
Andrei:	the (first) it's er it's (2) happy to be (xxxx) =	
Ray:	= <@ yes > (2)	
Mich:	but if Viktor died (1)	
Ray:	OK (1)	
Viktor:	no (.)	
Mich:	and er (2)	
Viktor:	sorry (1) one moment (2) ((*gets up and moves towards the flipchart*)) pre-died (2) pre-died =	
Mich:	= <@ after died>	

Thomas creates a hypothetical scenario to explain a point, much as a teacher might. It is interesting to note here that he picks up Michele's initial comment and Viktor himself builds on it by enacting his own death. Again, the contextualisation cues are exaggerated and physical in nature. Thomas's initial attempt to explain the situation through the use of an example has been collaboratively built upon to create a moment where the gesticulating, breathing, speaking Viktor is, at the same time, reduced to a corpse. It is noteworthy too how Michele takes pleasure in the hypothetical frame, pretending that he and Andrei are Viktor's sons who are about to inherit. There is no outright laughter here but much smiling and a sense of fun.

Viktor picks up the idea moments later when he decides to go to the flipchart to explain further and gives himself a few more moments of life in order to do so—"one moment, pre-died, pre-died". One can imagine that if Viktor were a native speaker of English, he would get up and say something like "Before I pop my clogs, let me just explain…" This blending of the real and imagined frames such that the dead can talk provides a sense of shifting ground, a place where things are not quite as they seem. In such a world, paper cups can be filled with vintage champagne, biros can be priceless gifts and one can be both language learner and party-goer at the same time. Such a world has the flavour of Bakhtin's notion of "carnival" where "…the laws, prohibitions, and restrictions that determine the structure and order of the ordinary, that is noncarnival, life are suspended" (Bakhtin 1984: 122–123, first published 1965). It is a world which allows the possibility of subverting the established order, at least on a temporary basis. It is to the manifestations of this subversion, made possible by the blending of different frames, to which we now turn.

4.2.1 Subverting the Established Order

Gordon (2002), in her study of the interactions between a mother and her daughter of two years and eleven months, notes how play frames allow the two to reverse roles, so that the daughter takes on the nurturing role and the mother plays the child. This reversal of the footing that the two take up to each other actually allows the mother, the figure of authority, to achieve particular strategic goals, such as getting her daughter to pick out a book for naptime. This particular example of role reversal between two individuals echoes wider societal instances of role reversal from history. For instance, in the ancient Roman festival of Saturnalia, masters would serve their servants at table, something which finds an echo in the medieval Feast of Fools where power was invested for a few hours in those who did not ordinarily have it. In the latter event, a member of the peasantry would typically assume the role of someone in the ecclesiastical hierarchy and openly preach subversion. However, although such festivities may seem to the modern eye to be tinged with the whiff of revolution, it is worth bearing in mind that they were sanctioned by the power structures of their times. So,

4 Exploiting Frames for Fun 93

it could be argued that, rather like the mother in her role reversal with her daughter in Gordon's research, such outlets were, in their way, an instrument of institutional control.

Subversive role reversal is prominent in the featured data, although here the role reversal is instigated, not by an authority figure as represented by the teacher, but by the students themselves. The frames available to the learners mean that they can, within their role-play, turn the normal world upside down. This can be seen in the roles that learners assign for themselves in simulations, allowing them to take up different footings with each other from those they usually have. The pleasure members of Group C derived from reversing roles can be seen when Joseph hands over to Sandro who is playing the team's company director:

EPISODE 5: OUR SOCIETY DIRECTOR

Joseph: the-our dir- our society director gonna summarise on our proposal and er @@@ =
Bilel: = our company GM =
Joseph: = @[@*
Sandro: [I'm going to* show you the-the last (1) area

The laughter springs from the fact that Sandro is the youngest in the group and yet, in this imagined world, he is the most senior of the team and has been elected as such by them. The others enjoy this inversion of the social norms, although Sandro's lack of reaction leaves open to question whether he does.

This episode finds a striking parallel in the exchanges of Group B when its members are deciding on which roles to assume in their simulated meeting. Nobody seems to be willing to chair the meeting:

EPISODE 6: YOU DIRECTOR

Viktor: Michele (.)
Mich: yeah (.)

94 D. Hann

Vitkor:	please (.)
Mich:	please (2)
Viktor:	you (3) director (.)
Mich:	I director =
Andrei:	=chairman =
Mich:	=no =
Andrei:	=big boss (.)
Viktor:	Michele (.) you Michele (.)
Mich:	[I*
Andrei:	[not* Michele (.) Mr Big Bo[ss*
Mich:	[I'm* young (.) I young (2) I'm more very young (1)
Andrei:	you only image (.) imagine (.) yeah (1) big boss (2) foot on table (.) cigar (.)
Viktor:	tod[ay you* can (1) you can be big boss
Mich:	[no (xx*)

Like his fellow Italian, Sandro from Group C, Michele is the youngest in his group by far (he was twenty at the time of the recording while the others were in their thirties and forties). Here, although the learners are not yet in the simulated role that they are about to take part in, Andrei evokes the hypothetical frame where Michele would assume the position of boss and conjures up the trappings of power to humorous effect. There is hyperbolic language here in Andrei's use of the term "Mr Big Boss", a form of address with a cartoon-like quality which he would not ordinarily use outside a play frame. As Carter (2004: 136) observes, hyperbole signals a recognition that something is contrary to the perceived facts.

The question of taking on and switching roles is one which will be returned to later where it is revealed how the learners assume the mantle of the authority figure within the classroom by purloining the words of their teacher.

The training room allows students the opportunity to play with their assigned roles within the frame of the simulation and within the outer frame of the language lesson itself. This play has a subversive element to it, albeit one which does not seriously seem to threaten the status quo.

4.2.2 Asserting the Established Order

BizLang is an organisation where there are few explicitly elaborated rules. However, two are mentioned to course participants at the outset of their stay. These are, firstly, to speak only English when communicating together during the course, even if participants share a common first language, and, secondly, to arrive on time for the training day and after coffee and lunch breaks.

At the beginning of the recording of Group A, Dieter and Koji as customers welcome Mario and Antoine to their office for a renegotiation of their contract (you encountered the end of this simulation in EPISODE 1). The start of the meeting is held up by Antoine going off to get himself a coffee. Upon his return, Dieter kicks off the meeting by greeting his guests:

EPISODE 7: YOU ARE A LITTLE BIT LATE

Dieter: um er we hope you have a nice trip to (2) er (1) to our company [and* =
Ant: [oh yes*
Dieter: = you have no problem you are a little bit late but er (1) it's not
[a problem*
Ant: ((*gesturing towards Mario*)) [his fault* his fault his fault =
All: = @@@@@[@*
Dieter: [we* welcome you

In this excerpt, Dieter manages to admonish Antoine for delaying the start of the simulation by bringing this fact into the role-play itself. This forces Antoine to deflect the criticism towards his colleague, Mario. As in the previous examples in this chapter, Dieter fuses the two worlds of the real and the make-believe. Although he uses this to uphold classroom procedures and, thus, the status quo, he also asserts his own authority over one of his fellow group members. After the role-play, Harriet, the group's trainer, mentioned to me that this episode is indicative of a rather fractious relationship that had built up between Dieter and Antoine over the course of their stay and which readily comes to the surface in this simulation. The exchanges illustrate, as noted previously (Sect. 2.4.1), that the play bite is not real but it is also NOT not real. From my experience of teaching at BizLang, any tensions that there are between-group members are manifest most readily in role-plays. The simulation allows Dieter to both joke with and reprimand Antoine at the same time.

The previous examples of the subversion and assertion of the established order that pertains in the outer frame of the language lesson through the exploitation of the inner frame of the role-play demonstrate that the research participants see role-play as a useful resource in the exercise of power. It can be hypothesised that this is because it allows speakers to push at boundaries in ways which would not otherwise be permissible. The fact that learners are ostensibly operating within a simulation gives them a fallback defence if their interlocutors take offence. "I was only in role", much like "I was only joking", is an assertion which is difficult to counter.

4.2.3 Releasing Tension When the Frame Dissolves

Bateson (1972: 182) observes that play is intrinsically labile or unstable: the play bite can become real; the football match can degenerate into violence. This applies as much to play-as-rehearsal as it does to play-as-fun. It was seen in the previously cited exchange how simulated situations often bring out any underlying tensions that can be found within a group. At such moments, the lamination of frames present in the classroom is de-layered or, as Goffman (1974: 359–360) would put it, "downkeyed" such that the participants' awareness that their role-play is embedded within a classroom frame disappears and the simulation becomes unkeyed. In other words, in their own minds, the simulation becomes real. An example of this can be seen in the negotiation between the members of Group A, where, as in the previous example, the tension between Dieter and Antoine surfaces. In the following exchanges, the customers, Dieter and Koji, have just indicated that they would be prepared to pay their suppliers, Antoine and Mario, 165 per unit:

EPISODE 8: HANDS UP!

Dieter:	((*pointing his finger like a gun*)) we are serious (2) we are serious (.) and when you say one times again we are not serious (1) you can go (2)
Ant:	go where? =
Dieter:	((*still pointing*)) = it's [right?*
Ant:	[@*@@@ =
Dieter:	=hands up =
All:	= @@@@

Here, Dieter's pointing finger is not accompanied by a smiling face that might indicate play. He is truly angry at Antoine's attitude and, at that moment, does not seem to be aware that he is in a language role-play but sees himself in a negotiation where his integrity has been impugned. There seems to be a real danger that the situation will become irretrievable when he points his finger at Antoine and tells him that he can go. As a BizLang colleague, Toby, subsequently observed, "they were getting quite swept away in the whole thing". Although Antoine attempts to defuse the moment with his riposte "go where?", it is, in fact, Dieter himself who manages to retrieve the situation by cleverly evoking another frame which recasts his utterances as mere play. He uses his already pointing finger to conjure up a world universally associated with it, that of the cowboy western or the gangster movie with his words "hands up". When children play at cowboys or gangsters, they often use the pointing finger to represent a gun. By changing the threatening gesture into one belonging to children's play, Dieter demonstrates that he is aware that he is in a simulated frame and, in that moment, the tension is released.

4.3 Conclusion

This chapter demonstrates how the research participants exploit and have fun with the play-as-rehearsal frame which is common in the language class, and especially so in the BizLang training room. Speakers are able to provoke laughter by using words and phrases that simultaneously refer to both the simulated frame and the language-lesson frame in which it is embedded. This blending of frames can be used for speakers' own social ends: it allows them to become authors and principals as well as animators of the words they utter; it allows them to pass judgement on the world around them by revealing a contrast between the real and simulated frames; it lets them choose the topic of interaction where otherwise they could not; it permits them to subvert or, indeed, asserts the established order and, finally, it allows them to rescue potentially embarrassing situations.

Through playing with frames, the learner can claim a voice which is their own. On the other hand, as Gordon (2008: 324) points out, this is a liminal world where "...footings of the participants may be uncertain, a world where frames can dissolve and pretence can evaporate". In other words, although there are a fluidity and give between frames which the learners can employ for their own playful ends, that very porosity also carries dangers which are potentially face threatening.

All the examples cited involve the use of language. However, the degree to which play is dependent on language varies in each episode. When Bilel offers a biro to David in EPISODE 3, the humorous incongruity of the moment is primarily generated by the physical prop, although the accompanying words—"here's our big gift from our company"—are vital in triggering humour. At the other end of the scale, when Dieter shouts "hands up!" (EPISODE 8), the humour of the moment relies heavily on his interlocutors' understanding of the associations which the words carry with them. In Chapter 5, language moves centre stage as the extent to which the participants play by using words and phrases which carry particular associations and connotations is investigated. These associations evoke different frames which the speakers compare and contrast for comic effect.

References

Appel, J. (2007). Language teaching in performance. *International Journal of Applied Linguistics, 17*(3), 277–293.

4 Exploiting Frames for Fun 99

Bakhtin, M. M. (1984). *Rabelais and his world*. Bloomington: Indiana University Press.

Bartlett, R. C. (1932). *Remembering: A study in experimental and social psychology*. Cambridge: Cambridge University Press.

Bateson, G. (1972). *Steps to an ecology of mind*. New York: Ballantine.

Brkinjac, T. (2009). *Humour in English as a Lingua Franca*. Saarbrucken: VDM Verlag Dr. Muller.

Carter, R. (2004). *Language and creativity: The art of common talk*. Abingdon: Routledge.

Cook, G. (1994). *Discourse and literature: The interplay of form and mind*. Oxford: Oxford University Press.

Cook, G. (2000). *Language play, language learning*. Oxford: Oxford University Press.

Goffman, E. (1974). *Frame analysis*. Boston: Northeastern University Press.

Goffman, E. (1981). *Forms of talk*. Oxford: Blackwell.

Gordon, C. (2002). "I'm Mommy and you're Natalie": Role-reversal and embedded frames in mother-child discourse. *Language in Society, 31*(5), 679–720. https://doi.org/10.1017/S004740450231501X.

Gordon, C. (2008). A(p)parent play: Blending frames and reframing in family talk. *Language in Society, 37*(3), 319–349. https://doi.org/10.1017/S0047404508080536.

Gumperz, J. J. (1982). *Discourse strategies*. Cambridge: Cambridge University Press.

Holmes, J. (2000). Politeness, power and provocation: How humour functions in the workplace. *Discourse Studies, 2*(2), 159–185. https://doi.org/10.1177/1461445600002002002.

Hoyle, S. (1993). Participation frameworks in sportscasting play: Imaginary and literary footing. In D. Tannen (Ed.), *Framing in discourse* (pp. 114–145). Oxford: Oxford University Press.

Lantolf, J. (1997). The function of language play in the acquisition of L2 Spanish. In W. R. Glass & A. T. Perez-Leroux (Eds.), *Contemporary perspectives on the acquisition of Spanish* (pp. 3–24). Somerville, MA: Cascadilla Press.

Lantolf, J. (2001). Introducing sociocultural theory. *Sociocultural theory and second language learning* (pp. 1–26). Oxford: Oxford University Press.

Linell, P. (1998). *Approaching dialogue: Talk, interaction and contexts in dialogical perspectives*. Amsterdam: John Benjamins.

Long, M. H., & Crookes, G. (1992). Three approaches to task-based syllabus design. *TESOL Quarterly, 26*, 27–56.

Morreall, J. (1987). *The philosophy of laughter and humour*. New York: State University of New York.

O'Halloran, K. (2006). The literary mind. In S. Goodman & K. O'Halloran (Eds.), *The art of English: Literary creativity* (pp. 364–389). Basingstoke: Palgrave Macmillan.

Rampton, B. (2006). *Language in late modernity: Interaction in an urban school*. Cambridge: Cambridge University Press.

Raskin, V. (1985). *Semantic mechanisms of humor*. Dordrecht, Holland: D. Reidel.

Sacks, H., Schegloff, E. A., & Jefferson, G. (1974). A simple systematics for the organization of turn-taking in conversation. *Language, 50,* 696–735.

Sinclair, J., & Coulthard, M. (1975). *Towards an analysis of discourse*. Oxford: Oxford University Press.

Skehan, P. (1998). *A cognitive approach to language learning*. Oxford: Oxford University Press.

Tannen, D., & Wallat, C. (1993). Interactive frames and knowledge schemas in interaction: Examples from a medical examination/interview. In D. Tannen (Ed.), *Framing in discourse* (pp. 57–76). New York: Oxford University Press.

van Lier, L. (1988). *The classroom and the language learner: Ethnography and second-language classroom research*. Harlow: Longman.

5

Evoking Frames Through Associated Language

It has been noted how the research participants use the particular environment of the language classroom in order to blend the frames of reference available to them for comic effect. Exploiting the "play" between frames gives the learners the licence to subvert the usual power dynamic and to break free, however temporarily, of the roles assigned to them by the classroom context. In this process, language is used as a means of positioning the participants in a particular framework. For instance, Bilel's "here's our gift from our company" (EPISODE 3) clearly places the words within the simulated role-play while the gift itself—a humble biro—remains stubbornly outside it in the outer frame of the classroom interaction itself. The humour is derived from this juxtaposition. Nevertheless, the relationship between the words and the frame is very different from that in Dieter's "hands up!" (EPISODE 8). In the latter case, the evocation of the play frame is largely dependent on the phrase which is inextricably linked to the schema of a western or gangster movie and, in turn, to that of children's play. The language does not so much refer to a current frame of interpretation, such as those of the lesson and the simulation, but actually summons one into existence because the words themselves encode their own particular

© The Author(s) 2020
D. Hann, *Spontaneous Play in the Language Classroom*,
https://doi.org/10.1007/978-3-030-26304-1_5

102   D. Hann

framework. This chapter explores the ways participants use words to activate previously encountered frames with which they are associated, thus allowing those frames to become available for play.

5.1   Theoretical Perspectives on Language, Context, Play and Learning

This section examines further the theoretical underpinning to the relationship between language and frame. In so doing, it draws upon the ideas of two influential thinkers from the twentieth century, Saussure and Bakhtin. There then follows an examination of the data where the movement of a word or phrase with all its associations into a novel context allows that word or phrase to be "rekeyed", thus changing the meaning of an interaction. Furthermore, recontextualised words in the data are often associated with a previous speaker who, in Bakhtinian terms (1981), is "voiced" for the current speaker's own communicative ends. Recontextualised language metonymically refers to and stands for other frames, thus highlighting humorous contrasts and gaps between elements of the evoked frames and those of the moment. Associations are often particular to the group and, as such, carry a specific social resonance. Throughout the analysis, the important social functions that the individual episodes fulfil are commented on.

5.1.1   The Relationship Between Language and Its Context of Use

Saussure (1959) posited a theory of language built around the idea that the linguistic sign is arbitrary. This arbitrary nature, coupled with the fact that languages do not name existing categories in the physical world but articulate their own, dictates that linguistic signs only have meaning in relation to other linguistic signs in the language system. This non-essentialist conceptualisation of language makes meaning inherently fluid and unstable. In order to explore this, and how meanings are transformed with use, the interaction between language and its

5 Evoking Frames Through Associated Language   103

context of use needs to be interrogated. In the early twentieth century, the Russian literary scholar Mikhail Bakhtin (1981), although drawing upon Saussure's non-essentialist notion of language, rejected the idea that the language system is a reified synchronic code which speakers simply draw upon to communicate. He rooted the study of language firmly in its socio-historical soil and maintained that, as a word or phrase has no essence beyond that with which users endow it, its meaning is profoundly influenced by the contexts in which it is encountered by individual speakers. Of course, no two contexts are exactly identical (Pennycook 2007) and, consequently, a particular word within the sign system of a language carries the flavours of previous uses. Because of this, language is heteroglossic (multi-voiced) by its very nature. Furthermore, Bakhtin maintains that every instance of a word's reuse changes it. As the literary theorist, Terry Eagleton (1983: 129) puts it:

> It is difficult to know what a 'sign' originally means, what its 'original' context was: we simply encounter it in many different situations, and although it must maintain a certain consistency across those situations in order to be an identifiable sign at all, because its context is always different it is never absolutely the same, never quite identical with itself.

The fluidity at the heart of language suggests that its meanings are always provisional. Thus, an exchange between a pre-pubescent boy and girl may be viewed purely as an innocent exchange between children or as the first tentative step in establishing a boyfriend/girlfriend relationship (Maybin 1994: 139–140). How the two participants view their conversation will, to a large extent, be determined by exchanges to come, a point which illustrates another Bakhtinian concept, that of language's dialogical nature (Bakhtin 1981: 276–277): all utterances respond to previous utterances and anticipate their own response. Of course, there is no guarantee that interlocutors will come to a shared understanding of any particular interaction.

Despite Bakhtin providing a persuasive argument for showing that meaning is not fixed and is shaped by its contexts of use, it would be a mistake to see it as completely fluid. After all, even the Eagleton quotation above admits to a "certain consistency" across situations for any sense to be made of a word or utterance. Widdowson (2004: 70), despite seeing the analysis of language as meaningless without a consideration of its particular context of use, provides a useful brake on the tempting notion that language meaning is simply what the speaker wants it to be. He views semantically encoded meaning "…as constituting a range of delimiting coordinates". Nevertheless, it should be noted with regard to L2 speakers of a language, their knowledge of the conventionally understood meanings of words is generally less secure than that of their L1 counterparts.

5.1.2 The Relationship Between Language, the Speaker and the Social Group

The distinctiveness of particular types or styles of talk among different social groupings demonstrates that speakers are not merely subject to language "rules" but have a degree of agency that allows them to use it as a resource in their own image-making. Word meanings are not just given but can be manipulated to the user's own ends. However, it has already been noted that it would be a mistake to view individual speakers as having complete freedom to generate what meanings they will with the language. Indeed, Bakhtin himself views language use as very much a socio-historical process which is constrained by what has gone before:

> Language is not a neutral medium that passes freely and easily into the private property of the speaker's intentions; it is populated, overpopulated – with the intentions of others. (Bakhtin 1981: 274)

Because Bakhtin views language within a broad societal context, it is no surprise, as noted above, that he is interested in the ways in which the different groupings within society find expression through habitual patterns of usage which, in turn, establish their own linguistic norms. This is pertinent to the language learners in the featured study who have to endeavour to establish their own collective cultural identity within the short time span that their course allows them.

5.1.3 Recontextualisation in a Bakhtinian Conceptualisation of Language

The previous discussion brings to the fore the intimate relationship between language, its speakers and its contexts of use. The notion of context needs to be clarified as it is not easy to define in the fluid and amorphous stream of experience. The concept of frame (Sect. 4.1) is useful here as it de-limits the context. The frame is a psychological construct, something determined in people's heads rather than in their physical surroundings. It tells the interactants what is happening at any given moment. It is local and essentially interactive in nature, allowing frames to change even when the physical environment does not do so. My focus is on how language is used to manipulate interlocutors' frames of interpretation where the movement of a word or phrase from one frame with which it is associated to another transforms it into something else. I refer to this movement as "recontextualisation", something which Linell (1998: 154) describes as:

> ...the dynamic transfer-and-transformation of something from one discourse/text-in-context (...) to another. Recontextualisation involves the extrication of some part or aspect from a text or discourse, or from a genre of texts or discourses, and the fitting of this part or aspect into another context.

In the broadest sense, all language is recontextualised and recontextualisable, even, it could be argued, neologisms. Indeed, a language learner cannot be said to have mastered a feature of a language, be it a word, phrase or grammatical construction, until he or she is able to take it from the context in which it is first encountered and then use it in another. Given that all the language we hear around us is recontextualised, it is not necessarily the case that this transforms a frame. In order to determine what sort of recontextualisations leads to reframing, a notion from linguistic anthropology, that of "entextualisation" is useful. Bauman and Briggs (1990: 73) define the concept as:

106   D. Hann

> ...the process of rendering discourse extractable, of making a stretch of linguistic production into a unit - a text - that can be lifted out of its interactional setting.

This makes the elements of the text bounded, so that, for example, words within the extracted text become a unified whole. An example might be a common word or phrase which may stand out when used, intentionally or not, in a particular context. So, I also take the text to be bounded in another way in that it is, in the mind of the speaker who recontextualises it, linked to its original interactional setting. To be entextualised, the text "...can be detached from one discursive context and fit [sic] and grafted into others" (Eisenlohr 2010: 321). As Eisenlohr's words make clear, entextualisation can be regarded as part of a process which encompasses "decontextualisation" (taking a text out of a particular context) and "recontextualisation" (putting it into a new one). Indeed, from the observer's point of view, recontextualisation is the only evidence that a text has been entextualised and de-contextualised. An example of this process in action can be seen in Trester's (2012) research into a troupe of improvisers whose exchanges she analyses. She notes how their backstage and frontstage performances largely depend on entextualisation, decontextualisation and recontextualisation:

> ...performers pay attention for opportunities to hang on to texts, and by noticing them, render them extractable (entextualising them), moving them from the original interactional context in which they were used (decontextualising them), and looking for an opportunity to use them again (to recontextualise them). (Trester 2012: 238)

The notion of recontextualisation is inextricably linked to that of "intertextuality", a term coined by Kristeva (1980) and based on Bakhtin's ideas about the inherently heteroglossic and dialogical nature of language. Intertextuality is to do with the way in which texts incorporate previous texts and reshape them by so doing. Intertextuality, therefore, is realised through recontextualisation. To take Trester's example of the improvising performers, their skill (and presumably their audience's appreciation) lies in the ability to weave intertextual references from

5 Evoking Frames Through Associated Language   107

their prior talk into their current utterances. For these improvisations to carry any weight, the recontextualisations must carry associative links with what they have already said. They cannot simply contain words which the audience has heard somewhere before!

Trester notes that intertextuality invariably signals a shift in frame, that is, a change in participants' understanding of what is going on at any given moment. Indeed, "intertextuality can at times be the only signal that a frame shift has been enacted (that a game has begun)" (Trester 2012: 240). Furthermore, as the bracketed words at the end of the previous quotation indicate, reframing can be playful and previous talk can be rekeyed as something humorous.

In a Bakhtinian account, as discussed above, the movement of a word or phrase from one frame to another affects the meanings of those words or phrases which are transposed. The result is that interactions are reframed as something else. One can imagine, for example, Maybin's girl and boy (1994: 139–140) evoking elements of their past exchange to lay claim to a particular meaning to that exchange and, so, a particular status for their relationship as either playmates or girlfriend and boyfriend. Tannen (2006) shows how the meanings of family arguments can subsequently be rekeyed and reframed as something humorous. Words and phrases of previous exchanges are repeated—recontextualised—and their significance is consciously altered, something which is discussed below.

At this point, it is helpful to clarify the definitions of concepts which are closely interconnected and are pertinent to the analysis to come:

* Recontextualisation—the movement of language from one frame with which it is closely associated to another.
* Entextualisation—the process by which a text is "chunked" and rendered potentially extractable from its original context and co-text.
* Decontextualisation—the process by which a text is decoupled from its original context.
* Intertextuality—the result of recontextualisation where a chunk of language is entextualised, de-contextualised and recontextualised into another setting.

108   D. Hann

- Reframing—a change in what the discussion is about, often triggered by the recontextualisation of a word or phrase.
- Rekeying—an activity becomes something patterned on that activity, for example, an argument is rekeyed as a humorous exchange. The rekeying is often signalled by a change in the tone of voice, indicating "…a change of emotional stance" (Tannen 2006: 601). Rekeying inevitably results in reframing.

The reason for focussing on the movement of language from a context with which it is identified to one where we do not usually expect to find it is that it has the potential to be regarded as humorous and playful. We now turn to why this might be so.

5.1.4 Recontextualisation and Humour

It could be argued that wordplay, which typically manifests itself in such behaviour as punning, is a form of recontextualisation: it involves taking language out of one interpretative framework and putting it in another, such that its ambiguities are highlighted.

We hear recontextualising play in everyday interaction and see it in magazine and TV advertising. An example is a cartoon which features a barman, leaning over his bar and saying to a private detective and his female client, "The guy you're looking for waltzed out of here an hour ago". The humour arises from the fact that the woman is dressed in a tutu and ballet shoes. Our schema or script for a detective story includes the fact that the word "waltzed" is typically used metaphorically by its characters. However, our expectations of this are thwarted by the picture which allows the meaning to be realised literally. An exchange associated with tracing a crook or a cheating husband is transformed by the recontextualisation into one about finding a dancing partner. However, play involving recontextualising and reframing without necessarily exploiting ambiguous meanings is also common. It has already been noted how, in a particular game show, someone's name not only refers to a particular person but also metonymically stands for a shared experience (Sect. 2.4.3).

5 Evoking Frames Through Associated Language   109

Recontextualising language often produces a sense of incongruity. The notion that incongruity lies at the heart of humour has a strong tradition among humour theorists—see Morreall (1987) for an overview of the field. It is noteworthy that a particular recontextualisation may only have meaning and humour for someone present throughout a particular discussion, producing a sort of fleeting in-group reference point to which people who were not there are not privy. This indicates a possible reason why humour is such a common feature in the language repertoire of different social groupings—their shared experiences allow the incremental build-up of meanings whenever language associated with those experiences is uttered. Of course, particular meanings based on shared experience may fade and die while others persist and become part of the group's identity. It could be hypothesised that my research participants' relative lack of exposure to the TL makes words and phrases more susceptible to taking on particular shared meanings which persist.

Unsurprisingly, given that Bahktin sees the meanings of language as infused with the voices and intentions of previous speakers, he is interested in the ways in which speakers consciously manipulate the words of others. He sees an utterance in which, for example, a narrator quotes a previous speaker as a form of "double-voicing", as it carries the intentions of both speakers. When the meaning of the former contrasts with that of the latter, he categorises this as "vari-directional double-voicing" (Bakhtin 1984a: 193). This is often ironic and humorous in intent (DaSilva Iddings and McCafferty 2007; Rampton 2006b). The words of the original speaker are rekeyed. In the classroom setting, many people have memories of pupils from their schooldays who mimicked the words and mannerisms of their teachers. It seems highly unlikely in my research setting that learners would dare such a face-threatening act. However, the degree to which they voice others as part of their playful repertoire is an area of interest in the study.

The recontextualisation of language, then, can reframe the meaning of an interaction, often turning it into something humorous. The humour is triggered by the juxtaposition of interpretative frameworks and by the uttering of others' words where they are overlaid with the speaker's own intentions. However, this explanation of the enjoyment

110   D. Hann

to be had in the conscious act of recontextualising language can only partly explain its appeal.

5.1.5 Recontextualisation, Language Learning and Language Play

If speakers never use a word or phrase beyond the context in which they first meet it, then there is, of course, no proof that they have understood it, let alone incorporated it into their active language repertoire. Unsurprisingly, when we acquire a language, including our first, the process of reusing the language we hear is by no means smooth or unproblematic. We have to learn the extent and limit of the meanings of specific words and phrases. We need only reflect upon the amusement and affection unintentionally generated by first language learners when they inadvertently generalise the meaning of a word beyond its universally accepted semantic limits to appreciate that learners often overextend meanings. An example would be a young child going through a period of calling all animals "cat" until eventually learning that cats are just one type of animal (e.g. Kay and Anglin 1982). Beyond semantic meaning, speakers also need to learn about the appropriateness of language in particular situations. The child who asks about Granny's varicose veins in front of a roomful of strangers shows that learners do not always get this right.

This aspect of learning puts the L2 speaker in a position akin to although not identical with that of the child acquiring its first language. Adult learners may well have a breadth and depth of life experience that can help them in many ways when learning another language. However, they have not encountered particular uses of the TL in various contexts and are not able to draw upon the accumulated flavours of meaning that such experience allows. Meaning, therefore, already less fixed in a Bakhtinian framework than we might usually regard it, is even more unstable in the minds and mouths of L2 speakers, especially in the early stages of acquisition. This could be regarded as a disadvantage for someone wishing to play with the connotations and associations that lie behind language but who is unable to do so through lack of exposure to such meanings.

5 Evoking Frames Through Associated Language   111

A further disadvantage for the non-native speaker can be seen in the evocation of others' voices. A narrator, for example, in quoting the words of another, may reproduce a particular accent, inflection or way of speaking which can heighten the ironic or humorous effect of vari-directional double-voicing. It is notoriously difficult for L2 speakers, even those who are fluent in the language, to identify, let alone mimic a particular accent or way of speaking. This suggests that they would avoid any form of double-voicing. However, the data in the featured study indicate that this is not the case.

Although the language learner is burdened by a number of disadvantages when recontextualising language, it could be argued that some of these drawbacks actually have the potential to enhance the opportunities for HLP. As alluded to previously (Sect. 2.5), the very fact that non-native speakers are less familiar with a language than adult native speakers might allow them a fresher perspective on it, giving them the chance to play with its sounds and shapes in similar ways to children experimenting with their first language. Secondly, the speaker's status as a non-native might actually work to their advantage in terms of how their utterances are received, at least in a supportive environment. There seems to be evidence that speakers in intercultural exchanges take a lenient attitude to each other's attempts at humour (Bell 2007). Furthermore, the very effort and mental dexterity needed for a learner of the language to successfully transpose a word or phrase from one context to another could be appreciated for those factors alone, transforming what would otherwise be a mundane comment into an example of wit:

> While in native speaker discourse, the satisfactoriness of talk typically lies in its nonroutine nature, its particular wittiness and harmoniousness, which makes it the achievement of somes rather than anys, in non-native speaker discourse, even the routine may be problematic, with the result that its successful bringing-off can appear a noteworthy accomplishment that provides grounds for mutual satisfaction. (Aston 1993: 239)

Finally, the very limitation on the linguistic resources accessible to non-native speakers means that locally emergent expressions which,

112   D. Hann

among native speakers would not usually outlive the conversation in which they first appeared, could be hypothesised to be more likely to become part of the group's active repertoire of humorous reference points. In other words, the comparative narrowness of associations that a word or phrase may have for the learner is likely to make its recontextualisation that much more significant, evoking a previous context of use, one likely to be shared with their fellow learners. In such circumstances, it is a metonym for that shared experience, a figurative expression of common ground.

5.2 Evidence of Recontextualisation for Playful Purposes

Having considered the way in which language carries with it flavours of its previous contextualised uses and how the transfer of language to new contexts can trigger humour, we now look at the ways in which my research participants recontextualise previously encountered language for their own communicative and comedic ends.

5.2.1 Taking Ownership of Learnt Language and Evoking Shared Experience

Being able to incorporate new words and phrases into their active repertoire is a significant moment for language learners. During the morning when Group B were recorded, the meaning of the word "impressive" becomes a subject for debate among the participants. Only one of their numbers, Takeshi, feels confident of its meaning when it first comes up for discussion. He gives the example of the painting of Monet's Water Lilies which he had seen in Paris as something which he found impressive. The group's teacher, Ray, then asks the rest of the group for examples of things that they had found impressive during their stay in London. At first, they complain about the rain which is "bad impressive", but then Viktor mentions something which has left a more favourable impression on him:

5 Evoking Frames Through Associated Language   113

EPISODE 9: YESTERDAY PUBS

Viktor:	but pubs (2)
Andrei:	@@[@*
Viktor:	[yest*erday pubs (4) very good (1)
Andrei:	yes (1)
Viktor:	good [impressive*
Andrei:	[good* [impressive*
Ray:	[was very* [impressive*
Viktor:	[was* very impressive (.)
Ray:	good was very impressive (.) yesterday's pub was [very impressive*
Viktor:	[was very* impressive (1)
Thom:	((*gives thumbs up*)) < @ I agree with you >

Ray attempts to get the learners to decouple the word "impressive" from Takeshi's anecdote and use it to refer to another context. As mentioned previously, without such decoupling and reuse, no learning can be evidenced. Viktor's mention of pubs is significant. An inkling of the group's professed relationship with alcohol has already been seen in EPISODE 2 (Sect. 4.1.4). On that occasion, Viktor's miming of raising a glass of champagne prompts a discussion among its members of the group's drinking habits. It is clear that the collective enterprise of going to the pub forms an important part of the group's sense of shared identity. This does not necessarily extend to all its members. Ray told me that Takeshi did not always join the others in the evening. Neither, from the evidence of the data, does he play as much as they do. Interestingly, when Viktor mentions yesterday's pub (or it may indeed be "pubs"—whether the group made a night of it is unclear), Andrei immediately backs him up. This is significant, not only because he and Thomas reinforce the group's collective identity as hard drinkers, but also because Viktor employs the newly learnt piece of lexis in order to do so, albeit with a non-standard intensifier "good". This provides clear evidence of a learner taking possession of an element of the TL and using it for his own ends as he evokes the group's shared socialising.

114   D. Hann

As mentioned on various occasions, the participants on a BizLang course cannot assume that they share cultural reference points. As a result, among the few allusions which they can safely expect to be successful are those to experiences they have had together. In the previous chapter, the playful blending of frames has already been remarked upon. In the exchanges highlighted below, the learners evoke previous experiences by using language associated with them. One such occasion occurs in Group A's lively negotiation (see EPISODES 1, 7 and 8). In order to make sense of the exchange below, it needs to be understood that, prior to the role-play, the group had practised comparative forms and these had been reinforced in the language laboratory using the examples of different makes of car. Antoine cleverly draws on this shared experience at a moment in the negotiation where the suppliers' team (of which he is one) have made a price offer which the customers have rejected as too high. Nevertheless, Antoine remains undeterred:

EPISODE 10: YOU WANT COMPARE A VOLVO WITH A FERRARI?

Ant: your price on the other price of other car [is different*
Dieter: [so* so you will say us
          you want [the*
Ant: [you* want compare a Volvo with a Ferrari? =
Others: = @[@*@@
Dieter: [no* so you will us say that we have (1) you will take us the
          same price as last year

Antoine triggers laughter and defuses a rather tense situation by cleverly evoking the previous laboratory drill while simultaneously alluding to the quality of his company's product (presumably, he is implicitly likening it to the prestigious Ferrari). Of course, it is significant that an outsider hearing the interaction for the first time would find it puzzling, not because the language used is incorrect—although there is a slight grammatical error—but because the reference to a previously shared learning experience is, by its nature, exclusive. The wit of

5 Evoking Frames Through Associated Language 115

Antoine's utterance lies in its ability to evoke the previously shared context through the reproduction of a phrase which, nevertheless, remains congruous to the current communicative moment. It is also interesting that Antoine does not use a phrase which the learners had to repeat in the laboratory. Rather, he attempts to reproduce the trainer's cue for the language drill. He, therefore, consciously voices the figure of authority and, as in previously analysed exchanges, gently subverts that authority in the process. The reaction of collective laughter can be explained, at least in part, by the purchase that the recontextualised phrase has for the learners. The laboratory session is still fresh in their minds and probably so is the grammar session that preceded it. This fresh association, coupled with the phrase's use by Antoine in a new and unexpected context, produces amusement. It is also noteworthy that the words, like many recontextualisations featured in this chapter, already have the potential to be entextualised—rendered extractable from their original context— by the teacher providing them as a readily reusable chunk of language. In this case, they were originally realised as a laboratory cue. In other cases, the recontextualisations are of phrases which the teacher had explicitly taught as useful language for the learners to master.

Another moment where the group's shared learning experiences are evoked occurs some ten minutes after the episode above. As the negotiation continues, the customers (Koji and Dieter) drop the bombshell that they are developing their own in-house product which, on the face of it, suggests that they are not tied to their suppliers (Antoine and Mario). This prompts some interesting exchanges which to an outsider are unremarkable. However, to the participants, they are pregnant with added meaning:

EPISODE 11: GOOD QUESTION

Dieter: I [call* tomorrow with the (.) I call tomorrow with [the*
Mario: [how*   [how* long
        does it take to (.) to be (1) [to*=
Ant: [(xxx)*

Mario:	=to produce ourself-yourself?
Dieter:	p-pardon?
Mario:	ho[w*
Ant:	[how* long time to produce (1) @@ do you need yourself? =
Mario:	= how long =
Dieter:	= oh it's very quickly very quickly (.)
Koji:	good question (.)
All:	@@@@

In fact, the group's trainer, Harriet, informed me that they had been practising questions about duration earlier that day. Laughter is precipitated by Antoine's efforts to get the form right. Koji's reply— "good question"— seems to refer neatly both to the form of Antoine's question and to the negotiation context itself. In fact, in their pre-negotiation preparation, Dieter and Koji had realised that they did not have enough time to develop their own product before their current agreement with the suppliers ran out. Thus, the latter's response is an acknowledgement of the pertinence of Antoine's enquiry as well as its attempt at grammatical well-formedness. It could be argued here, rather as with Antoine's voicing of the trainer's laboratory cue in the previous episode, that Koji is assuming the mantle of authority by taking on the role of trainer in giving praise to the linguistic efforts of his fellow learner. After all, teachers typically give their students encouraging back-channelling feedback when the latter produce target words and phrases. So, as seen with the data in Sect. 4.2, the learner manages to blend the two frames of the simulation and the lesson by producing a phrase which simultaneously refers to and can be applied to both.

In the last two analysed episodes, voicing is used as a means of blending frames and evoking shared experience. It is this phenomenon which is focussed on in more detail in the next section, where language which has been taught as having a particular communicative intention is infused with the speaker's own meanings, triggering irony and humour.

5 Evoking Frames Through Associated Language   117

5.2.2 Subverting Learnt Language for the Speaker's Own Intentions

It has already been noted that at the heart of Bakhtin's account of the nature of language is the idea that it is forever being recycled and reshaped by use. He sees all language use as involving the voicing of previous speakers (Bakhtin 1984a: 193). When the speaker introduces a semantic intention which is opposed to that of the original, then he characterises this as vari-directional double-voicing. The vari-directional nature of the utterance is often signalled through tone of voice or other cues. This concept seems to relate closely to Goffman's (1981) footing, the alignment that a speaker takes up in relation to the words that he or she utters.

The simulated negotiation featured in the last two analysed episodes contains a couple of moments which are noteworthy for vari-directional double-voicing. During a particularly heated series of exchanges between Dieter and the representatives of the other party, Antoine and Mario, Koji interjects:

EPISODE 12: LET'S SUM UP

Dieter: before we give a price (1) we will (.) show you a picture from the situation [from Koenig*
Mario: [another picture?*=
Ant: = another picture no =
Dieter: = please can you let me speak [xxx*
Ant: [you know you need a picture to speak about the price? (1)
Mario: speak the price [and then talk about the picture*
Ant: [@@@* (.)
Dieter: OK um (.) we have no problem to finish the er [conversation*
Ant: [it's not to* it's not to finish =
Koji: = let's sum up =
All: = @@@

118   D. Hann

The group has grown somewhat tired of Dieter's loquaciousness, and the simulated meeting provides Mario and Antoine with the cover they need to vent their feelings about this. Koji, Dieter's partner in the role-play, finds a way to defend him by cleverly utilising a phrase—"let's sum up"—explicitly taught as a means of structuring and clarifying one's message in the feedback after a previous simulated meeting. The contrast between this taught function and its use as a way of shutting up the other party in the negotiation seems to provide the source of the humour which everyone appreciates. Conveying a meaning which is opposed to that for which it was originally taught can also be seen moments earlier when Mario interrupts Dieter:

EPISODE 13: SORRY, MAY I STOP YOU FOR A MOMENT?

Dieter:	and you didn't can lost (1) and you didn't can (last) (.)
Mario:	sorry (.) may I-may I stop you (.) for a moment (.)
Dieter:	[yes*
All:	[@*@@@

Mario's contribution produces seemingly disproportionate laughter from everyone in the room and even Dieter joins in. Again, the humour seems to lie in the contrast between Mario's real meaning and the phrase used. "Sorry, may I stop you for a moment?" had been taught as a polite form of taking the floor in part of the same feedback package with "let's sum up" (see EPISODE 12). The humour seems to come from the contrast between the surface meaning of the phrase and what is really meant. Interestingly, in neither case is the irony signalled clearly by any shift in intonation, although, in this case, Mario subtly enhances the comedy with a brief pause before he says "for a moment". Nevertheless, as Kotthoff (2003: 1389) points out, the cues to signal irony can be purely contextual. Both these extracts show the learners using language ironically. These examples are not so different from the way in which a native speaker might take an overtly polite phrase such as "Can you possibly see your way clear to…?", associated with a particularly delicate request as a means of asking an everyday favour such as passing the salt. In both the episodes, the gap between what is said and what is meant

5 Evoking Frames Through Associated Language 119

is simultaneously the source of the ironic humour and the potential defence against any riposte to it, as the speaker could point to the surface meaning and refute the implied meaning. What is also noteworthy is the fact that this ironic flavour allows the learners to take ownership of the recontextualised language. Rather like Viktor using the words of the recorded dialogue for his own ends (see EPISODE 2), both Koji and Mario break free of the role of mere animators and become principals of the words they utter.

An interesting example of the process in action whereby a group takes charge of the meaning of a particular phrase and uses it to evoke a shared experience while also teasing one of its members can be seen at the beginning of Group B's training day when they are revising language from earlier in the week. Their teacher, Ray, has been trying to elicit the phrase "miss the target" which the group had first encountered a couple of days previously by asking for the opposite of "hit the target". In the original context, they had been discussing graphs which they had produced pertaining to their jobs:

EPISODE 14: YESTERDAY YOU MISS

Mich:	the target? =
Ray:	= hit the target? (.)
Andrei:	((*whistles*)) =
Mich:	= errr (.) miss the target (.)
Ray:	yeay (.) bravo well done (.) miss the target good (.)
Viktor:	((*puts his hand on Michele's arm*)) yesterday you miss (.)
Andrei:	mmm-hmm (.)
Mich:	miss the target? =
Andrei:	= yeah you promise- you promised a drink everybody (1)
Ray:	aa[hh yes*
Andrei:	[remember yeah* ((*whistles*)) (.)
Mich:	err (.)
Ray:	<@ and? > (1)
Mich:	on lunch (.) [very good lunch*
Ray:	[at at lunch* (.)
Andrei:	imagine (.) not-not only to drink < @ and feed > =

Others: = [@@*@@
Mich: [no sorry*
Viktor: ((*over continuing laughter*)) I don't [understand*
Mich: [(I don't* understand) (1)
Andrei: popularity (2) ((*points at M*)) not only to drink (1) and plus
           to feed ((*gestures eating*)) (2) feed (.)
Ray: feed? (.)
Thom: ((*also simulates eating*)) mangiare (.)
Mich: plus (2) I-I promised (.) one drink (.) for [each person*
Ray: [yeah yeah yeah* this
           is a single [drink*
Mich: [a single* drink for each person (.) if you want (.)
           table dance (.) lunch(.) dinner (1)
Others: @@[@@*
Mich: [well (2) < @ I'm stupid* > (.)
Ray: we didn't- we didn't win the lottery (.) come on (.) OK =
Others: = @@@@

Michele missed the target the day before by not standing his round at
the pub. Obviously, the above exchange would be puzzling to an outsider for a couple of reasons. Firstly, the phrase "miss the target" is, by
native standards, semantically misapplied. It is extended to encompass
a context (the pub) with which it is not usually associated (except perhaps when playing darts!). Here can be seen an example of overextension, much as a child might overextend a meaning when learning a first
language. However, the phrase is, within the group, pragmatically successful: Andrei immediately follows up Viktor's opening and everyone
seems to understand what he is referring to (except, briefly, Michele
himself). Secondly, an outsider would not know about the original context to which the group alludes. Much of the pleasure of the moment
seems to derive from this reference to a shared experience. It would not
be surprising if this episode were discussed again at some later stage
(maybe at the next pub visit) and become part of the group's active repertoire of reference points.

The episode shows how a learnt phrase is employed for the
group's own social ends. "Miss the target" had been learnt in the

5 Evoking Frames Through Associated Language   121

serious-minded context of a discussion of business trends. The group recontextualise it and imbue it with their own intentions, thus reframing, indeed hijacking, an exchange which is originally about revising job-related vocabulary as a teasing reprimand to one of their number about his social obligations.

Another noteworthy element of the recontextualisation is that it alters the structure of talk here, much as the structure of talk was disrupted in EPISODE 2 during a comprehension exercise. These exchanges take place in a revision phase of the class. As such, the opening exchanges follow the classic IRF structure of Sinclair and Coulthard's (1975) model. Ray asks Michele a question (Initiation). After an initial check, Michele answers (Response) and then Ray provides him with feedback (sometimes called Follow-up). This structure is then interrupted by Viktor's "yesterday you miss" which is quickly taken up by Andrei: "you promise you promised a drink…". This restructuring of the talk can be seen as a subversion of the power dynamic in the group, albeit sanctioned by the teacher who encourages the group to develop their anecdote by prompting with an "and?" when Michele's initial promise to the group is first mentioned.

5.2.3 Using Language Associated with the Trainer

Voicing of the trainer has already been witnessed as a means of fusing the simulated frame with the outer frame of the language lesson (see EPISODES 10 and 11). There are other moments outside simulated role-plays where the learners take on the voice of the trainer. Within the classroom setting itself, authority is typically embodied in the figure of the teacher. Within the framework of the lesson, the person in this role has, within reason, the power to tell the students what to do, at least with regard to the objective of improving their second language skills. Of course, the teacher's authority does not go unquestioned in every context (e.g. Rampton 2006a), but the BizLang classroom is rarely one that witnesses real rebellion. However, this does not mean that it is one which is immune to forms of power play between teacher and learners and among the learners themselves. Assuming the role of teacher is one

122   D. Hann

means the learners have of claiming power, however fleetingly and symbolically. Just such an episode can be found in the phase of Group B's lesson of which EPISODE 2 forms a part. The group are repeating from a recording that provides some of the background to a meeting in which they will participate:

EPISODE 15: REPEAT!

Ray: OK Takeshi (.) here we are (2)
TAPE: ((*Knock, knock*)) *ladies and gentlemen* (.)
Andrei: ((*knocks on table*)) @@@ repeat (2)
Tak: ((*knocks on table*)) ladies and gentlemen =
Others: = @@@@

Andrei takes the procedure, now familiar to the group, whereby the trainer asks the students to repeat what they hear on a recording, and he turns it into an absurdity. He firstly adopts the role of unthinking student, simply repeating what he hears. However, in this case, he does not repeat a particular word or phrase but imitates the knocking sound from the recording. This, of course, has no merit in terms of helping with his language acquisition. After knocking on the table, he immediately changes footing and assumes the role of the group's trainer, asking his colleagues to repeat and, in so doing, passes judgement on the usefulness of the exercise itself. He would probably deny that he had any such intention. However, part of the fun of the episode is its subversive dimension, however ritualistic that might be. It is noteworthy that Takeshi, the most reserved and least playful of the group on the evidence of the collected data, enthusiastically joins in by rapping on the table. As a BizLang trainer, I have used the particular pre-meeting dialogue that features here on a number of occasions and Andrei's exhortation to repeat is not the first time in my experience that a student has reacted as he does.

Another moment where one of the learners mouths words which are associated with the group's trainer, happens in the same group. It is later on the same morning of the listening exercise, and the group members are deciding who will chair a simulated meeting for which they have

5 Evoking Frames Through Associated Language 123

been preparing. There is a general reluctance to take on the responsibility that chairing entails:

EPISODE 16: TAKE ONE AND PASS THEM ON

Ray: so (1) whose turn to chair the meeting (3) whose turn (1) you were yesterday in (2) who's next (.) who's next (.)
Andrei: Viktor (2)
Viktor: mm? (.) no (1)
Andrei: yes (1)
Viktor: Takeshi (2)
Andrei: Takeshi no (.) Michele (.) Michele no (.) Andrei (.) Andrei no (x) @@ =
Ray: = and roll around round two (.)
Mich: take one and pass them on (1)
Viktor: <@ take one and pass them on > =
Others: = @@@

At first glance, Michele's last contribution—"take one and pass them on"—makes no sense yet is appreciated by the others because it evokes something that their teacher, Ray, had said regularly over the week when passing out papers to the group. It could represent another example of overextension (see EPISODE 14), where the meaning of the phrase has been stretched beyond its usual semantic boundaries. It seems that Michele may well have wanted to convey the idea of passing the buck, although this is not recoverable from the data alone. However, like the previous example, it shows that there is a strong impulse to reuse language and test out the limits of its meanings. Michele's utterance carries with it associations with its past uses, a dialogical dimension which has an important social function as it produces a shared laugh of recognition among those present even though they may not have a secure grasp of its semantic meaning.

A further example of a learner assuming the trainer's role is taken from Group C. It is the beginning of the day and Bilel and Joseph are explaining to Harriet and David how, on the previous evening, they had come to miss the London gig of their fellow group member, Sandro, a

124   D. Hann

keen musician. The narrative has become recriminatory in nature, with Joseph and Bilel blaming each other for being late for Sandro's performance. However, the exchanges are never less than good humoured. In this excerpt, they have just talked about their visit to the British Museum which preceded their attempt to get to Sandro's gig. After the museum, Joseph called his wife:

EPISODE 17: YOU SHOULD

Joseph: after the British Museum I call her (.) and say maybe I-I will call
          you later (1) maybe I will go to see Sandro (1)
Bilel: ((*points at Joseph*)) you spoke with your wife in French (.) I hear
          you (2)
Joseph: ((*shrugs shoulders*)) < @ yeah > =
Bilel: ((*continues to point*)) = I heard you (.) you should (1)
Joseph: ((*smiles*)) you should =
Bilel: = you should =
Joseph: = [speak*
Bilel: [speak* with your wife in English

Here, Bilel recontextualises a structure that the group had practised the day before. The modal form "you should" had been used to generate various examples of commands and strong advice. Bilel takes on the role of the authority figure by assuming that of the teacher and using the role for his own ends. In the BizLang context, as previously mentioned, the English only rule is one of the few that is explicitly reinforced with students during their stay. Perhaps because it is difficult for him to modify his accent or voice quality in English, Bilel accompanies his words with finger wagging, lending the episode a pantomimic quality which signals that it is humorously keyed and should not be taken too seriously. Joseph reacts in the light-hearted spirit in which it was meant and, despite being the object of the rebuke, smiles and prompts Bilel with the correct form. Both students take clear pleasure in the process of recontextualising language from the previous day's lesson. Interestingly, Bilel asserts power through a teacher–student role reversal whereby he reinforces institutional power while, at the same time,

5 Evoking Frames Through Associated Language — 125

asserting his own power within the group. Humour allows him to do this in a way which would not otherwise be possible. It is reminiscent of Dieter's rebuke to Antoine when arriving late for his simulated meeting (see EPISODE 7) and is carnivalesque in nature (Bakhtin 1984b: 112–113).

The ambiguity that play allows means that Bilel's assertion of power does not really threaten the authority of the teacher. Indeed, in this case, it could be said to be reinforcing it. In fact, there are no moments in the data which suggest any serious bid to usurp the institutional power embodied in the teacher's role. In part, this may be because the power dynamic in an organisation like BizLang is rather different from that in the state sector such as the schools in which Rampton (1999, 2006b) researches. In the latter, it is clear that real power is manifested in the educational institution and its staff. The children are subject to it and, however much they might undermine or demoralise its representatives, they can never completely overthrow its power over them. In BizLang, on the other hand, who holds power is a more open to question. Although the staff generally dictate the learning agenda, the students are also the organisation's clients, retaining the prerogative to go elsewhere if they are not happy with the service provided.

5.2.4 Evoking Assumed Shared Knowledge Through Associated Language

Unsurprisingly, the course participants assume that they share schemata for particular situations and events, even when they have not experienced those situations and events together. Dieter's utterance "Do you want a glass of champagne?" (EPISODE 1) only works as a dual reference to the simulated frame and classroom frame that he is simultaneously operating within if his fellow group members understand that successful negotiations are sometimes sealed with a drink. Similarly, his exclamation of "hands up!" as he points at his adversaries (EPISODE 8) is only successful as a means of releasing tension because his interlocutors grasp that the phrase is intimately connected to and metonymically stands for a children's game of Cowboys and Indians or Cops and Robbers.

126   D. Hann

Another episode, again involving Dieter, exemplifies the impulse to find common ground by making a specific intertextual reference which he presumes the others will understand. At one point in the simulated negotiation in which he is taking part, he sums up the dynamic of the meeting as he sees it:

EPISODE 18: SAME PROCEDURE

Dieter: and so I think it is a normal situation (.) you want the highest price and we want the (.) smallest price it's a normal thing (2) it's (a thing) every year (.) same procedure as every year (2)

Here, he quotes from a TV sketch that, despite being in English, is well known in the German-speaking world and is shown annually during the Christmas and New Year holidays on the networks there.[1] The sketch features the catchphrase "the same procedure as every year", and it is to this that Dieter refers (something he confirmed to me in the coffee break later). Needless to say, this goes unrecognised by the other group members at the time. Indeed, Harriet, the BizLang colleague who viewed some of my raw data, was also unaware of it. This is noteworthy because the speaker uses a phrase which is relevant to the communicative needs of the moment in the simulated frame. At the same time, he attempts to activate another potential framework to which the group could refer and possibly play with by using an associated phrase to metonymically stand for the TV sketch. However, this recontextualisation has no purchase for the other students because it holds no resonances for them. As a result, the moment passes unnoticed by everybody except me as I'd heard this sketch referred to by other German students on previous courses. There is a noticeable silence which ensues where it could be hypothesised that Dieter is waiting for a reaction from the other group members that does not materialise. This contrasts tellingly with the same speaker's successful evocation of western or mobster films in EPISODE 8.

---

[1]See https://en.wikipedia.org/wiki/Dinner_for_One (accessed 13.06.2019).

5.3 Playing with the Semantic Properties of Language

This chapter has revealed the ways in which learners use the resources available to them. They creatively blend the frames that the language classroom provides. They also use learnt language to evoke shared experiences. However, as posited at the beginning of the volume, the kinds of wordplay which L1 speakers sometimes indulge in (e.g. Carter 2004; Chiaro 1992; Crystal 1998) are not much in evidence. Figurative play among the research participants tends to be metonymic in nature, where a word or phrase stands for a previous, usually shared, experience. Even so, there is some evidence of play with the literal and metaphorical meanings of words and it is to these that the discussion now turns.

In the following example, Takeshi from group A has just been talking about something which he has found "impressive" in a recent visit to Paris (see the discussion that introduces EPISODE 9). Under the teacher's prompting, he checks whether the others have understood what he has been saying:

EPISODE 19: I'M ON THE LEFT OF YOU

Tak: thinking (2) ((*points to head*)) impression ((*looks at others*)) (4)
Thom: the first impression(.)
Ray: are you with me? (.)
Tak: are you with me? (2)
Andrei: yeah yeah (.) I'm on the left of you (.) Michele on the right of you (.) [we're here*=
Viktor: [@@@*
Andrei: = don't worry (2)
Ray: joker on the left (.)
Others: @@@@

Here, Andrei plays with the literal and metaphorical meanings of Takeshi's question. Measured in terms of native-speaker wit, this is a rather laboured pun. However, in the context of his and the group's language level, it is an impressive piece of wordplay although it produces little laughter until the teacher's contribution. Indeed, a couple of BizLang colleagues who witnessed the recorded exchanges interpreted Andrei's words as hurtful to Takeshi. Robert commented "laughter is nervous laughter by the others… he crossed the line" while another, Ruby, remarked with regard to this exchange, "what hit me particularly was the just very very subtle relationship between laughter and cruelty". Both Ray's contribution and the group's reaction to it are also noteworthy here. Firstly, "joker on the left" is an intertextual reference to a song from the early 1970s which also features in a famous torture scene in the 1992 film *Reservoir Dogs*. The fact that the teacher uses it here shows that the impulse to join in with play is a strong one for many people. In fact, it is unlikely that all those who laughed would have understood the allusion. However, they still laughed. In part, they might have enjoyed the surface meaning of Ray's words but the laughter was probably also indicative of one of its social functions—to please its receiver. Indeed, evidence elsewhere (Bell 2007) suggests a certain tolerance of attempts at humour among native and non-native speakers where the social benefits of laughter can override any actual understanding of humorous language play.

Interestingly, the second example of clear wordplay involves the very same clarification phrase "I'm with/not with you". Group C are preparing for a simulated meeting which involves allocating equipment and staff to new offices. At the beginning, they are ascertaining how much equipment and how many staff they have:

EPISODE 20: WITHOUT

Bilel: twenty-three people (.) we have twenty-three people (.)
Sandro: no (.)
Bilel: wha? (3) what (2)
Joseph: you have two salemen (.) two secretaries (.) two technical [assistants*
Sandro: [not twenty*-three (.)
Bilel: how much (.)
Joseph: one two three (1) four five (4) seven =

5 Evoking Frames Through Associated Language 129

Sandro:	= twelve =
Joseph:	= nine =
Bilel:	= twelve OK (1)
Joseph:	twelve yes twelve (.)
Bilel:	I check only if you're with me or [not*
Joseph:	[@*@@ without (.)
Bilel:	<@ without (.) OK >

Bilel initially gets some of the information wrong. However, he covers himself by pretending that his mistake was in fact a strategy to check on the others' understanding. In doing this, he uses the phrase "if you're with me or not". Joseph then plays between the idiomatic/metaphorical meaning and the literal meaning to create an absurd response. Significantly, Bilel repeats it. On seeing this, my colleague, Geraint, said:

> if a very linguistically adept and deft native speaker did that, if a kind of Mick Smith (a work colleague) said that, we'd all kind of arch our eyebrows and go 'clever bit of word play, clever bit of wordplay, Mick'. But from a D level from a D level non-native speaker, it looks kind of just OK, as a bit resourceful but maybe it was more than that.

This again raises the question of native privilege and the notion of the L2 speaker's reduced personality (Harder 1980). However, although there is the danger that some non-native speaker wit may go unacknowledged, the fact that only two instances of punning are present in this data and that they both involve playing with the same expression suggests that native-like wordplay is rarely attempted by learners at the lower end of the proficiency scale.

5.4 Conclusion

This chapter has shown the resourcefulness of the research participants in using what they have available to them in order to play. The analysis shows that the learners exploit the simulated and language learning frames of the classroom, often blending them to invert established roles or to create absurd scenarios. They also use recontextualisation as a means of generating humour. The locus of their humour and play lies primarily in the process of transposing words, phrases or other communicative elements from one context with which the learners associate them to a different context. It does not lie in playing with the ambiguity of semantic meaning within the words and phrases themselves which is common in some native speaker play and is the focus of Raskin's (1985) analysis. In the process of recontextualisation, the learners often use certain words and phrases to metonymically stand for shared experiences of which the words were originally a part. The importance of shared experience points to the social and cultural dimension to such play. However, an investigation into the sociocultural element of HLP is very restricted if its development is not traced, especially given its incremental nature which allows in-group references to accumulate as a potential resource bank for future exchanges. This expression of group identity through shared humorous reference points is a phenomenon which has been noted by researchers in the talk among groups of native speakers (e.g. Carter 2004; Coates 2007; Holmes and Marra 2006). For this reason, the next three chapters are dedicated to analysing the play of a pair of learners and their teacher over two continuous days of their course together, as the role of HLP in the establishment of relationships and in-group culture is tracked and analysed.

References

Aston, G. (1993). Notes on the interlanguage of comity. In G. Kasper & S. Blum-Kulka (Eds.), *Interlanguage pragmatics* (pp. 224–250). New York: Oxford University Press.

Bakhtin, M. M. (1981). *The dialogic imagination*. Austin: University of Texas Press.

Bakhtin, M. M. (1984a). *Problems of Dostoevsky's poetics*. Minneapolis: University of Minnesota Press.

Bakhtin, M. M. (1984b). *Rabelais and his world*. Bloomington: Indiana University Press.

Bauman, R., & Briggs, C. L. (1990). Poetics and performance as critical perspectives on language. *Annual Review of Anthropology, 19,* 59–88.

Bell, N. D. (2007). How native and non-native English speakers adapt to humor in intercultural interaction. *Humor, 20*(1), 27–48. https://doi.org/10.1515/HUMOR.2007.002.

Carter, R. (2004). *Language and creativity: The art of common talk.* Abingdon: Routledge.

Chiaro, D. (1992). *The language of jokes: Analysing verbal play.* London: Routledge.

Coates, J. (2007). Talk in a play frame: More on laughter and intimacy. *Journal of Pragmatics, 39*(1), 29–49. https://doi.org/10.1016/j.pragma.2006.05.003.

Crystal, D. (1998). *Language play.* London: Penguin Books.

DaSilva Iddings, A. C., & McCafferty, S. G. (2007). Carnival in a mainstream kindergarten classroom: A Bakhtinian analysis of second language learners' off-task behaviors. *Modern Language Journal, 91*(1), 31–44. https://doi.org/10.1111/j.1540-4781.2007.00508.x.

Eagleton, T. (1983). *Literary theory: An introduction.* Oxford: Basil Blackwell.

Eisenlohr, P. (2010). Materialities of entextualization: The domestication of sound reproduction in Mauritian Muslim devotional practices. *Journal of Linguistic Anthropology, 20*(2), 314–333. https://doi.org/10.1111/j.1548-1395.2010.01072.x.

Goffman, E. (1981). *Forms of talk.* Oxford: Blackwell.

Harder, P. (1980). Discourse as self-expression—On the reduced personality of the second-language learner. *Applied Linguistics, 1,* 262–270.

Holmes, J., & Marra, M. (2006). Humor and leadership style. *Humor, 19*(2), 119–138. https://doi.org/10.1515/HUMOR.2006.006.

Kay, D. A., & Anglin, J. M. (1982). Overextension and underextension in the child's expressive and receptive speech. *Journal of Child Language, 9,* 83–98.

Kotthoff, H. (2003). Responding to irony in different contexts: On cognition in conversation. *Journal of Pragmatics, 35*(9), 1387–1411. https://doi.org/10.1016/S0378-2166(02)00182-0.

Kristeva, J. (1980). *Desire in language: A semiotic approach to literature and art.* New York: Columbia University Press.

Linell, P. (1998). *Approaching dialogue: Talk, interaction and contexts in dialogical perspectives.* Amsterdam: John Benjamins.

Maybin, J. (1994). Children's voices: Talk, knowledge and identity. In D. Graddol, J. Maybin, & B. Stierer (Eds.), *Researching language and literacy in social context* (pp. 131–150). Clevedon: Multilingual Matters.

Morreall, J. (1987). *The philosophy of laughter and humour.* New York: State University of New York.

Pennycook, A. (2007). "The rotation gets thick. The constraints get thin": Creativity, recontextualization, and difference. *Applied Linguistics, 28*(4), 579–596. https://doi.org/10.1093/applin/amm043.

Rampton, B. (1999). Dichotomies, difference, and ritual in second language learning and teaching. *Applied Linguistics, 20*(3), 316–340. https://doi.org/10.1093/applin/20.3.316.

Rampton, B. (2006a). Language crossing. In J. Maybin & J. Swann (Eds.), *The art of English: Everyday creativity* (pp. 131–139). Basingstoke: Palgrave Macmillan.

Rampton, B. (2006b). *Language in late modernity: Interaction in an urban school.* Cambridge: Cambridge University Press.

Raskin, V. (1985). *Semantic mechanisms of humor.* Dordrecht, Holland: D. Reidel.

Saussure, F. de. (1959). *Course in general linguistics.* London: Peter Owen.

Sinclair, J., & Coulthard, M. (1975). *Towards an analysis of discourse.* Oxford: Oxford University Press.

Tannen, D. (2006). Intertextuality in interaction: Reframing family arguments in public and private. *Text and Talk, 26*(4–5), 597–617. https://doi.org/10.1515/TEXT.2006.024.

Trester, A. M. (2012). Framing entextualization in improv: Intertextuality as an interactional resource. *Language in Society, 41*(2), 237–258. https://doi.org/10.1017/S0047404512000061.

Widdowson, H. G. (2004). *Text, context, pretext: Critical issues in discourse analysis.* Oxford: Blackwell.

6

A Case Study: Overcoming Failure in the Search for Common Ground

6.1 Rationale for Recording a Group Over a Continuous Period

I mention at the beginning of this book that the idea for my research was born out of my long experience of teaching English as a foreign language. I often found that when I first started teaching a group whose members had already been together for a number of days, I could expect to hear in-group language and references which trigger laughter and whose meaning was not necessarily immediately accessible to me. The exclusive nature of such behaviour is commonly recognised and has been noted in research contexts such as the workplace (Holmes 2000: 159) and the adult numeracy classroom (Baynham 1996: 194).

By the nature of humorous in-group language, its meaning arises in its context of use. As Boxer and Cortés-Conde (1997: 277) point out, "[i]n situational humour being there becomes a very important part of getting it". However, being there at any one moment is not enough. As my own experience of puzzlement when taking over a group shows, the humour's exclusive quality has grown out of the learners' shared experiences. So, it is not just a question of being there but also of having

© The Author(s) 2020   **133**
D. Hann, *Spontaneous Play in the Language Classroom*,
https://doi.org/10.1007/978-3-030-26304-1_6

been there. This provides a strong rationale for recording and analysing interactions over a continuous period that encompass more than one activity or one session.[1] True, my own extensive knowledge of BizLang's classroom practices and routines together with post-recording discussions with a group's trainer can provide insights into the types of shared experiences and language that the learners draw upon in order to play. Nonetheless, recorded data of these shared moments and how they are subsequently played with provides even more compelling evidence of the phenomena that are the focus of this research. Furthermore, an extended recording enables an investigation into how in-group reference points and language develop and change with each instance of use. Analysing interactions over a continuous period not only allows for an investigation into play's incremental nature but also an examination of the frequency, duration and distribution of playful episodes, and the likelihood of their occurrence in or around particular types of classroom activity.

The data analysed in previous chapters indicates that, despite the challenge of communicating in a language over which they do not have mastery and despite lacking the cultural common ground which facilitates the formation of a cohesive social unit, learners are adept at forging social links. Play is an important means of evoking their limited shared experiences together. So, for instance, learners exploit the frameworks of interpretation that a classroom in particular makes available in order to call forth experiences that they have had together. It has been noted how learners exploit the lamination of frames where the role-play represents "…the innermost layering, wherein dramatic activity can be at play to engross the participant" (Goffman 1974: 82) while, in the outermost layer, the role-play can be viewed as a mere vehicle to a learning end. Learners often blend frames to comic effect by highlighting the contrast between the real world and the simulated one (e.g. EPISODE 3). These contrasts can create a world of carnival (Bakhtin 1984),

---

[1] By "session" here, I am referring to an unbroken period in the classroom. Although there is no formalised timetable at BizLang, teachers and their groups usually have short breaks from the classroom every hour and a half to two hours.

a place where the most junior members of a group can assume power (e.g. EPISODE 5) and where the impossible becomes possible, such as the dead rising again and speaking (see EPISODE 4). In this blending of frames, learners not only mix the available here-and-now frameworks that a particular moment supplies but also bring in references to their preceding shared experiences. These can include nights out together in the pub (EPISODE 14), language laboratory drills (EPISODE 10) and other learning experiences. In this, the role of language is important in that words and phrases associated with one context of use are recontextualised, often producing an incongruity which is humorous in effect. These shared moments are more easily traced and their development analysed when learners are recorded for a continuous period together.

6.2 Background to the Case Study

Two people were recorded on a one-week "blend" course. A blend consists of three days in a group followed by two days of one-to-one training. I taught the pair for the opening phase of their course and recorded them continuously on their second and third days, giving them their first day to settle in rather than recording them from the outset. They then each had different trainers for their final two days.

An objection that might be put forward is that my taking part in the exchanges under scrutiny compromises my position as researcher. In fact, I would say that being actively involved in the interactions gives me a privileged insight into their nature. Furthermore, the observer's paradox is lessened by the fact that the interactions were recorded by a continuously running camera rather than a mute observer sitting in a corner. This holds especially true in the relatively intimate context of three people together in a room. It is also important to add that nearly all of the play was instigated by the learners themselves. This is not to say, however, that my presence did not influence the playful behaviour of the two learners or, indeed, that I did not participate in noteworthy episodes of play. My role in the playful behaviour evident in the data will be analysed in Chapter 8.

My selection of particular episodes as worthy of analysis is informed, in part, by the patterns which had emerged among the three groups I had recorded previously. So, in choosing particular exchanges to analyse, I was sensitive to any manipulation by the learners of the frames available to them in the classroom and the recontextualisation of language. The significance of these recontextualisations became apparent over the course of the two days as particular words and phrases were recycled for humorous purposes and became part of the in-group repertoire (see Chapter 7). Of course, of themselves, neither exploiting frames nor recontextualising language constitute HLP, so accompanying laughter and other contextualisation cues (Gumperz 1982: 131) such as exaggerated prosody and body language were also important in identifying significant exchanges. However, not all the episodes that feature in the case study chapters contain features such as repetition or contextualisation cues. Indeed, some do not contain HLP at all. Recording over two days gives particular exchanges retrospective significance because they are subsequently referred to and eventually lead to HLP. Looking back over the data allowed me to identify patterns and trace significant play to its source in a way which would not have been possible otherwise. Finally, I was also interested in uncovering unsuccessful attempts at play, although, by their nature, many of these may have gone unnoticed. However, dysfluencies, silence and a lack of response to playframe cues were potential indicators of such moments.

The two learners were initially classified as low C in BizLang terms which, roughly speaking, translates more widely into something like "low intermediate". In terms of the CEFR (see Sect. 3.1.3), they would fall into the B1 standard of Independent User, being able to understand and talk about most aspects of subjects with which they were familiar. Although they could be said to have more grounding in the language than some of the participants featured in this research, their general level of English was such at the time of the recording that wordplay as it is commonly understood was usually beyond their capability.

The two learners were Juan and Marek (see Sect. 3.2.5). Juan was the more outgoing and playful of the two. They had not met prior to the course and neither had been to BizLang before, although both had previously visited London. Their use of English in their jobs was usually,

6 A Case Study: Overcoming Failure in the Search ... 137

although not exclusively, with fellow L2 speakers, and they could be said to be part of the world of global communication where ELF is the preferred mode of interaction (Seidlhofer 2011).

Everything that happened in the classroom was filmed on a video camera placed on the corner of the table in the classroom. This amounted to about twelve hours of recordings, including moments where I was not present. Approximately forty-five minutes of classroom time was lost where, unbeknown to me, the camera did not record because its memory card was full. Despite this minor mishap, the data captures the ever-evolving culture within the classroom and the role in that process of the linguistic behaviours that are the focus of this research.

6.3 The Obstacles to Play as Revealed by the Data

I now turn to the analysis itself. In this chapter, I look at the failures in play that I was able to pinpoint and the insights these gave into the obstacles to play. I also explore two main resources that are used to overcome such obstacles—paralinguistic resources and the structures and sounds of the language itself.

6.3.1 Lack of Mastery of the Structures and Phonology of the TL

As has been mentioned previously, L2 speakers at the lower level of proficiency face a problem with attempting the kind of play that is commonly witnessed among native speakers (e.g. Carter 2004) involving, as they do, a knowledge and exploitation of the sounds, morphology and semantic properties of English. Some researchers in the field point to what they perceive as a need for such mastery in order to play in the TL (Tarone 2002: 293). Furthermore, the learners also lack the common cultural reference points upon which so much play is based and which allows a lot of what is meant to go unstated. The assumed need for such knowledge has also been seen by some as a prerequisite to the use and appreciation of play (e.g. Chiaro 1992: 122; Davies 2003: 1363–1364).

The risks involved in attempting to play in a language over which one does not have mastery inevitably means that some speakers avoid doing so. By their nature, such missed opportunities do not show up in the type of data I have collected. Furthermore, failed attempts at humour may easily go unnoticed by interlocutors and researchers alike. However, some significant moments of failure did come to light in the data. The first of these occurs during the revision session at the beginning of Tuesday's training where David is going over some useful lexis which the group had encountered on their first day:

EPISODE 21: LOSERS

Juan: our main competitors (4) are (.) are? Accenture and EBM (.)
David: good good =
Juan: = IBM (.)
David: IBM good (.) give me another word for competitors (2)
Juan: another one? =
David: = yeah (.)
Juan: Infosys (.)
David: no no (.) for competitors (.) the word (.)
Juan: ah (1) rivals =
David: = rivals (.)
Juan: ((*raises eyebrows*)) losers (.)
David: rivals yeah (.)
Juan: @@ (.)
David: rivals OK

Here, Juan says something which is witty by native speaker standards but which is lost simply because his pronunciation means that neither David nor Marek reacts to what he says, even though he signals that he is in play mode through his smile and his raised eyebrows (Bell 2007a: 39). This signal subsequently alerted me to Juan's attempt at play but it was only after going over the recording on a number of occasions that

6 A Case Study: Overcoming Failure in the Search ... 139

I was able to catch that he utters the word "losers". Juan seems to suffer fleeting embarrassment—hence, the laugh—from this communication breakdown. There are other moments where Juan's unclear enunciation of words causes moments of non-understanding or misunderstanding. However, he usually attempts to repair problems when they arise and perhaps this persistence is a trait which marks him out as a playful learner.

It is not only pronunciation which thwarts attempts at play. Another revealing moment comes during a simulated meeting where Juan is breaking the ice with a visitor. The exchanges are recoverable from the feedback session where the recorded simulation is played to the learners and paused at moments where the teacher wants to comment. In the simulation, Juan asks whether his guest had seen an event from beyond the simulation in the real world, the football game the night before, a game in which his team, Barcelona, lost. His guest says that he went to bed early so did not see the match:

EPISODE 22: I WOULD HAVE GONE BACK TO SPAIN

Tape: ((Juan's recorded voice)) *don't worry(.) if I know in advance the result I can (.)<@ go to sleep> (.)*

Juan: @@

David: ((*stops playback of the recording*)) I think I understand what you meant I think I- are you saying if I had known the result (.)

Juan: I have (.)

David: if I had known the [result*

Marek: [@@@*=

Juan: = I have I have

All: @@@[@*

David: [<@ I would have* gone to bed yeah > =

Others: = @@@ =

David: = yeah =

Juan: = I would have (.) <@ (gone) back to Spain > =

David: = <@ [gone back to Spain yeah yeah OK* >

Others: [@@*@

140   D. Hann

The third conditional tense is beyond Juan's grammatical capabilities, and in the feedback, David provides him with the language which he needs, although he still struggles to master it. The exchange is also noteworthy because Juan actually manages to retrieve the situation with his punchline—"I would have gone back to Spain"—during the feedback session. This is something he had been unable to do during the actual role-play. Notice too how all the participants including Juan himself laugh at his attempts to master the structure. This laughter seems to be a mixture of both amusement and, at least in Juan's case, embarrassment. The relationship between play and language "errors" is one which we will return to.

These two episodes show how the lack of mastery of the phonology and grammatical structures of the TL can thwart or, at least, hamper attempts at play.

6.3.2 Searching for Common Cultural Ground

Although, as will be seen, common ground is developed between members of the group in the process of sharing a learning experience together, there are other attempts by Juan to search out connections and commonalities in terms of experiences, viewpoints and cultural references from beyond the immediate context, much as anyone would when meeting other people for the first time (Brown and Yule 1983: 11). What is noteworthy about these attempts is that Juan figuratively relates these references from outside the classroom to their shared experiences within it.

All three episodes identified refer to internationally recognised products of the American media—a PC game, a TV series and a Hollywood film. These are worth looking at briefly as they not only illustrate this search for shared cultural connections but bring out other themes which are characteristic of the data from this group and others. The first occurs in the middle of the Tuesday morning, the second day of training and the first of recording, where the group are listening to a pre-recorded business dialogue:

6 A Case Study: Overcoming Failure in the Search ... 141

EPISODE 23: I REMEMBER A PC GAME

Tape:	*all doom and gloom* (2)
Juan:	doom and gloom (.)
David:	doom and gloom (.) yeah =
Juan:	= I remember a (.) I remember a (.) PC (.) game =
David:	= ahh [called Doom something?*
Juan:	[named Doom* (.)
David:	Doom yeah =
Juan:	= and I understand now the (1)
All:	@@[@*
Juan:	[you know* Doom (1) [<@ terrific>* terrific game terrific game (.)
David:	[that's right *
Juan:	very bloody(.) bloody? (.)
David:	yeah (.) violent and bloody yeah (.) OK (.) doom (.)
Juan:	sorry (.) doom

Juan relates the story in the listening exercise to a PC game called Doom. The amusement seems to come from the nature of the link forged between the violent computer game and a comment in the recorded dialogue about prospects for a particular industry through the phrase "doom and gloom". It is Juan's unfinished phrase "and now I understand the..." which triggers the laughter as the common nature of the worlds of business and of blood-letting violence seem to dawn on him. This link is hardly novel, given that many everyday metaphorical expressions used in business relate its activities to warfare. Interestingly, the fact that Juan fails to finish his sentence does not hamper the impact of his utterance. Indeed, it could be argued that it enhances it because much humour lies in what is left unsaid or in the gap between what is said and what is meant, leaving the audience to complete the sense (e.g. Coates 2007: 32). Furthermore, it is also noteworthy that he apologises after making the reference, suggesting that he is aware that his initial comment about the PC game might be perceived as off task.

A second reference to the American media is made again by Juan, and again, at the end of a comprehension exercise which takes the form of instalments of a business story. David is just handing out the transcript of the dialogue which they have been listening to:

EPISODE 24: DO YOU REMEMBER FALCON CREST?

Juan: but I'm I'm waiting for the- I'm waiting for the end of the history (.)
David: well (2) you're here for five days (.)
Juan: yes oh =
David: = the story has five parts as you can see so who knows (.) maybe @ (.)
Juan: OK (.) we will continue with the history? OK ((*mops brow in mock relief*))
David: absolutely absolutely (.) [OK alright*
Marek: [@@@* =
Juan: = this is a film (.) a Falcon [Crest* (.)
David: [@@*
Juan: do you remember Falcon Crest? (.)
David: <@ I remember Falcon Crest yes>

As in the first example, Juan relates a classroom activity to the world beyond by likening the business story they have been using as a means of improving their listening skills to a well-known American soap opera about feuding families from the 1980s. Again, the comparison is a humorous one and, it could be argued too that it is slightly subversive in nature as there is an ironic flavour to the utterance with a contrast between what is said and what is meant. Juan's superficial eagerness to hear the rest of the story can be interpreted as meaning the opposite, thus representing an evaluation gap between the superficial and real meaning of his utterances (Kotthoff 2003: 1390). This impression is reinforced by the exaggerated gesture of mopping the brow.

Finally, at the end of the last day of group training, as everyone is preparing to leave, Juan alludes to the Spielberg film Minority Report, a

6 A Case Study: Overcoming Failure in the Search ... 143

thriller set in a dystopian world where the authorities know every detail of their citizens' lives. During the brief exchanges below, David starts to remove a couple of sheets of flipchart paper from the wall on which are written key dates and events in Marek's private and professional life. These had been used on the very first training day and subsequently as a vehicle for consolidating and practising certain tenses in English:

EPISODE 25: MINORITY REPORT

David: shall I- shall I remove your life from the wall? (.)
Marek: from the wall? [yes please*
Juan: [ooh ooh* (2) the Minority Report (.)
Marek: don't worry

Juan's reference to the film does not draw any strong reaction from David or Marek. However, it is noteworthy for a number of reasons. It has commonalities with the previous examples cited: Juan refers to a product of the American media and links it to a shared classroom activity, in this case a primarily grammatical exercise. The plastering of details of Marek's life on the classroom's walls is likened to the totalitarian nightmare that the film portrays. As with the previous allusion to Falcon Crest, this link can be seen as carnivalesque in nature (Bakhtin 1984: 122–123) as it blends the potentially mundane world of language learning activities and the fantasy world of sci-fi film. As in examples of the data from the other groups in the research, the subversion here speaks of carnival rather than rebellion as Juan's comparison is not to be taken seriously.

The attempts at finding common ground that feature in this section all involve likening the classroom activities or the business world featured within them to violent video games, overblown TV series or dystopian sci-fi films. As such, they are figurative and hyperbolic in nature, characteristics which are indicative of creativity and playfulness (Carter 2004: 119ff.; Coates 2007: 45). However, although more successful than Dieter's attempt to allude to a cultural reference (see EPISODE 18) in that they mostly trigger some amusement from the other two group members, they are not taken up and developed. In fact, there is no compelling evidence that Juan's fellow learner, Marek, recognises any of these references—Falcon Crest may not have been broadcast in Eastern Europe before the fall of the Iron Curtain! What is more, it soon became apparent that allusions to shared experiences were much more successful in terms of the participants deriving pleasure from them as they clearly carried much more resonance. In fact, the most engaging area of shared interest outside the classroom for Marek and Juan, both in terms of the number of times they refer to it and the passion with which they talk about it, is football. By the beginning of their second day together, they have already spoken about the sport on a number of occasions and, as the following analysis of various interactions demonstrates, it features heavily in their conversation, especially during play frames. Juan is a Barcelona supporter, and the important game between Chelsea and Barca which took place on the evening of the second day of their course, sandwiched between the two days of recording, is a recurring theme, both in its anticipation and its aftermath.

6.3.3 Overcoming Obstacles to Play: Body Language and Other Resources

One of the means by which learners can compensate for the challenges of attempting to play without mastery of a TL is to draw upon resources from beyond the language itself. As in the previous data, there is some significant use of body language and physical props as resources in play episodes. Its use has already been noted as both a contextualisation cue (Gumperz 1982: 131) for a play frame—Viktor toasting his fellow group members using a paper cup (EPISODE 2), Viktor playing dead to illustrate a hypothetical scenario (EPISODE 4) and Dieter using his pointing finger as a gun (EPISODE 8)—and as a means of pointing out contrasts between the simulated frame and the real one—Bilel proffering a cheap biro as a gift to his honoured guest (EPISODE 3). This exploitation of non-linguistic resources is hardly surprising, given the speakers' limitations in English. Indeed, it features in the data from the pair of learners in the case study: both Juan and Marek use physical resources to play or as a means of signalling and enhancing their play.

6 A Case Study: Overcoming Failure in the Search ...   145

The first instances of such play can be seen in the revision session at the beginning of the second day of the course. Part of this includes going over some of the social questions one might ask when first meeting someone:

EPISODE 26: OR YOU PRESENT A QUIZ

David: ask me? nationality (2)
Marek: what's your nationality (.)
David: yes (.) police officer (3) [police officer *
Marek: [@@* (1)
David: ((*mimes taking notes*)) what's your nationality? (2)
Juan: police officer? =
David: = police officer (3)
Juan: ah @@[@*
David: [what's your nationality?* OK =
Juan: = or you present a quiz ((*shuffles the cards he has on the desk in front of him*)) =
All: = @@@

There are a number of noteworthy points in these exchanges. Firstly, Marek's initial question "what's your nationality?" is socially inappropriate for a conversation, although forgivable given David's initial cue. In Goffman's terms (1974: 128), his utterance unintentionally projects an alignment between the speaker and his interlocutor which puts them on the footing of interrogator and interrogated. This footing actually reframes what is already a keyed conversation into something more likely to happen in a police station than a social gathering.[2] David points this out through mime rather than language. The incongruity between the intention and realisation of the utterance causes Marek to laugh. It takes Juan a moment longer to understand what is happening, but once he does so, he builds upon the play frame that the teacher has

---

[2]The conversation is keyed in Goffmanian terms in the sense that the question, typically a means of asking for information, is actually a means of practising a grammatical structure.

146   D. Hann

opened up by using the blank cards on the desk to reframe the inter-action still further as a quiz. The gap between what is said and what is meant is a recurring theme in this data, and it is one which will be revisited.

The second piece of physical comedy happens a minute or so later during the same revision session and has a number of commonalities with its predecessor:

EPISODE 27: ARE YOU MARRIED?

David: family? (.) what's a question you would ask (.) family? (2)
Marek: are you married? =
David: = yes OK are you married (.) it's quite direct (.) are you mar-ried (.) it's perfectly good grammatically (2)
Juan: it's quite direct? =
David: = it's quite direct (3) are you married ((*mimes taking notes*)) =
Others: = @@[@*
Juan: [what about* your family? =
David: = yes (.) do you have family? repeat (.)
Juan: do you have family? =
David: = yeah and you can answer that question any way (.) you can say yeah I've got brothers and sisters or (2) I'm married or whatever it is (.) but I think er (.) are you married is fine but (.) it's a question (.)
Juan: <@ are you married?> ((*mimes taking off his ring and putting it in his pocket*)) =
Others: = @@@

These exchanges echo the previous ones in a number of ways. Firstly, the initial question put by Marek is socially inappropriate, something which David points out and, when Juan needs further clarification, David again mimes taking notes, suggesting once more that Marek's question aligns the speaker to his interlocutor in terms of interrogator and interrogated. Although both learners laugh at David's mime, the moment for further humour seems to pass before Juan brings in his

6 A Case Study: Overcoming Failure in the Search ... 147

own mime—taking off his wedding ring. This takes up David's observation that the question is too direct but, unlike the teacher's mime, frames it as something which sets up a relationship between speaker and listener of potential adulterers rather than interrogator and interrogated. As with the preceding episode, the teacher deems a question inappropriate and points this out through mime that demonstrates the discrepancy between what the speaker means by the question and what it actually means to the listener. This gap between intention and impression is taken up by Juan and, again, played with through mime.

There is a third significant episode where, in this case, Marek uses gesture and body language playfully which is then developed further by Juan. These exchanges happen at the beginning of the third day of training. The group has been discussing the football match between Chelsea and Barcelona from the previous evening, and Juan, a fan of the Spanish side, has been cursing his team's luck after they hit the woodwork a number of times during the game. At this point, he decides to tell a story:

EPISODE 28: SQUARE

Juan: I want to tell you a good history a good history about the goal (.) you know the history of Barcelona with (.)the Euro Euro Cup? (3) Barcelona (.) play the final of Euro Cup (.) I think forty years ago? =
David: = right (.)
Juan: or forty-five years ago in Berne (2)
David: yeah (.)
Juan: beside of (.) against Benfica =
David: = Benfica right OK (2)
Juan: in this in this in this (.) time of football history =
David: = yeah =
Juan: = the post and the bar (.) are (2) no no no round no circle (.) ((*forms circle with fingers*))
David: OK (.)
Juan: it's (2) they are um (2) ((*traces a square in the air*))

148   D. Hann

David: square? =
Juan: = square (.)
David: square =
Juan: = square (2) in this final <@ Barcelona team in this final > (.)
         only in this final (.)Barcelona team (.) shot three times to the
         post (2) and a square post =
David: = it comes back out OK =
Juan: = return the ball outside (3) since this match =
David: = yeah =
Juan: ((*traces circle*)) = the posts have been changed to (.)
David: [round *
Marek: [@@@* =
Juan: = round (1)
Marek: < @ do you think that [from yesterday *
Juan: [because this because this* (.)
Marek: from yesterday evening <@ the post and bar will be > (.)
         ((*gestures with his hands to show a shrinking bar*))
All: @@[@*
Juan: [plastic plastic* ((*gestures ball bouncing in off a flexible
         post*))
All: @@[@*
David: [yes OK* =
Juan: = since yesterday, the posts will be(2) plastic (.) <@
         flexible > =
All: = @@@

Marek builds on the true story that Juan tells in order to create a hypothetical and cartoon-like scenario where the posts and bar of a goal are
shrunk to almost nothing to accommodate the needs of the Barcelona
team. Juan then develops the play further by imagining a world where
the materials of the goal facilitate shots bouncing in off posts and bar.
Both learners use gesture to convey their message in a way which prevents the exchanges from losing momentum as they undoubtedly would
if the interlocutors had to draw exclusively on their own limited lexical resources. Indeed, the speed of the interaction in this episode is one

6 A Case Study: Overcoming Failure in the Search ...   **149**

which Harriet remarks upon. On viewing the clip, she noted that "there's a nice collaborative, accelerating aspect to the humour…".

Although different in kind from the exchanges previously discussed, it has a number of commonalities with them: it sets up a hypothetical and amusing scenario which develops naturally out of preceding talk; it involves the development and co-construction of play, a collaborative dimension that has already been noted in research into native speaker play (e.g. Carter 2004; Coates 2007), albeit that the focus of such research has been on talk rather than mime.

It would be a mistake to see the use of gestures and body language as merely a means of compensating for the learners' comparative lack of linguistic resources. It is an integral part of the participants' toolbox of resources which is drawn upon in the process of socialising and projecting identity. It is not only a means of playing but also a contextualisation cue to frame accompanying language as play. As has been noted elsewhere in the literature (DaSilva Iddings and McCafferty 2007: 42), use of gesture can stand out as signifying carnival.

A final example of the strategic use of non-linguistic resources for playful purposes involves not the use of gesture and body language but that of a pictorial stimulus. The exchanges below occur about fifty minutes after those analysed in EPISODE 28. As becomes clear, the two episodes are intimately connected. The following exchanges take place in the context of a discussion of the word "euphemism". David has just explained that, when visiting the USA, he was puzzled when he first encountered the sign comfort station meaning toilet. Marek takes up the theme:

EPISODE 29: AND THIS IS FOR BARCELONA SUPPORTERS

Marek: in Poland you have (.) two marks (.)
David: yeah yeah (5)
Marek: ((*draws a triangle and circle in his notebook and shows the others*)) I always confuse (2)
David: and that is for (.) toilet? (.)
Marek: that is for woman and for for man (.) ((*points to the symbols*))

David:	oh really? (2)
Marek:	I didn't- I didn't- (.) I can't <@ I can't (.) remember what is what > =
All:	= @@@ =
Marek:	= <@ and I waited for (.) I waited* for someone who will =
David:	= OK =
Marek:	= who will (.) (come) in > =
All:	@@@[@@*
David:	[serious Marek (.) serious* (3)
Juan:	((*leans across and draws a square in Marek's notebook*)) and this is for Barcelona supporters =
All:	= @@@@@@

Marek's story triggers amusement for reasons which will be looked at later. What is noteworthy here is that Juan uses it as a means of connecting it to his own account of the history of the changing shape of goalposts. The two stories have nothing in common thematically except shapes. Juan's wit lies in his identification of this commonality, and, thus, his drawing of the square metonymically evokes his anecdote. It has been seen in previous data (e.g. EPISODES 10–17) and will be seen again in the data from this group that certain words and phrases are used to represent and evoke a particular shared experience. Through its telling, Juan's goalpost story has itself become part of that shared experience. In this case, a sign from a semiotic system other than language is used in exactly the same way as a particular word or phrase might be used to forge a link between the two anecdotes, although it would not be funny without the accompanying utterance. It could be argued that there is an absurdist incongruity in bringing together public signs for toilets and Barcelona supporters. However, it might be more accurate to regard it as what Brock (2017) calls "unexpected congruity": Juan's wit lies in finding a surprising commonality between his goalpost story and Marek's toilet anecdote which resides in shapes.

As noted previously with regard to in-group references, Juan's drawing and remark make no sense to anyone who has not heard the previous anecdote. As a consequence, it has at least the potential to take on significance as a marker of an emerging in-group culture. Indeed, Harriet's comments are revealing in this regard. Although she had viewed the preceding linked EPISODE 28, she did not make a connection between them: "The separate sign for Barcelona supporters I don't really get—don't quite understand why that is funny and what he's saying with that. Is this a running joke of some kind?".

Harriet's puzzlement shows the potential for such play to exclude those who are not in the know, making it a significant in-group marker. The incremental nature of play is explored in depth in the next chapter. There are further notable occasions in the data from this group where body language and other non-linguistic resources are used for comic effect by the learners.

We now turn to the use of the language itself and the ways in which the learners are able to exploit its properties for their own playful and creative purposes, despite the constraints imposed by their own limitations in it.

6.3.4 Playing with Structure and Sound

It has been noted in the literature on play among native speakers that people take pleasure in the sounds of the language (e.g. Cook 2000; Crystal 1998) and in the repetition of words and phrases (e.g. Carter 2004; Tannen 2007). Indeed, the two can be linked, given that repetition creates a certain rhythm which must, in part, account for its appeal. There is evidence of just such pleasure in the present data.

There are various moments in the two days where David corrects the learners' intonation or pronunciation of particular words or phrases. He then asks them to mimic his realisations of the target language. This often induces laughter. Of course, in part, this laughter may be the result of embarrassment or any number of other factors. However, it is not unreasonable to surmise that the sounds of English itself are foreign and pleasurable to the learners. Unlike their native tongue whose use has dulled their aesthetic appreciation of its sound qualities, the TL presents new and entertaining phonetic combinations to them.

152   D. Hann

This has similarities with the pleasure that young children take in nonsense rhymes and repetitions when acquiring their first language (Cook 2000). It could be argued that both children and L2 learners have a comparatively fresh perspective on the TL which allows them to see its potential for play in ways in which adult native speakers may not. An example of this pleasure in sound can be found when Juan is recounting how unlucky his football team, Barcelona, was in its game with Chelsea the evening before. The following exchanges form the preamble to Juan's anecdote about the history of the shape of goalposts (EPISODE 28). The extract is closely linked to some talk that occurs some fifteen minutes later, so the two series of exchanges will be looked at together:

EPISODE 30: WOODWORK

Juan:	erm (2) in two legs (.) two legs we shot [four times* (.)
David:	[yeah*
Juan:	to the ((*traces the shape of a goal*)) I don't know the name of the (.) goal (.) what is the name of the (.)
David:	yes, goal yeah so er (2) we say shots on target =
Juan:	= on target =
David:	= target (.) [is that* what=
Juan:	[no no*
David:	=you mean (.)
Marek:	on stands (.) on the stands (1) ((*traces shape of goalposts*)) on stands (.)
David:	ooh I see (.) I understand (.) you mean we- we (.) Barcelona (.) hit the woodwork (.)
Juan:	hit the? =
David:	= wood (.)work (.)
Juan:	wow (.) the woodwork (1)

In this instance, the word "woodwork" emerges from Juan's story and he returns to it shortly afterwards when David signals that it is time to get down to some serious study:

6   A Case Study: Overcoming Failure in the Search ...   153

EPISODE 31: WOODWORK 2

David: OK guys (1) work (1)
Juan: work =
David: = work (.) [alright*
Juan: [work* =
David: = um (.)
Juan: woodwork =
David: = good work (.) woodwork @@ =
Juan: =[disaster woodwork*
Marek: [@@@*

Juan's reference to "woodwork" in the second series of exchanges does not in any way follow on from David's utterances from a semantic viewpoint. It is the form of the word "work" which triggers his response, and he seems to be drawn to the alliterative quality of the sound. Indeed, a case could be put that, in his first encounter with the word, his response "wow the woodwork", whether consciously or not, highlights this alliterative element. Sound is privileged over meaning, much as it is in children's nursery rhymes (Cook 2000: 11ff.). Thus, the word itself becomes an objectivised plaything. Juan then uses it to refer to the story of Barcelona's bad luck in hitting the woodwork so often by modifying the word with "disaster". Thus, he reminds his audience of the dialogical flavour it has taken on in the context of its use within this group. This process of recontextualisation is an important one which will be revisited in the next chapter.

There are also significant moments of parallelism where Juan repeats particular structures for effect. One of these occurs at the end of an anecdote which he has been telling in order to illustrate how the English course has made him forget his Spanish:

EPISODE 32: YOU CAN FORGET

David: <@ so after one week in-> after one week in (2) BizLang you-
         you lose your first language OK @@@ (.)
Juan: but don't lose or forget my team (.) my football team =

David:	= don't forget your (.) no [no no*
Juan:	[never* =
David:	= never forget your football team (.)
Juan:	((*counts on fingers*)) @@ you can forget your family you can forget your language you can forget your work but not your football [team*
David:	[not your* football team

As can be seen, Juan uses the simple stem phrase "you can forget your…" and a series of substitute nouns. This cumulative pattern is then broken by the negative "..but not your football team", thus reinforcing his message.

A similar use of repetition by Juan can be found when David is setting up a negotiation and asks the learners about their own experiences of negotiating in their professional lives:

EPISODE 33: I NEGOTIATE WITH

David:	let's move on (2) fine (.) and what I want to do is (4) is run a meeting (2) with you (2)you said you negotiate (2) do you negotiate? (1)
Juan:	yes (.)
David:	who do you negotiate with? (2)
Juan:	I negotiate with (.) my bosses (.) with my team (.) with my customers (.) with my providers (.) with my partners <@ and with my family> =
David:	= @@@ OK good good =

Here, Juan answers David's question about who he negotiates with by using "I negotiate with my…" as the stem phrase, adding appropriate nouns related to his professional life. What seems to be his final word in the list takes a departure from the expected by adding something from his personal life, his family. Harriet sees this reference as part of the theme of the speaker belittling himself, a strategy that Juan often seems to employ: "When a man says he negotiates with his family – he is subverting his own authority".

6 A Case Study: Overcoming Failure in the Search ... 155

Juan's words humorously emphasise the fact that life is a constant negotiation, whether at work or not. It is noteworthy that, as with the EPISODE 32, he sets up a pattern and then changes it with this final line. In the former episode, this deviation from the established pattern takes the form of introducing a negative, while in EPISODE 33, he breaks with the semantic field—his world of work—which he has established. This echoes Carter's observations about how speakers creatively set up patterns through repetition and then break these patterns, phenomena he calls "pattern forming" and "pattern reforming":

> ...a pattern draws attention to itself. It is made more transparent because it involves a deliberate play on or with words and it is overt because it can involve a break with an expected pattern. (Carter 2004: 102)

Juan's use of repetition in this and the previously cited instance shows that he is able to indulge his penchant for rhetoric even though he is operating in a language other than his own.

Tropes such as hyperbole, irony and metaphor are seen as signs of creativity and playfulness among native speakers (e.g. Carter 2004: 119ff.; Coates 2007: 45). The use of irony by Juan has already been noted when he compares classroom activities to the stories from American TV soaps and films (see EPISODES 23, 24 and 25). It can also be found at other moments in the data. A simple example can be found at the beginning of the second day of the course when David is revising question forms:

EPISODE 34: WITH ONLY FIVE YEARS?

Juan: how long has you known (.) your wife? =
David: = good (.) good (.) I've known my wife for (1) 29 years (3) I think (2) 29 years (.)OK good alright (.)
Juan: with only five years? (1)
David: sorry?(.)
Juan: with only five years? =
David: = absolutely yeah (.) she was only five I was six (.) yeah [incredible*
Juan: [@*@

156   D. Hann

It is noteworthy here that Juan's utterance "with only five years" which deviates from native speaker norms is recast by David as "she was only five". However, it actually takes him a moment to understand Juan's remark. For someone without regular exposure to such non-standard features, this might have led to a breakdown in communication. However, in this instance, the learner manages, with the teacher's collaboration, to be gently ironic.

It has already been noted how Juan likens classroom activities to products of the American media. As well as making connections through cultural allusions, he also uses metaphor as a means of commenting on the nature of particular taught phrases. During the feedback from role-played telephone calls, David gives them the phrases "I'm afraid" and "the problem is" as a way of preparing one's interlocutor for bad news. This amuses Juan and he uses a word to describe these phrases which neither David nor Marek initially understands. Having failed to find the word in the dictionary, Juan is forced to explain it:

EPISODE 35: WHEN THE DOCTOR NEED TO OPERATE YOU

Juan: with the doctor when the doctor (.) need to operate you ((*gestures towards his arm*)) (3) before the (.) the operation (2) an assistant put you in (.) um (2) ((*gestures a mask over the face*)) anaesthesia @[@*
David: [OK* gives you an anaesthetic (.)
Juan: anaesthetic =
David: = yeah (.) anaesthetises [you*
Juan: [<@ an*aesthetise> @@@@@ =
David: = anaesthetise OK (.)
Juan: I'm af[raid*
David: [<@ I'm* afraid is> a way to anaesthetise yes

Juan seems to take pleasure in the metaphor and in the sound of the verb "anaesthetise", an aesthetic appreciation which seems to echo his reaction to the word "woodwork" as noted previously. Indeed, his liking for the word whether as a metaphor or simply for its sound is seen again the following day during a feedback session on a simulated meeting:

6 A Case Study: Overcoming Failure in the Search …   157

EPISODE 36: THIS A FORM OF ANAESTHETIC

Juan:	((recorded voice)) *as- as you know the standard (1) the standard size of the drums in the market (.) are 50 (.) 50 KG (.)*
David:	good good (.) and actually a simple expression as as you know is a good expression(.) especially in a negotiation OK (1) so she has to concede that point (.) as you know the standard size is 50 K (.) OK (1)
Juan:	this a form of anaesthet-etic @@[@*
David:	[yes absolutely* absolutely yeah

Juan's reaction to these words seems to be significant in a number of ways. Firstly, he obviously enjoys the words "anaesthetise" and "anaesthetic" for themselves. Although the equivalent words in Spanish are very similar, he seems to take pleasure in the ways they are realised in English. Secondly, the use of these words as metaphor is important because it suggests an outsider's perspective on the language. The fact that he can poetically liken everyday phrases such as "as you know" to an anaesthetic is indicative of a fresh perspective on TL and the norms of behaviour revealed through it, the type of perspective which, as I suggest earlier (see Sect. 2.5.2) is the stuff of a good humorist's armoury. Indeed, in my experience of language teaching, learners often comment on the "politeness" of British English, meaning its indirectness. A third reason for Juan's enjoyment of the word "anaesthetic" is that he has the opportunity to utter it again more than a day after its first use in the classroom. This recontextualising of language previously encountered and shared together is an important feature of play among these learners and the others in my research cohort. As stated previously, it forms an important part of the rationale for recording the interactions that take place over a two-day period and is the focus of the next chapter.

6.4   Conclusion

We have seen in this chapter's data that attempting to play in another language is a risky business. At times, a speaker's pronunciation or shaky mastery of grammatical structure can jeopardise any attempt at humour.

158   D. Hann

In addition, the search for common reference points is more likely to be challenging among people from different cultural backgrounds than it is among those who are able to share and draw upon a mutually understood reservoir of allusions from a nation's history, the media and so on.

Yet, despite these challenges, there is evidence here that Juan is able to exploit resources from beyond the language to be playful. He is also able to use the language itself to be gently ironic or to create effective rhetorical impact through parallelism. However, it is worth pointing out that the manipulation of structure in this data is not complex. There is, for example, no play with prefixes and suffixes as you might find in some native play (Crystal 1998: 30). Also, as Attardo (2000: 814) points out, irony is a completely pragmatic phenomenon rather than a semantic one, and there is no evidence of the exploitation of the semantic dimension of the language by these learners, such as the use of puns (Carter 2004: 90–97). Indeed, the meaning of certain words and phrases in play episodes comes from their significance in context rather than their dictionary definitions. This becomes clearer in the next chapter where we see how the learners' shared learning experiences are summoned up through the language associated with them. Thus, these manifestations of play through language are similar in nature to Juan's drawing of a square in order to evoke a previous anecdote (see EPISODE 29). Like this pictorial representation, words and phrases function metonymically and emblematically rather than linguistically (Blommaert 2010: 181) as speakers draw upon their previous utterances and exchanges in order to have fun.

References

Attardo, S. (2000). Irony as relevant inappropriateness. *Journal of Pragmatics, 32*(6), 793–826. https://doi.org/10.1016/S0378-2166(99)00070-3.

Bakhtin, M. M. (1984). *Rabelais and his world.* Bloomington: Indiana University Press.

Baynham, M. (1996). Humour as an interpersonal resource in adult numeracy classes. *Language and Education, 10*(2–3), 187–200. https://doi.org/10.1080/09500789608666708.

6 A Case Study: Overcoming Failure in the Search ... 159

Bell, N. D. (2007). How native and non-native English speakers adapt to humor in intercultural interaction. *Humor, 20*(1), 27–48. https://doi.org/10.1515/HUMOR.2007.002.

Blommaert, J. (2010). *The sociolinguistics of globalization.* Cambridge: Cambridge University Press.

Boxer, D., & Cortés-Conde, F. (1997). From bonding to biting: Conversational joking and identity display. *Journal of Pragmatics, 27,* 275–294. https://doi.org/10.1016/S0378-2166(96)00031-8.

Brock, A. (2017). Modelling the complexity of humour—Insights from linguistics. *Lingua, 197,* 5–15. https://doi.org/10.1016/j.lingua.2017.04.008.

Brown, G., & Yule, G. (1983). *Discourse analysis.* Cambridge: Cambridge University Press.

Carter, R. (2004). *Language and creativity: The art of common talk.* Abingdon: Routledge.

Chiaro, D. (1992). *The language of jokes: Analysing verbal play.* London: Routledge.

Coates, J. (2007). Talk in a play frame: More on laughter and intimacy. *Journal of Pragmatics, 39*(1), 29–49. https://doi.org/10.1016/j.pragma.2006.05.003.

Cook, G. (2000). *Language play, language learning.* Oxford: Oxford University Press.

Crystal, D. (1998). *Language play.* London: Penguin Books.

DaSilva Iddings, A. C., & McCafferty, S. G. (2007). Carnival in a mainstream kindergarten classroom: A Bakhtinian analysis of second language learners' off-task behaviors. *Modern Language Journal, 91*(1), 31–44. https://doi.org/10.1111/j.1540-4781.2007.00508.x.

Davies, C. E. (2003). How English-learners joke with native speakers: An interactional sociolinguistic perspective on humor as collaborative discourse across cultures. *Journal of Pragmatics, 35*(9), 1361–1385. https://doi.org/10.1016/S0378-2166(02)00181-9.

Goffman, E. (1974). *Frame analysis.* Boston: Northeastern University Press.

Gumperz, J. J. (1982). *Discourse strategies.* Cambridge: Cambridge University Press.

Holmes, J. (2000). Politeness, power and provocation: How humour functions in the workplace. *Discourse Studies, 2*(2), 159–185. https://doi.org/10.1177/1461445600002002002.

Kotthoff, H. (2003). Responding to irony in different contexts: On cognition in conversation. *Journal of Pragmatics, 35*(9), 1387–1411. https://doi.org/10.1016/S0378-2166(02)00182-0.

Seidlhofer, B. (2011). *Understanding English as a Lingua Franca*. Oxford: Oxford University Press.

Tannen, D. (2007). *Talking voices: Repetition, dialogue, and imagery in conversational discourse* (2nd ed.). Cambridge: Cambridge University Press.

Tarone, E. (2002). Frequency effects, noticing, and creativity. *Studies in Second Language Acquisition, 24*(2), 287–296. https://doi.org/10.1017/S0272263102002139.

7

Prior Talk: A Key Resource for Play

The importance of in-group references and shared experiences in understanding playful conversational behaviour has been noted in the literature on native-speaker humour (e.g. Baynham 1996; Coates 2007). Yet, as Gordon (2002: 684) points out, too often in the research into this facet of communicative behaviour, "…play episodes are not linked to prior interactions or utterances". There are exceptions. Tannen (2006), for instance, is able to trace how family arguments are subsequently rekeyed in a humorous frame as a means of re-establishing the speakers' shared family identities and values. However, such investigations are rare. In part, the logistical challenges of doing this kind of research help explain this gap. It is difficult to follow the development of particular ideas, events and the language that goes with them when speakers, in their daily lives, move from setting to setting and interlocutor to interlocutor. Even a seemingly enclosed space such as a classroom does not mean that its members do not meet in other contexts and at other times. In this regard, my research setting presents particular advantages as the class and their teacher are together all day and so provide a relatively enclosed environment for investigation (Sect. 3.1.2). Furthermore, the group's time together is not only relatively

© The Author(s) 2020
D. Hann, *Spontaneous Play in the Language Classroom*,
https://doi.org/10.1007/978-3-030-26304-1_7

161

162   D. Hann

self-contained but also short-lived. Indeed, in the case of Juan and Marek, they did not spend the evening between the two days of recording in each other's company, so it can safely be claimed that a large slice of their time together was captured on the classroom video camera. The evidence that emerges from that camera reveals that, as with the data from other classes, prior talk is a vital resource which the learners draw upon when playing. This is important, not only because it allows them to have fun but also because it is useful tool for building rapport and a sense of group identity. With this pair of learners, one of the features of the prior talk that they utilise for play is paradoxical in nature: they have fun with their own limitations as performers in the language.

7.1 A Thread of Play Woven Together to Create a Cultural Reference Point

This section traces the birth and development of play over two days which is based on a performance error by one of the participants. Instances where the learners exploit the errors that they themselves make have already been noted in the exchanges where Juan takes up and plays with David's observations about the inappropriate nature of the questions which Marek asks in EPISODES 26 and 27. Indeed, learner errors as a source of play are evident in other research into L2 learner interactions (e.g. Broner and Tarone 2001; Cekaite and Aronsson 2005). Errors are potentially memorable, especially for those who make them, primarily because of their face-threatening nature. Play is one means of laughing them off and showing an awareness of weakness, so enhancing the speaker's positive face (Dynel 2009: 1295).

The next eight episodes start innocuously enough when Marek and Juan take part in a recorded telephone role-play. The humorous thread is a particularly significant one in a greater tapestry of references which are woven together over the research group's brief lifespan. In this one, Juan, who you will have gathered, is the member of the group with the greatest proclivity for play, takes a dominant role. In order to provide a sense of progression, these episodes are presented chronologically and

7 Prior Talk: A Key Resource for Play   163

start when the feedback from the simulated telephone call, the scenario for which is the same for both Marek and Juan. These calls, and especially Marek's, become the subject of a number of subsequent playful exchanges. In the world of the simulation, the learners have to speak to a work colleague called Harry. Their objective is to ask Harry to send some figures earlier than planned because they are urgently required for analysis. The calls are recorded with David playing their interlocutor while speaking on the phone from another room. The following extract occurs after the role-plays, when the three members of the group are listening together to the beginning of Marek's recorded conversation. During the feedback, David occasionally pauses the recording, sometimes asks the pair to repeat what they have heard, comments on what has been said and, where appropriate, advises them on how they might say things more effectively:

EPISODE 37: IT'S NOT MY PROBLEM

David: ((recorded voice)) *because I'm afraid he's not very well* (.)
David: ((*pauses recording*)) I'm afraid he's (1)
Marek: not very well (2)
Marek: ((recorded voice)) *OK* (.)
David: <@ OK? (2) that's alright actually>(.) ((*turns to Juan*)) I'm afraid he's not very well (2)
Juan   ((*shrugs shoulders*)) <@ OK>=
David: = [OK*
Others: [@*@
David: I'm afraid he- =
Juan: = <@ it's not my problem (.) my problem is the figures >
All: @@@

In the simulation, Marek's initial response of "OK" to the news of Harry's ill health seems to signal a lack of interest. In fact, a common problem that learners in such phone calls have is that they are so preoccupied with communicating their own message that they often do not listen to or hear what their interlocutor is really saying. Juan plays with this moment by rekeying Marek's response as a deliberate act

164 D. Hann

rather than the result of shortcomings in performance. He does this by seeming to voice Marek as if in the simulation itself, thus carrying the intentions of both speakers, or "double-voicing" in Bakhtinian terms (Bakhtin 1984a: 193). In fact, this is an instance of "vari-directional double-voicing" which is ironic and humorous in intent (Rampton 2006a: 138). In this instance, Juan initially repeats Marek's "OK". However, he accompanies this utterance with a shrug to signal indifference. In so doing, he rekeys Marek's original utterance as indicative of this supposed indifference. Furthermore, in order to reinforce this rekeying, Juan adds "it's not my problem. My problem is the figure". Ostensibly, this is a face-threatening act where Juan seems to be making fun of Marek. Even so, it is unclear whether the first-person possessive pronoun in "my problem" refers to Marek or to Juan himself. In fact, it emerges as the telephone calls are revisited over the course of two days that Juan's utterance is one born of the impulse to laugh with rather than at Marek. This episode seeds the idea that the two learners are insensitive to the predicament of their interlocutor, Harry. What happens moments later is instructive from this viewpoint. The group is still listening to Marek's call:

EPISODE 38: MMM-HMM

David: ((recorded voice)) *um (1) and so yeah I'm afraid he's- he's not very well he had to go home (2)*
Marek: ((recorded voice)) *mmm-hmmm* (.)
All: *@@@@@@*

Juan and Marek both laugh when they hear the latter's original monotone reaction. It seems very unlikely that this would have occurred if it had not been for the previous episode priming them for it. Although this brief episode contains no play, it reinforces the comic potential in the idea of the learners' seeming lack of interest in Harry's predicament. It is only a matter of another five or so minutes before this potential is actually realised in play in EPISODE 39. During the feedback, David has just paused the recording and explained the meaning of "short-staffed":

7 Prior Talk: A Key Resource for Play 165

EPISODE 39: BUT BEFORE YOU DIED

David: we're short-staffed (1) OK (5)
David: ((recorded voice)) *as you can imagine* (.)
Marek: ((recorded voice)) *yeah yeah* =
David: (recorded voice)) = *yeah* =
All: = @@@ =
Juan: ((*dismissive hand gesture*)) = < @ yeah yeah > (2)
David: <@ yeah yeah yeah OK > =
All: = [@*@@ =
Marek: = [(xxx)*
Juan   = <@ but before you (died) you can (xx) and send me the fig-
        ures please > =
All: = @@@@@ =
David: = you're having a heart attack now? (.) oh really? (.) OK (.)
        send me the figures first =
Others: = @@@ =
Juan: = please (.) ((*raises hands in placation*)) please

As with his previous utterance "mmm-hmm", Marek's "yeah yeah" triggers laughter. However, on this occasion, Juan transforms Marek's seeming indifference into cold-hearted callousness as he plays out a scenario
where the latter presses for a favour while his interlocutor breathes his
last. This is reinforced by a dismissive hand gesture. The absurdity of
the created scenario is added to by Juan as he juxtaposes incongruous
elements, imagining the need to remember the social niceties in such
an exchange by adding "please". Interestingly, it is again Marek's mistake which Juan is happy to exploit here. Marek laughs freely at these
episodes rather than taking offence. In part, this seems to be because
Juan's contributions give the impression that he is humorously pointing
to their common predicament, something that becomes explicit some
hours later at the end of training, when the group is packing up and
disbanding for the day:

166   D. Hann

EPISODE 40: THE CALL EXERCISE WAS VERY FUN

Juan: the (.) the (.) the call exercise was er was very fun @@@ <@ was very very fun > (2)
David: the core exercise (.) did you say? (.)
Juan: the? (.)
David: the what exercise? (.)
Juan: the call (.)
David: oh the call (.) yeah yeah =
Juan: = was very fun (.) for me (2)
David: yes I think we had a (2) a slight identity crisis but (1)
Marek: < @ yeah we had > (2)
Juan: < @ and you have the video> =
David: = < @ I have (.) I have all the evidence I need > =
Others: = @@@@@@ =
Juan: = Harry is dead (.) OK =
All: = @@@@@@
Juan: ((*continues over laughter*)) <@ where is my figure (.) my fig (.) I have no computer (1) OK (2) it's your problem > (2)
David: <@ fantastic >

It is noteworthy here that Juan explicitly says how much he enjoyed the telephone calls. Yet, as his comment about the video suggests, he is aware of the way in which the simulations highlight the learners' own shortcomings when communicating in English and, thus, have the potential to embarrass and even humiliate. Despite this, he takes pleasure in evoking the moment through reconstructing and voicing the conversations. Again, he utters something which was not said in the simulations themselves—"Harry is dead". However, this reinforces a scenario which, of course, is an invention of his own making (see EPISODE 39). Furthermore, he evokes his own particular telephone call when Harry told him that the computer was down. It is noteworthy here that "OK" is beginning to assume a metonymic status, representing the seeming indifference to their interlocutor that both he and Marek display during their phone conversations. In this regard, the related concepts of entextualization and recontextualization are relevant. In this case, the entextualized unit is the word "OK", rendered

7 Prior Talk: A Key Resource for Play 167

memorable and extractable by the play around it in EPISODES 37 and 39. This is then taken from its original context and recontextualized in yet another of Juan's invented dialogues. The laughter that Juan triggers in Marek and David is precisely because of the significance it has accrued with each recontextualization. Furthermore, the utterance "it's your problem", like "OK", explicitly embodies the attitude that he and Marek inadvertently create during the telephone conversations rather than echoing anything they actually say at the time of the calls.

It is noteworthy that Juan seems to actively seek out moments where he can indulge in self-denigrating humour. This seems to be an important strategy in terms of positive face which requires that the individual's "wants be desirable to at least some others" (Brown and Levinson 1987: 62). It has been noted previously (Boxer and Cortés-Conde 1997: 281; Norrick 1993: 47), such behaviour can actually enhance the speaker's positive face by showing him or her not to be a threat and to be approachable. In addition, admitting to such failures shows a certain composure and control in that it demonstrates self-awareness, even under stress (Dynel 2009: 1295). Furthermore, by sharing their weaknesses with others, speakers implicitly send out the message that they have trust in their audience (Holmes 2000: 170). The self-denigrating nature of much of the humour between this pair is further evident in the anecdotes they tell each other. Immediately following on from EPISODE 40 are a series of exchanges as the group takes leave of each other which shows Juan blending the simulated world and the here-and-now of reality. David refers to the important football game that evening between Chelsea and Barcelona already featured in previous play episodes (e.g. EPISODES 28 and 29) which Juan is planning to watch in the pub later:

EPISODE 41: TOMORROW JUAN IS GOING WITH HARRY

David: OK guys (.)
Juan: <@ (xx xx) > (.)
David: so have a good eveni- are you beginning to feel nervous? (1) is the stomach going? (2)
Juan: yes (2) [I'm concentrate*

Marek:	[@@@*
David:	how long have you got (.)
Juan:	I'm concentrate (2)
David:	mm (.) it'll all be over tomorrow (.) If er (.) we will know the result if- if Juan doesn't turn up tomorrow [morning*
Others:	[@*@@ (2)
Juan:	I have butterfly in my [stomach*
David:	[butterflies in* your stomach (3)
Marek:	<@ don't laugh > @@[@*
David:	[it's a* serious matter (.)
Marek:	in every case (.) <@ in each case (.) [(xx xx)*
Juan:	[it's possible tomorrow* Juan is going with Harry (.)
David:	<@ OK > =
Juan:	= [OK?*
Marek:	[@*@@ =
Juan:	= you understand me? @@[@*
David:	[to have* the afternoon off you mean? =
Juan:	= yes =
David:	= yeah OK

David speculates that Juan may not show up for the next day's class if his football team lose. Juan then brings in the details of Marek's previous simulated telephone call with Harry where the latter had to go home because he was not feeling well. Juan's wit lies in making the connection between that simulated scenario and the possible consequence of his team losing, and the humour is triggered by the blending of the two. This ability to blend frameworks of interpretation for comic effect blurs the fictional and the real, where boundaries become fuzzy and the footing between participants is shifting and ambiguous, making them reminiscent of Bakhtin's carnival, where the established social order is suspended (Bakhtin 1984b: 122–123).

A significant element of the series of references to the learners' simulated telephone calls is that they carry over to the next day's training. Unsurprisingly, they re-emerge during the revision session on the following morning when the students are taken through the learning points which had emerged in the previous day's learning activities.

7 Prior Talk: A Key Resource for Play 169

Revision is a feature of many language classrooms, and in this case at least, it allows the learners to "re-play" the fun they had previously had with the telephone simulation. At this point, David is reminding them of the need to listen actively and provide appropriate reactions when on the phone:

EPISODE 42: OOOH… OK

David: so I think the main point there (.) and I think we mentioned this (.) just that reaction OK (.) just more reaction (1) Harry's ill (3)
Marek: ((*smiles*)) [how is he ill*
Juan: ((*smiles*)) [ooh (.)* oooh (.)
David: oh really?
Juan: oooh OK (.)
David: <@ OK>=
Juan: = oh [I'm sorry*
David: [@@*@ he's dead (.) OK (.)
Juan: <@ poor Harry (.)>where are my figure

There is a three-second gap between David's first prompt and the simultaneous reactions of Marek and Juan. They both utter their words simultaneously and smile as they do so. The juxtaposition of the initial reaction of concern with the seeming indifference of the follow-up word in "oooh OK" symbolises the gap between what was meant by the learners in their telephone calls and what was said. This recurs in "poor Harry… where are my figure". As noted with previous examples, these voicings make no attempt to accurately reflect what was said in the calls. In fact, in the original conversations, one criticism that could be levelled at the learners is that they did not utter words of sympathy such as "oooh" or "poor Harry". Thus, through these evocations, Juan is not recreating the event but demonstrating an awareness of the indifference that he and Marek originally and inadvertently communicated. He does this with humour by juxtaposing contradictory phrases, the first being words of sympathy—"poor Harry", followed moments later by those which actually indicate a callous self-interest—"where are my figure". Another point worth mentioning here is that the vocal realisation of what could be called "the indifferent OK" has progressively become more stylised with each repetition. Juan delivers it with a flat monotone that helps to contrast it with its co-text. This entextualises it, allowing it to be decoupled from its textual environment and primed for recontextualisation elsewhere. One of the reasons for the distinctive and stylised delivery may be the fact that "OK" is such a common filler in everyday talk that it is necessary to differentiate the use to which Juan puts it in these exchanges from the other frequent instances where it is uttered. It would not be fanciful here to say that such a quality shows that it is beginning to assume one of the characteristics of the language of ritual in its "stylised intonation contour" (Du Bois 1986: 317). As such, it is indicative of a distinctive linguistic repertoire that is emerging within the group. That "OK" has come to be part of the pair's collective identity (the nature of which is discussed below) becomes explicit some time later that morning when they are doing a comprehension exercise together, part of which involves listening to and repeating elements of a pre-recorded dialogue:

EPISODE 43: AND FOR US OK

Tape: *really?* (.)
Marek: really? =
David: = yeah second most useful word in English (.) really (2) what's the most useful word in English? (.)
Juan: sorry =
David: = absolutely (1)
Marek: @[@@*
Juan: ((*gestures to himself and Marek*))[<@ and for us* OK >=
Others: = @@@

By now, the flat delivery for "OK" is already established. However, what seems more significant is Juan's use of the collective pronoun when referring to himself and Marek in relation to the word—"and for us OK". "OK" has become part of who they are, something emphasised by the accompanying gesture. The final references to the telephone calls

7 Prior Talk: A Key Resource for Play 171

and to the special status of "OK" in the collective culture and identity of the pair occur, aptly enough, very near the end of Juan and Marek's training time together. David explains to them both that he will be speaking to the teachers who will be tutoring each of them over the final two days of their stay:

EPISODE 44: BE CAREFUL WITH THE OK

David: I've (.) written a little email but I will speak to them this evening to say who you are (.) OK (.)
Others: @@@@@@ =
Juan: = <@ be careful> (.)
David: just to- yeah (.) I will I will give them a warning(.) [yeah (.) prepare them for*
Others: [@@@* =
Juan: = < @ good guys but but not (.) so much pol- polite> =
Others: = @@[@*
Juan: [don't worry* =
David: = <@don't worry don't worry (.) don't take it personally (.) OK (.)
Juan: be careful with the OK =
Marek: = @@@ <@ OK >

Both learners laugh at the prospect of David speaking about them to their respective future teachers. Juan pinpoints their use of "OK" as something that characterises them both. He does this by voicing David in the imagined conversation to come. As in EPISODE 43, the use of the collective pronoun to associate them both with the expression is significant, as is the distinctive realisation of "OK". Unlike the previous examples of Juan re-enacting the telephone call, he does not reframe their use of "OK" as indicative of an indifferent attitude. Indeed, his reference to them being "good guys" implicitly concedes that their use of the term shows up their shortcomings when using English rather than revealing anything about their characters. Throughout the exchanges featuring the use of "OK", Juan's humour lies in pretending that he and Marek were intentionally rude and, in so doing,

172   D. Hann

acknowledging that they were, in fact, unintentionally so. In the preceding episodes, we see the gradual development of the significance of the word "OK", until it becomes an integral part of the pair's identity. In this regard, my BizLang colleague, Harriet, observes:

> There is that 'running joke' feel to this… there is a voicing, reliving of the earlier conversation, a reinvention.. and it has become a 'humour touchpoint'.. all they will need to say is 'OK' for the rest of the week, and they will have this release of laughter. There's a joy in discovering these touch points, and playing on them.

Juan uses "OK" to represent their collective shortcomings in the telephone simulation. He evokes the conversation by re-enacting it. However, it has been noted before that reported speech in everyday conversation is, in effect, a construction (Tannen 2007: 132). Juan's re-enactments are not attempts at an accurate recreation of what was originally said but creative and symbolic constructions of his own making, for social and humorous ends. It is noteworthy that the errors that are playfully exploited in the data can be categorised as performance mistakes. They involve pragmatic shortcomings in the learners' reactions to particular moments. They do not involve errors with formal properties of the language, such as tense, word order or semantic meaning. Furthermore, they cast doubt on Aston's (1993: 229) assertion that "[r] ole-played interactions are without effective social consequences, since the relationships between characters are, in the final analysis, fictional and temporary". In one sense, role-plays are indeed fictional and temporary. However, the comment fails to take account of the lamination of frames (Goffman 1974: 82) pertaining at any one time in a classroom simulation which allow real relationship work to be undertaken in imagined scenarios.

7.2   Playing with Errors, Playing with Identities

As well as the "OK" thread of humour generated by a simulated telephone call, that same call is the source for another humorous thread which the group plays with and revisits. This one arises out of a

7 Prior Talk: A Key Resource for Play   173

confusion over role-play identities rather than the pragmatic error which triggered the "OK" thread. Like the "OK" thread, it is significant in terms of the nurturing of a collective group identity.

Its source lies in Marek's call to the character Harry to ask him to send on some figures early because their boss, Jens, urgently requires an analysis of them:

EPISODE 45: I WOULD LIKE TO SPEAK TO JENS

David: ((*on phone*)) *hello sales?* (1)
Marek: hello Marek Jugas speaking (2) how are you Jens (1)
David: *sorry? who do you- who would you like to speak to?* (2)
Marek: er (2) Marek Jugas speaking and I would like to speak to- to Jens (1)
David: *to Jens?* =
Marek: = yeah (.)
David: *I'm afraid that this is the UK sales* =
Juan: ((*points to paper in front of him with information about the scenario*))
Marek: = <@ sorry (.) sorry I- I- I made a mistake> =
David: *= OK no problem no* [*problem*
Marek: [sorry sorry (.) I'm looking for (2)
Juan: Harry =
David: *= Harry* =
Marek: = for Harry sorry for [Harry*
David: [*for* Harry oh right right (.) I'm very sorry (.) I'm afraid you're out of luck*

It is not untypical for learners in simulations such as this to lose track of the different roles in the scenario. Here, Marek mistakenly asks to speak to his hypothetical boss (Jens) rather than his colleague (Harry). Juan is sitting next to Marek during the call. His status is not straightforward as, within the inner frame of the telephone call, he is not there. On the other hand, in the outer rim of the language lesson, he has, in Goffman's (1981) terms, the role of "official audience", his presence being sanctioned as part of the learning experience. During the call, he points to the right name on the sheet in front of him and, when that does not work, actually intervenes during the simulation with a prompt.

174   D. Hann

There is no play during this episode, merely the laughter of embarrassment when Marek realises his mistake, and he remains on task despite
this fleeting distraction.

At the end of this same call, a brief exchange occurs between Marek
and Juan before David returns to the training room, having stooged on
the phone from another location:

EPISODE 46: I'M HELMUT

Marek: ((*on phone*)) OK (.) nice to hear you and- and- and I will wait
         for- for your call =
David: ((*at the other end of the line*)) = *alright then (.) thanks very much (.)*
         bye bye =
Marek: - thank you (.) bye (2) ((*replaces receiver*)) @[@@@*
Juan: [@@@* =
Marek: ((*puts hand to forehead*)) = <@ and so (am I)? I'm Helmut > @[@*
Juan: [where
         is* the bl- the bloody Harry @[@@@@@*
Marek: [@@@@@*

One of the main aspects of note here is that Marek misremembers the
nature of his own mistake, actually thinking that he had confused his
own identity rather than that of his interlocutor (in the background
information that the learners receive about the scenario, the character
whose position he assumes is called Helmut). This is significant in that
it is this idea that he had not known who he was which he develops in
later references. However, it is also interesting to note how Juan reacts.
His utterance of "where is the bloody Harry?" can be seen as an act of
solidarity where he puts the blame for the confusion onto the interlocutor in the simulated frame. My colleague Harriet reflected on this
episode:

> Juan makes it a collaborative laugh by saying "bloody Harry" - it's then
> confirmed as a "we're in this together" - the "bloody Harry" for me is the
> key here. As well as showing sympathy for Marek, that's a subversion of
> the exercise - and, being possibly more disrespectful than they would be
> with the trainer in the room - it's a very uniting moment.

7 Prior Talk: A Key Resource for Play 175

The first time that Marek refers to his confusion of identities occurs only moments later when David returns to the classroom:

EPISODE 47: I CAN'T CHANGE MY IDENTITY
((*David returns to the room*))

Marek: I'm sorry David (.) [< @I can't... I can't change my identity*>
Juan: [@@@* =
David: = < @ it doesn't matter (.) it doesn't matter > (.) that's OK (.) that's fine that's [fine *
Marek: [< @it was* - it was surprising for me > (1)
Juan: he wants to (2) talk with er (.) Jens and say (.) you can- you need forget your figures and your analysis goodbye (.) ((*gestures putting phone down*))
David: < @ forget it (.) forget it >

A feature of these exchanges is that Juan voices Marek in an alternative outcome to the telephone call. Here, he imagines a situation where Marek's asking for Jens is not a mistake but actually what he wants to do. This reframing of an event where the accidental is re-imagined as a deliberate act occurs in the "OK" thread and is worthy of comment. The rekeying of a conversation as something different has been noted in the literature on native speaker interactions. As previously mentioned, Tannen (2006), for instance, looks at the ways in which family arguments are reframed in a humorous key for the sake of harmony and as part of the way in which the family unit projects itself to the world beyond it. Juan here does not really think that Marek actually wanted to speak to his boss in order to tell him to forget his analysis. However, his act can be seen, like that in EPISODE 46, as one of solidarity with his fellow learner. Again, Juan gives to Marek implicit support through this rekeying. Furthermore, Juan uses voicing here as he does on a number of occasions in this data, a phenomenon which will be revisited later in this chapter.

Some twenty minutes after this episode, the group are listening to Juan's telephone simulation during feedback and David is just reminding Juan and Marek about the particulars of the role-play scenario:

176   D. Hann

EPISODE 48: MY NAME IS

David: what's happening tomorrow? (4)
Juan: what's happens (.)
David: yeah what's happening tomorrow (.) tomorrow I'm? (.)
Juan: tomorrow Wednesday? =
David: = yeah yeah (.) no no (.)
Juan: ah tomorrow = ((*gestures towards piece of paper related to the role-play*))
David: = in this - [in this situation * (.) I'm getting confused (.)
Marek: [(xxx) *
Juan: [well *
Marek: < @my name is > @[@@*@
David: [<@ my name is *

David's question "what's happening tomorrow" is misinterpreted by Juan because the two of them are referring to different frameworks of interpretation and, thus, different time frames: David to the simulated frame of the telephone call context, Juan to the real world. This confusion is taken up by Marek, who seems to use the phrase "my name is" to metonymically stand for his own confusion during the simulated call that he had to make. It is significant that he not only perpetuates the myth that he confused his own identity but also uses a phrase which was never spoken in the original call as a means of doing so. Thus, an utterance which was never said in the conversation to which it refers comes to represent an occurrence that never happened. Here can be seen the potential that a phrase has to become part of the cultural mythology of the group (I comment further on myth in the conclusion to this chapter). In fact, it does not attain such a status as it is not said again, although, as will be seen, there are words and phrases which do acquire a mythological standing.

Finally, some forty-five minutes after the original identity mistake by Marek, Juan refers to it again when David is explaining the phrase "you're out of luck" to the two learners:

EPISODE 49: NO JENS NO HARRY

Juan:	luck? =
David:	= you're out of luck (2)
Juan:	and what mean? (3)
David:	OK (.) first of all notice (.) when I said it I packaged it with this little phrase I'm afraid (.) just to prepare the ground (.) if you're out of luck (.) you have no luck (2) you're unlucky (.) OK (.) in other words Harry is not here (.) [OK? *
Juan:	[@@ *@ =
David:	= I'm afraid you're out of luck (.)
Juan:	< @ nay Jens no (1) no Harry > @@[@ *
David:	[<@ no Harry *(.) no Jens >

The accumulated references to Marek's original identify confusion intensify the learners' amusement. As Harriet remarks about this particular episode "I think they are just at the point of any mention of Harry bringing back the giggles". The original mistake by Marek triggers a number of references to it over the next hour, and in these various instances can be seen the potential for such errors to trigger play and to be incorporated into the group's pool of shared allusions. Harry's name has become synonymous with, or more accurately, metonymic of the confusion over identities that Marek originally had, much as the word "OK" comes to stand for the learners' performance shortcomings. The name evokes not merely this rather commonplace slip-up but a myth which has subsequently been built around it where, variously, Harry is impossible to get hold of (EPISODE 46) or where Marek wants to challenge his hypothetical boss, Jens (EPISODE 47). These stories seem to have developed through moves by Juan to protect Marek's face.

As the source of both the humorous threads involving the word "OK" and the case of mistaken identity, the telephone role-play establishes itself as a comedic resource which Juan draws upon. A final example of the topsy-turvy, mixed-up and carnivalesque world that he creates is shown again in the middle of the final day's group training where the group are about to watch a video of themselves in another simulation which they have just taken part in where they welcome a visitor to their respective offices:

178 D. Hann

EPISODE 50: WHO'S THAT?

Tape: ((*sound of knocking on the door*))
Others: @@[@ =
David: ((*pauses recording*)) [OK so I'm just going to play it back
Others: = @@@@@@ (.)
Juan: who's that =
David: = who's [that*
Others: [@*@@
Juan: (xx)? =
All: = @@@ =
Juan: = <@ or Harry> =
All: = @@@

In this case, the two frameworks that Juan blends are not those of the real and the simulated frames but, in fact, two simulations-the telephone call and the role-play meeting. Once more, Juan evokes the telephone call scenario with Harry. This evocation carries with it all its accumulated associations of Marek's identity crisis and the pair's seeming indifference to their interlocutor which have already been explored in this chapter, thus confirming Harriet's observation that Harry's name alone has become a touchstone for laughter.

7.3 Recontextualising Learnt Language

The recontextualisation of words and happenings by the learners helps them to shape their experiences on their own terms. Similarly, using language for their own purposes allows them to take possession of it. For example, the simple and ubiquitous discourse marker "OK" is imbued with special meaning through the learners' play. Indeed, it could be argued that learners cannot be said to have truly learnt a vocabulary item until they've recontextualised it, that is, used it for their own ends. Needless to say, one of the reasons that people attend courses such as those provided by BizLang is that, as part of their objective to improve their performance in English, they want to extend their vocabulary base. The reuse of learnt language in a context other than the one in which it was first encountered can be seen, especially among L2 speakers at the lower end of the proficiency spectrum, as a form of wit, such as Viktor's use of "impressive" in EPISODE 9. In the data obtained from Juan and Marek, there is clear evidence, especially with the former, of attempts to reuse new language that is encountered in the classroom. This recontextualisation of language also seems to be a way to make connections to shared experience through the words and phrases that the group have practised or learnt together. This can be seen when the class is listening to a dialogue on the Tuesday morning. At one particular moment, they are practising the social responses to "Are you free for a drink?", an expression that appears in the recorded dialogue that they are listening to and repeating:

EPISODE 51: ARE YOU MARRIED?

David:	sorry I'm afraid not (.) repeat =
Juan:	= I'm afraid not =
David:	= yeah ((sighs)) (2) I can't (.) repeat (.)
Juan:	I can't (.) are you married? [<@ no>
David:	[@@@

These exchanges occur about an hour after the learners had been practising social questions when Juan had mimed taking off his own wedding ring as he asked the question "are you married?" (EPISODE 27). It is noteworthy here that he once again suggests a covert motivation in the question, giving the same situated meaning to the utterance as when he first says it. The original miming of taking his ring off as he said the phrase seems to have helped entextualise it for further use. It is also significant that his use of the question allows him to break free of the rigid format of exchanges imposed upon the learners at that moment where they are required to repeat the phrases David feeds them. Once again, in Goffman's (1981: 144) terms, Juan is no longer merely the animator of words, but their author.

Another episode illustrates the impulse to recontextualise and shows how it relates to quick-witted humour. During the morning revision

180   D. Hann

programme, the language of schedules comes up and David practises it with the group:

EPISODE 52: AHEAD TO THE SCHEDULE

Marek: how far (.) are you behind schedule (.)
David: good what's the opposite (.) we are? (2) we are early (.) we are? (.)
Juan: how are you behind (2) are you (4) how are (.) no (.) how are (.)you ahe-ahead (.)[of* the schedule =
David: [good*   = good (.) how (.) far are [you ahead* of the schedule (.)
Juan: [how far*
David: repeat (.) how far (.)
Juan: how f- how far are you (.) ahead to the schedule =
David: = good

Here, the teacher strictly controls the language which the learners utter through prompts and through the simple directive to repeat. The learners are animators of the words they utter, and they are "the sounding box" (Goffman 1981: 144) that relays the words. Often, in certain types of language classroom, the student has little opportunity to move beyond this role (Rampton 2006b). Yet Juan takes possession of this phrase an hour or so after the above exchanges, when the group are about to take a short break from a comprehension exercise that they are doing:

EPISODE 53: WE ARE AHEAD THE PROGRAMME

David: good OK (.) let's- that's the end of the first scene (1) no real problems there actually (1) maybe it's too easy for you (3) maybe I'll give you something more difficult tomorrow (2)
Juan: (nah)(1)
David: maybe not (.) anyway OK (.) [let's have a break (.) after*
Juan: [but but* our English is improving =
David: = of course absolutely yeah (.) twenty-four hours =
Marek: = @@@ =
Juan: = <@ we are ahead the programme> =
David: = @@@

David's observation about the comprehension exercise possibly being too easy for the group prompts Juan to say that their English is improving. This could be taken ironically and David's response "twenty-four hours" suggests that he takes it this way. In other words, the notion that the group's English has shown improvement in just one day seems to be improbable. Juan then decides to take the phrase he had learnt earlier and applies it to the moment: "we are ahead the programme". Although his entextualisation of "we are ahead the + noun" is grammatically erroneous, the mere ability to recontextualise the phrase appropriately is appreciated by David who laughs in response. By using the phrase for his own purposes, Juan aligns himself to the phrase as its author (Goffman 1981: 144).

We have already seen how Juan recycles the word "OK" for comedic effect. Indeed, it can be surmised from the data I have collected from this group and others that the chances of a phrase outliving its initial context of use are probably higher among L2 speakers than L1 speakers. Their active repertoire of language is inevitably less extensive, and so, they are more likely to draw upon those words and phrases that make up their pool of shared language. Something similar to the fate of the word "OK" happens with a particular phrase which features on a number of different occasions over the two days of recording. This series of occurrences make up the final part of my analysis of recontextualisation in this group.

One particular phrase is introduced as David is going over the simulated telephone call (the same call that triggers the "OK" thread of play). Together, the group are listening to Marek's call:

EPISODE 54: THESE THINGS HAPPEN

Tape: ((David's recorded voice)) *unfortunately (.) yeah we- we (.) there has been this virus going around the office (.)*
Tape: ((Marek's recorded voice)): *no it's no problem as I would like to (2)*
David: ((*stops recording*)) yeah good no problem (.) these things happen (.) repeat (1)
Juan: this is happen =
David: = these things happen (1)

182 D. Hann

Juan:	ah (.) these thing (.) these things happen (.)
David:	these things happen (1)
Marek:	these things happen =
David:	= yeah happen so sometimes people get a virus or whatever (.) these things happen (.)
Juan:	these things happen =
David:	= yeah (2)
Juan:	OK (6)
David:	((*at the flipchart*)) OK (.) we've run out of paper (2) these things (1)
Juan:	these things happen (.) don't worry (.)
David:	good OK (.) give me two seconds (.) I'll get some more paper =
Juan:	= OK ((*David leaves room*))
Others:	((*look at each other*)) @@@

David introduces Marek and Juan to the phrase "these things happen" as part of a pool of phrases which can be used to signal an empathetic attitude to one's interlocutor's situation. As is often the case in the language classroom context, the participants are asked to repeat the new phrase. One reason why this particular episode might stick in the mind and stimulate subsequent uses of the phrase is that David runs out of flipchart paper at the moment he is going to write it up for the group. He uses this unexpected occurrence to prompt Juan to say the phrase in response to the moment.

There is no further reference to the phrase until the following morning, during the day's revision session. In fact, the group has just finished going over the language that arose from the telephone calls when Juan decides to utter the phrase "these things happen":

EPISODE 55: THESE THINGS HAPPEN 2

David:	good OK (.) then um (4)
Juan:	((*looking at his notes from the day before*)) these thing happens (1) ((*turns to Marek*)) these things happen (.)

David:	these things happen (2) Barcelona hit the woodwork four times (.) these [things happen*
Juan:	[these things* happen (2)<@ it's not possible but happen > =
All:	= @@@

Juan's use of "these things happen" does not actually follow on from the previous talk. He is obviously attracted to the phrase for some reason and decides to give it an airing before the opportunity to do so disappears. David then links it to Barcelona's defeat the evening before which, in turn, causes Juan to joke about the impossible happening. It is perhaps this linking of the phrase to the football game which causes him, consciously or not, to use it during a simulated meeting with a visitor to his office an hour or so later. Here, David plays the visitor:

EPISODE 56: THESE THINGS HAPPEN 3

David:	I hear that it was a bad result for Barca last night (.)
Juan:	sorry? =
David:	= it was a bad result for Barca (1)
Juan:	is? =
David:	= it was a bad result for Barca last night (.)
Juan:	it was a bad result? yeah very bad very bad =
David:	= I'm sorry (.) sorry to hear that (.) yeah yeah =
Juan:	= don't worry (2) these things [happen*
Marek:	[@@*
David:	these things happen (.) this is true =
Marek:	= @@@

The use of the phrase here reveals, through the reaction of the people present, that it is beginning to assume a particular status among the group. Marek, an onlooker in the simulation, silently laughs when Juan first utters it and all laugh on David's repetition of it. Indeed, when the recording of the meeting is played back, this triggers even more laughter. Again, as hypothesised earlier, it seems that the rituals and routines of the language classroom, where new language is revisited and practised on more than one occasion, increase the chances that particular words and phrases can attain a social and cultural significance within a group.

A final use of the phrase comes when David is priming the pair for an exercise in expanding their vocabulary for budgets by discussing their own involvement in budgeting in their jobs. Juan has just explained that the French bosses in his company seem to accept the Spanish office setting their budget late because the whole Spanish market is always late as a matter of course:

EPISODE 57: THESE THINGS HAPPEN 4

David: if the customers are also late then you're not late (1) this is the thing yeah (1)
Juan: this- this (1) this could be the reason (.)
David: yeah yeah (2) alright (.) what [I want*
Marek: [these* things happen =
Juan: = [these things happen (.) yes of course of course*
David: [these things absolutely (.) these things happen* (.) these things happen =
Marek: = @@[@*
Juan: [OK* =
David: = this is the phrase you're going to go away with

This time it is Marek who comes out with the phrase. His interjection is not witty by native-speaker standards as he seems to overextend the phrase's meaning to comment on people's behaviour rather than events beyond their control. Even so, the reaction to it is significant. As soon as he utters "these things happen", there is a choral response from Juan and David. This reflects the position that the phrase now holds within the group. Furthermore, Juan links it to that other phrase with a privileged status within this particular social unit, "OK" delivered in a monotone (see EPISODES 37–44).

As in any community then, however small and ephemeral it may be, an in-group language seems to emerge spontaneously from the experiences and associated words and phrases that its members share. Of course, in a language classroom, the reuse of words and phrases holds a particular significance anyway, as it represents a barometer of the learners' success within their community of practice. Furthermore, the nature of the classroom's activities, with its repetitions and revisions, together with the limited linguistic resources of the learners present, means that words and phrases as they are recontextualised, are more likely to become significant within a language-learning group than they might do in other social settings.

7.4 Conclusion

Some might question whether the utterances featured in this chapter are humorous or have very much to do with language. After all, on the face of it, the reuse of "OK" or "these things happen" hardly seems linguistically inventive. However, such an observation would not take account of the way in which the language is used metonymically. It is distilled to represent the learners' shared experiences together and their shared limitations in the TL. As such, its significance can only be truly appreciated by those within the group. Furthermore, Juan especially is able to recreate dialogue for humorous (or perhaps I should say, recreational) purposes and nimbly moves between and exploits different frames. Through his recreations, Juan highlights Hazlitt's observations about the heart of comedy lying in the gap between the ways things are and the way they ought to be (Morreall 1987: 56). Juan's use of the word "OK" represents the difference between the English level he has reached and the level he strives for as he re-imagines the unintentional impression the word creates as an intentional self-centred response to his interlocutor's plight. Also, by turning this gap into comedy, he cathartically transforms the learners' potentially negative experiences into positive ones which they can literally laugh off. Indeed, he is able to take his and Marek's shortcomings in performance and make them part of their playful repertoire. In doing so, he takes control of a learning situation in which he might otherwise feel helpless. So, despite the learners' pratfalls, or indeed, maybe because of them, Juan is able to declare in all sincerity that "the call exercise was very fun"(EPISODE 40).

186   **D. Hann**

This psychological dimension to play helps explain why it can be found in the seemingly unpromising context of an intensive hot-housing English-for-Business course as well as the more informal, relaxed settings where it is usually thought to thrive (Carter 2004: 165). The data here, like Holmes' (2000, 2007) investigations among L1 users in the workplace, seems to suggest that humorous play can relieve tension, indicating that work and play are perhaps not as mutually exclusive as some might think and, indeed, as Cook posits (2000: 150), may overlap.

In terms of the group's culture, Juan's stylised realisation of the word "OK" shows how allusions to shared experience can be ritualized with their repetition. As such, they begin to symbolise a common history and sense of community. Although it is primarily Juan who plays in the featured episodes, his play is validated by the other members of the group: David sometimes builds on his contributions, and both David and Marek demonstrate their appreciation of them through laughter. In the latter's case, this appreciation is despite Juan's potentially face-threatening act of making fun of Marek's mistakes. Juan transforms his references to these mistakes into an act of solidarity with his fellow learner by making clear that Marek's shortcomings are also his own. In addition, Juan's reconstructed dialogues create a mythology rather than a history, one that the learners feel free to revisit. As Armstrong (2005: 111) comments when discussing the importance of myth in human history, "a myth (…) is an event that—in some sense—happened once, but which also happens all the time". For the learners in this group, the myth of their indifferent attitude on the telephone is one which endures for the length of their stay together. In this mythologizing process, the word "OK" is an integral part: the event which "happens all the time" is one evoked by its frequent recontextualisation, allowing the original context to be re-imagined every time it is referred to. Play, therefore, seems to be central to the process of making a community of practice with its own culture, one with an emergent history, language, mythology and ritual. It is noteworthy that the typical language class often has role-plays and revision sessions, making it an environment which is rich with possibilities to playfully recycle and recontextualise language items as part of the culture-building process. The humorous language play featured above is not simply of a type that L2 users fall back on because they lack the verbal dexterity of an L1 quipster. As Baynham (1996: 194) comments on the native-speaking adult numeracy classes that he investigates, "[t]here are examples in the data of exchanges that clearly refer to ongoing, in-group, joking, the full meaning of which it is hard for the analyst/outsider to gain access to". Indeed, the incremental nature of much play can be evidenced not only in social groups such as language classes or family units, but also in contexts where the in-group may be far more ephemeral. The example from the radio programme "Just a Minute" (Sect. 2.4.3) shows how humour depends on preceding talk or events within the programme. Prior talk, then, is a significant ingredient in humorous language play.

Much of the play that features in this book is instigated by classroom learners. Indeed, a large part of the pleasure that participants derive from HLP is that it is a realisation of the process of taking ownership of the learning situation and of the target language itself. This begs the question of what role the teacher has in relation to classroom play, a subject which is turned to in the next chapter.

References

Armstrong, K. (2005). *A short history of myth*. Edinburgh: Canongate.

Aston, G. (1993). Notes on the interlanguage of comity. In G. Kasper & S. Blum-Kulka (Eds.), *Interlanguage pragmatics* (pp. 224–250). New York: Oxford University Press.

Bakhtin, M. M. (1984a). *Problems of Dostoevsky's poetics*. Minneapolis: University of Minnesota Press.

Bakhtin, M. M. (1984b). *Rabelais and his world*. Bloomington: Indiana University Press.

Baynham, M. (1996). Humour as an interpersonal resource in adult numeracy classes. *Language and Education, 10*(2–3), 187–200. https://doi.org/10.1080/09500789608666708.

Boxer, D., & Cortés-Conde, F. (1997). From bonding to biting: Conversational joking and identity display. *Journal of Pragmatics, 27*, 275–294. https://doi.org/10.1016/S0378-2166(96)00031-8.

Broner, M., & Tarone, E. (2001). Is it fun? Language play in a fifth-grade Spanish immersion classroom. *Canadian Modern Language Review, 58*(4), 493–525. https://doi.org/10.3138/cmlr.58.4.493.

Brown, P., & Levinson, S. (1987). *Politeness.* Cambridge: Cambridge University Press.

Carter, R. (2004). *Language and creativity: The art of common talk.* Abingdon: Routledge.

Cekaite, A., & Aronsson, K. (2005). Language play, a collaborative resource in children's L2 learning. *Applied Linguistics, 26*(2), 169–191. https://doi.org/10.1093/applin/amh042.

Coates, J. (2007). Talk in a play frame: More on laughter and intimacy. *Journal of Pragmatics, 39*(1), 29–49. https://doi.org/10.1016/j.pragma.2006.05.003.

Cook, G. (2000). *Language play, language learning.* Oxford: Oxford University Press.

Du Bois, J. W. (1986). Self-evidence and ritual speech. In *Evidentiality* (pp. 313–336). Norwood, NJ: Ablex.

Dynel, M. (2009). Beyond a joke: Types of conversational humour. *Linguistics and Language Compass, 3*(5), 1284–1299. https://doi.org/10.1111/j.1749-818X.2009.00152.x.

Goffman, E. (1974). *Frame analysis.* Boston: Northeastern University Press.

Goffman, E. (1981). *Forms of talk.* Oxford: Blackwell.

Gordon, C. (2002). "I'm Mommy and you' re Natalie": Role-reversal and embedded frames in mother-child discourse. *Language in Society, 31*(5), 679–720. https://doi.org/10.1017/S004740450231501X.

Holmes, J. (2000). Politeness, power and provocation: How humour functions in the workplace. *Discourse Studies, 2*(2), 159–185. https://doi.org/10.1177/1461445600002002002.

Holmes, J. (2007). Making humour work: Creativity on the job. *Applied Linguistics, 28*(4), 518–537. https://doi.org/10.1093/applin/amm048.

Morreall, J. (1987). *The philosophy of laughter and humour.* New York: State University of New York.

Norrick, N. R. (1993). *Conversational joking: Humour in everyday talk.* Bloomington: Indiana University Press.

Rampton, B. (2006a). Language crossing. In J. Maybin & J. Swann (Eds.), *The art of English: Everyday creativity* (pp. 131–139). Basingstoke: Palgrave Macmillan.

Rampton, B. (2006b). *Language in late modernity: Interaction in an urban school.* Cambridge: Cambridge University Press.

7 Prior Talk: A Key Resource for Play   189

Tannen, D. (2006). Intertextuality in interaction: Reframing family arguments in public and private. *Text and Talk, 26*(4–5), 597–617. https://doi.org/10.1515/TEXT.2006.024.

Tannen, D. (2007). *Talking voices: Repetition, dialogue, and imagery in conversational discourse* (2nd ed.). Cambridge: Cambridge University Press.

8

Humorous Play and Its Implications for Classroom Practice

Imagine for a moment that you are a teacher being given the lowdown on a group of students you are about to teach for the first time. If the members of the class are described to you as "playful", how does that make you feel? Your first reaction may be to think that they could be fun to teach. Or you may think that you need to stay on your toes in order to keep them focused and on track. Or, of course, both thoughts may occur to you more or less simultaneously. This brief scenario illustrates the often multifaceted and ambiguous nature of play, characteristics which make the relationship between the teacher and classroom play a particularly interesting and complex one. This relationship is one which is, in some ways, foregrounded in my research setting, where as previously mentioned, there is nothing in the classroom setting which can occur away from the gaze or earshot of the teacher while she or he is present.

In the data analysed in the preceding chapters, it is clear that spontaneous play has the potential to disrupt the official classroom agenda. For example, Viktor's proffering of a paper cup full of "champagne" in EPISODE 2 and the same student's playful reminder to Michele that he did not buy a round in EPISODE 14 both interrupt the IRF structure of talk in operation at the time. On the face of it, many of the instances of play examined take the learners' attention away from the pedagogical

© The Author(s) 2020   **191**
D. Hann, *Spontaneous Play in the Language Classroom,*
https://doi.org/10.1007/978-3-030-26304-1_8

focus at that moment. This is hardly surprising, given that, as previously discussed, humorous play, by its nature, is a stepping out from the norm. Furthermore, although there are no instances in the data of the course participants threatening the authority of the teacher, there are occasions where humorous play is used to undermine fellow learners in a group, whether it's Mario's ironic use of a "polite" phrase to shut up Dieter in EPISODE 13 or the play on the literal and metaphorical meanings of "are you with me" by Andrei in EPISODE 19 which was judged by some observers of the exchanges to be face threatening to his fellow group member, Takeshi (Sect. 5.3). Again, this is to be expected, given that pushing at boundaries and norms seems to be part of humorous play's DNA. This double-edged nature of humorous play is one which, on the face of it, some teachers may be wary of allowing into the classroom.

Despite the inherent riskiness of humorous play, there are clear advantages from the pedagogical viewpoint of allowing or even encouraging it in the classroom setting. The data in this book backs up that found in much of the literature that humorous play can be a very important social glue. It can help students not only to project their own identities but also to forge a collective group culture. In terms of language acquisition, I can't make any specific claims from the evidence of my data, especially as the investigative time frames were so brief. However, the very fact that such play seems to enhance the learners' enjoyment of the learning process must be a good thing. Juan's observation that "the call exercise was very fun" (EPISODE 40) is the sort of observation that all teachers enjoy hearing. In addition, as previously discussed, the existing literature tentatively points to HLP's particular benefits. Tarone (2000), for example, hypothesises that play can lower affective barriers to learning, reduce stress and broaden learners' social repertoire by allowing them to experiment with new voices. She also posits (Tarone 2002) that the repetition of particular words and phrases which language play often involves can facilitate the learning of those items. Bell's (2005) study of the playful behaviour of three advanced non-native speakers of English indicates that one of her research participants remembered a particular piece of vocabulary because of the playful context in which she first encountered it. Engagement in play seems to encourage the use of more complex and varied linguistic forms (Pomerantz and Bell 2007). It is also worth pointing to evidence of the positive effects of humorous play from beyond the field of second language acquisition. Psychological research highlights its benefits for well-being and social cohesion (Martin and Kuiper 2016).

Despite regarding HLP as an important ingredient to the success of a language classroom, a viewpoint supported by the data in this book, I am not advocating the incorporation of play into the classroom curriculum, although there are those who do (see Sect. 8.1). In fact, the data throws into relief the possible issues surrounding such an endeavour. It shows how the students strive to own the humour which is generated, something which is hard to reconcile with a deliberate teacher-instigated introduction of play into the classroom agenda. Furthermore, the featured exchanges reveal the in-the-moment, unplanned and spontaneous nature of play, something which can develop incrementally to assume a cultural significance within a group of learners. Finally, in this regard, the premeditated incorporation of humorous play into the curriculum runs against the grain of its subversive nature. The exchanges featured in the preceding chapters reveal students and their teacher making fun of themselves, making fun of each other and making fun of the activities they undertake in the classroom (I say more about the teacher's role in these endeavours later in this chapter). Although this subversion is played out within very safe bounds, it is nevertheless difficult to reconcile with play as an official activity.

Before examining what light the data throws on the role of the teacher in play episodes, it is useful to consider the literature to date (such as it is) which examines the teacher's relationship to humorous play in the language classroom.

8.1 The Literature on the Language Teacher's Role in Play

It has already been noted that there are advocates of incorporating humour into the language curriculum (e.g. Berwald 1992; Deneire 1995; Schmitz 2002). Bell (2009) highlights that much of this literature takes no account of natural interaction. It also promotes the teaching of typographies of humour which fail to understand play's complexity and vitality. Bell and Pomerantz (2014) point to the fact that this vitality reflects the ever-evolving nature of language itself, a notion heavily influenced by Bakhtin's (1981) understanding of language as dialogical (Sect. 2.4.3). However, despite legitimate demands for an approach which takes account of language play's complexities, even those suggestions by Bell (2009) and Bell and Pomerantz (2014) for bringing humour into the second language classroom are primarily based on activities around the comprehension of, rather than the generation of, humour. They advocate activities around analysing comedy clips, sensitising learners to contextualisation cues or speculating on the meanings of newly coined words. There also seems to be an underlying assumption in these proposals that the teaching of humour and play in a TL is a means of exploring and understanding a target culture more fully. A persuasive argument can be made for such an approach in, say, a class of immigrant learners in a host country, but it becomes problematic with students who are learning a language in order to do business internationally or to enhance their chances of employment, motivations which are particularly pertinent to learners of English. Given that English has global currency, which target culture would a teacher aim to sensitise such students to through humour? It could be argued that an exploration of, say, British humour may be an interesting means of interrogating different cultural norms and encouraging students to reflect on their own culturally shaped viewpoints and attitudes. However, such an exploration would, in my view, not be humorous but would be *about* humour, and would constitute a potentially useful but essentially serious activity.

Humorous play is, by its nature, a spontaneous, in-the-moment phenomenon. The literature on such play among learners in the second language classroom is not extensive but has been growing (e.g. Broner and Tarone 2001; Cekaite and Aronsson 2005; Pomerantz and Bell 2007; Sullivan 2000). However, given the teacher's pivotal role in what happens in the classroom setting, investigations which focus on the teacher's effect on play remain surprisingly few and far between. There are studies which show how teachers, if not necessarily encouraging

8 Humorous Play and Its Implications for Classroom Practice   195

humour, permit and validate its use by students and sometimes contribute to humorous turns (e.g. Lehtimaja 2012; Pomerantz and Bell 2011; Reddington and Waring 2015). In those where the teacher's influence is foregrounded or acknowledged to be important, the research tends to be conducted in classes with a shared first language (e.g. Forman 2011; Sullivan 2000; Van Dam and Bannink 2017). This is significant as the shared language, together with common sociocultural reference points, gives the learners resources for play which are not accessible to multilingual, multicultural classes.

Two studies are of particular interest when looking at the teacher's role in play because they investigate language classrooms where the teacher is the primary play instigator. Despite their contrasting cultural settings—a Thai university (Forman 2011) and a Dutch secondary school (Van Dam and Bannink 2017)—both feature teachers who flit in and out of their institutional roles, sometimes making fun of the classroom exercises themselves. In Forman's study, the teacher even makes fun of the students he is teaching. These findings are of particular interest here as they chime with the some of the analysis to come.

Although planned intervention in the classroom in order to promote HLP carries inherent contradictions, good pedagogical practice should create an environment where play can be allowed to flourish. So, I am advocating the need for a heightened awareness among practitioners of the potential for play in the classroom and, when appropriate, to allow and encourage it. In this regard, a good starting point for a teacher is to know what sorts of classroom activities do and do not attract playful behaviour.

8.2   The Timing and Rhythm of Play Episodes

Recording learners continuously for two days allows an investigation into when play episodes occur in relation to the rhythms of the classroom timetable. This can throw light on which types of classroom activity and which stages within these activities attract language play and the extent to which specific behaviours can be related to particular activities.

196 D. Hann

Below is a table relating those episodes of play discussed in case-study Chapters 6 and 7 to the classroom activities with which they co-occur. The categorising of episodes is not an exact science, given that the behaviours witnessed are multifunctional. Furthermore, there are playful episodes which occur in the raw data which are not included in this book because they exemplify behaviour which I identify elsewhere. So, the table is, in part, a subjective reflection of my identification of play. Despite the fact that not all episodes that can be classified as playful are included, there are still 32 instances of play over the two days in the table below. Aside from those, those moments which are triggers to subsequent play are shown in brackets. This is some indication of how central play is to these participants' learning and socialising experience (Table 8.1).

8.3 Observations About the Rhythm and Pattern of Play

It is interesting to note that a good deal of the play clusters around the very end of training on the two days as the learners are winding down and packing to leave. There is also a concentration of playful behaviour at the beginning of the Wednesday (the second day of recording). This pattern seems to relate to some extent to Holmes's observation (2000: 179) that a lot of the humour she encounters in workplace interactions occurs at the beginnings and ends of the serious business of meetings. Similarly, humour seems to top and tail the business of learning, much as small talk does to more serious activities (Goffman 1981: 125). Much of the humour that features at the beginning and ends of the training day results from reflections on the day's activities and events. It is perhaps no surprise then that revision exercises and feedback sessions also attract playful behaviour. After all, these are the occasions which are designed for the class to reflect upon preceding activities and, more especially, the learners' performances during them. The telephone simulation in particular triggers a rich vein of play which endures over the two days: the "OK" thread and the play around mistaken identity.

8 Humorous Play and Its Implications for Classroom Practice 197

Table 8.1 The timings of play

TIME	EPISODE	CATEGORY	CLASSROOM ACTIVITY
Tuesday			
First Session			
15 mins	26 Or you present a quiz	Non-linguistic resources	Revision
17 mins	27 Are you married?	Non-linguistic resources	Revision
30 mins	34 With only five years	irony	Revision
31 mins	21 Losers	Failed humour	Revision
	(52 Ahead to the schedule)	Recontextualisation trigger	Revision
1 hr 30 m	53 We are ahead the programme	Recontexualisation	Comprehension,
Coffee break			
Second Session			
6 mins	51 Are you married?	Recontextualisation	Comprehension
7 mins	23 I remember a PC game	Cultural reference	Comprehension
1 hr 17 m	(45 I would like to speak to Jens)	Error trigger	Telephone simulation
1 hr 24 m	46 I'm Helmut	Error comment	Telephone end
I hr 26 m	47 I can't change my identity	Error play	Telephone end
Lunch break			
Third Session			
7 mins	48 My name is	Error play	Telephone feedback

198   D. Hann

Table 8.1 (continued)

9 mins	35 When the doctor need to operate you	Metaphor	Telephone feedback
31 mins	49 No Jens no Harry	Error play	Telephone feedback
33 mins	37 It's not my problem	Error play	Telephone feedback
34 mins	(38 Mmm-hmm)	Error trigger	Telephone feedback
41 mins	39 But before you died	Error play	Telephone feedback
51 mins	(54 These things happen)	Play trigger	Telephone feedback
Coffee break			
Fourth Session			
I hr 20 m	40 The call exercise was fun	Error play	Winding down
1 hr 21 m	41 Tomorrow Juan is going with Harry	Error play	Winding down
End of day			
Wednesday			
First Session			
4 mins	(30 Woodwork)	Trigger for play/ narrative	Small talk
6 mins	28 Square	Non-linguistic resources/narrative/blending	Small talk
15 mins	31 Woodwork	Recontextualisation	Small talk
36 mins	42 Oooh. OK.	Error play	Revision of telephone

8 Humorous Play and Its Implications for Classroom Practice   199

Table 8.1 (continued)

39 mins	*55 These things happen*	Recontextualistion	Revision of telephone
56 mins	<u>29 And this is for Barcelona supporters</u>	Non-linguistic resources/narrative	Background to comprehension
Coffee break			
Second Session			
4 mins	<u>43 And for us OK</u>	Error play	Comprehension
37 mins	24 Do you remember Falcon Crest?	Cultural reference	End of comprehension
I hr 04 m	*56 These things happen*	Recontextualisation	Meeting simulation
I hr 10 m	36 This is a form of anaesthetic	Metaphor	Meeting feedback
I hr 12 m	<u>50 Who's that?</u>	Blending frames	Meeting feedback
I hr 25 m	22 I would have gone back to Spain	Blending frames	Meeting feedback
Lunch break			
Third Session			
17 mins	32 You can forget	Repetition of form	End of general feedback
24 mins	*57 These things happen*	Recontextualisation	Prelude to trend/budget language session

200   D. Hann

Table 8.1 (continued)

59 mins (tape ran out)	33 I negotiate with	Repetition of form	Prelude to negotiation
Coffee break			
Fourth Session			
53 mins	44 <u>Be careful with the OK</u>	Error play	Winding down
59 mins	25 Minority Report	Cultural reference	Winding down

Table Key

Different styles of underlining and italics show episodes that are connected, either by theme or recontextualised word/phrase

<u>The telephone simulation</u>

<u>The goalposts story</u>

These things happen

<u>Are you married</u>

<u>Play with sound</u>

<u>Ahead of the schedule</u>

(triggers for later play)

As noted before, feedback allows for the self-denigrating humour that is a hallmark of the observed play. It also places a distance between the speakers and their performances as they become an audience to those performances. As noted previously, by making fun of their own errors, learners acknowledge them and, by being able to identify their nature, take a first step towards rectifying them. The nature of the classroom timetable allows for this revisiting of language and the activities associated with them on frequent occasions.

There is play not only in the aftermath of simulation s but also during them, and it can be seen, for instance, in the blending of frames

8 Humorous Play and Its Implications for Classroom Practice 201

which sometimes occurs, a phenomenon already seen in data from the other groups in the research. However, it is interesting to note that the learners remain very much on task during the actual telephone calls which produce so much subsequent play.

The comprehension exercises produced few moments of play. One attempt by Juan to blend the frame of the recorded dialogue to that of the lesson went unnoticed at the time: he responds to a "thank you" in the recording with his own "you're welcome". The others occur when he compares the comprehension exercises to products of the American media—a TV series (EPISODE 24) and a PC game (EPISODE 23). Again, these are reflective in nature, commenting on the nature of the exercises themselves rather than playing with them. Indeed, it is interesting to note that the initial phase of the listening exercise where the learners work together on comprehension questions while listening to the recording produce no play whatsoever, despite the fact that the authority figure as embodied by the trainer is not present at these times. A vocabulary-building session where David takes them through the language of budgets and trends is also devoid of play.

So, the above suggests that this pair of participants take their learning seriously. Unsurprisingly, play episodes occur at more relaxed moments in the day that mark the time at the beginning and the end of activities. However, they also frequently occur at those times where the class is looking at and reflecting upon the learners' performances. These occurrences seem to show that play is a means by which the learners acknowledge their shortcomings in the language while, at the same time, demonstrating that they can overcome them. So, play is not a sign of learners switching off from the learning process but a stage in the learning cycle where language items and other learning points can be reflected upon and played with.

In terms of the occurrences of recontextualised language, apart from "OK" and "these things happen", none of them endure for more than one repetition. However, this does not mean that the potential to play with particular words or phrases disappears. For example, it is easy to imagine that the words such as "woodwork" can hold significance for Juan and Marek for the duration of their five-day stay at BizLang should one of them care to reintroduce them in the other's company.

The table shows the importance of reference threads which weave themselves into the whole learning experience.

The tentative lesson that can be drawn from looking at the rhythm of play over the recorded two days of Juan and Marek's training is that learners should be given the leeway to play, as and should they want to, around the official learning events of the day, such as role-play, vocabulary-building and comprehension exercises. The students' play framed the events, coming in the revision and reflection sessions of the day. Indeed, those play episodes that did occur during learning events tended to happen in the comprehension sessions which, it could be argued, were a form of reflection and revision in any case, occurring after the students had listened to a recorded dialogue together as the teacher went over the dialogue with them. Play seemed to be a means by which the learners could both play with the language and reframe their own shortcomings in humorous and positive terms.

The next section examines the way in which play can be allowed or, indeed, encouraged by looking at examples from the research data, some of which have already been discussed in previous chapters.

8.4 The Roles Teachers Might Assume in Play Episodes

The data is not presented here in chronological order, but rather, organised in terms of the different roles that the teacher takes up in order to facilitate play. Given play's incremental nature, the sequencing of events is explained where this is significant.

8.4.1 The Teacher as Scaffolder for Play

Regardless of humorous play, part of the language teacher's role is to facilitate the learners' communication in the TL, and this often involves scaffolding what they are trying to say. The concept of scaffolding relates to sociocultural theory, a cognitive framework of learning whereby a more knowledgeable other (represented in the classroom by the teacher)

8 Humorous Play and Its Implications for Classroom Practice 203

provides the learner with the assistance they need as they move towards autonomy (Lantolf 2000). We saw in EPISODE 22 how Juan struggles with third conditional structures. At the time he attempted the structure in a simulated role-play where he was breaking the ice with a visitor. The exchanges are recoverable from the feedback session where the recorded simulation is played to the learners and paused at moments where the teacher wants to comment. In the role-play itself, Juan's guest has just commented that he hadn't seen the previous evening's football game because he had gone to bed early:

EPISODE 22: I WOULD HAVE GONE BACK TO SPAIN

Tape: ((Juan's recorded voice)) *don't worry(.) if I know in advance the result I can (.)<@ go to sleep> (.)*
Juan: @[@*
David: ((*pauses the recording*)) [I think* I understand what you meant I think I- are you saying if I had known the result (.)
Juan: I have (.)
David: if I had known the [result*
Marek: [@@@*=
Juan: = I have I have
All: @@@[@*
David: [<@ I would have* gone to bed yeah >=
Others: = @@@ =
David: = yeah =
Juan: = I would have (.) <@ (gone) back to Spain >=
David: =<@ [gone back to Spain yeah yeah OK* >
Others: [@@*@

The use of the third conditional clearly proves to be a step beyond Juan's proficiency in the language, so David provides the scaffolding for Juan to accomplish his witticism. A number of aspects of this episode are noteworthy here, one from the role-play itself and another from the feedback exchanges. In the role-play, Juan incorporates the real-world event of the football game into the simulation. During the course of the two days of recording, as you have seen, a football game between

204   D. Hann

Juan's team, Barcelona and Chelsea featured heavily. As both Marek and Juan were football fans, David frequently linked the language he was teaching to the football game in order to give that language more purchase. This may be one reason why Juan blends the real-world and simulated frames through reference to it. In the feedback, as noted in Chapter 6, it is significant that Juan actually rejects the language proffered by his teacher "I would have gone to bed", opting for an alternative punchline "I would have gone back to Spain". A further aspect of David's reaction to Juan's struggle with the language's structures is noteworthy, but I will return to it shortly.

Another moment where scaffolding is significant in play is evident in EPISODE 34 where the students are revising grammatical tenses:

EPISODE 34: WITH ONLY FIVE YEARS?

Juan: how long has you known (.) your wife? =
David: = good (.) good (.) I've known my wife for (1) 29 years (3) I think (2) 29 years (.)OK good alright (.)
Juan: with only five years? (1)
David: sorry?(.)
Juan: with only five years? =
David: = absolutely yeah (.) she was only five I was six (.) yeah [incredible*
Juan: [@*@

Juan's gentle irony—"with only five years"—in response to David's observation that he has been married for 29 years is momentarily lost on his interlocutors. It takes David a moment to retrieve the meaning and recast it as "she was only five, I was six". This prevents Juan's humour from failing and allows him to laugh in response. These sorts of recastings are typical of the interventions which teachers routinely carry out in any teaching day. However, they carry particular significance in play episodes as they allow such play to succeed and prevent the momentum of play from stuttering to a standstill. At the same time, some interventions by the teacher may disrupt such momentum, and it is interesting to note that the data from the case study and the other groups reveals that the teachers do not interrupt for such things as minor grammatical errors (e.g. EPISODE 53) or lexical overextensions (e.g. EPISODE 16), giving priority to play over language accuracy at such moments.

8.4.2 The Teacher as Role-Shifter

It is unsurprising that the teacher scaffolds the learners' communicative attempts and prudently allows inaccuracies when the occasion suggests that fluency rather than accuracy should take priority. Another aspect of his behaviour is the way he takes on different roles and voices. The following interaction features in Chapter 6. The group is revising the social language which may be used when finding out more about someone on first acquaintance:

EPISODE 26: OR YOU PRESENT A QUIZ

David:	ask me? nationality (2)
Marek:	what's your nationality (.)
David:	yes (.) police officer (3) [police officer *
Marek:	[@@* (1)
David:	((*mimes taking notes*)) what's your nationality? (2)
Juan:	police officer? =
David:	= police officer (3)
Juan:	ah @@[@@*
David:	[what's your nationality?* OK =
10 Juan:	= or you present a quiz ((*shuffles the cards he has on the desk in front of him*)) =
All:	= @@@

Here, David is attempting to elicit a phrase such as "where are you from?" from the learners, although it could be argued that he deliberately sets up a trap which Marek falls into by tempting him to use the socially inappropriate "what's your nationality?". David then indicates that this is a police officer's interrogational question and then generates the scenario by miming the taking of notes. It takes Juan a moment

206 D. Hann

to catch on to what's happening but David's mime encourages him to produce a scenario of his own where the errant phrase might be used. The juxtaposing of different frames of reference (in this case, the polite social meeting, the police interrogation and the quiz) often has comedic potential and lies at the heart of humour's incongruity. The teacher here sets up the conditions for frame-blending, acting as a primer for such play. It is also noteworthy that this frame-blending involves taking on another role other than the officially designated one of teacher. Acting out the role of police officer is something David does again in EPISODE 27 to indicate the inappropriateness of "are you married" as a conversational opener. Again, Juan reacts in kind by using mime to respond playfully.

The assuming of different identities by the classroom teacher is one noted by Van Dam and Bannink (2017) in their data, behaviour which seems to promote an emerging culture of play. This can be related to Bakhtin's (1984) notion of carnival where established roles are suspended. It is also noteworthy that David's initiation of play through the physical mode of mime is echoed by Juan when he enters the play frame.

8.4.3 The Teacher as Teaser

One striking feature of the data is that the students make fun of their own mistakes and, indeed, each other's. However, the most surprising finding in terms of the teacher's behaviour is the number of times that David joins in or, indeed, instigates the ridicule.

Looking back at EPISODE 22, one of the interesting features of the exchanges is the reactions of Marek and David to Juan's attempts to produce a conditional sentence. Some of the exchanges are reproduced below:

EPISODE 22: I WOULD HAVE GONE BACK TO SPAIN

David: if I had known the [result*
Marek: [@@@*=
Juan: = I have I have

All:	@@@[@*
David:	[<@ I would have* gone to bed yeah > =
Others:	= @@@ =
David:	= yeah =
Juan:	= I would have (.) <@ (gone) back to Spain > =
David:	= <@ [gone back to Spain yeah yeah OK* >
Others:	[@@*@

Both Marek and David laugh freely at Juan's efforts and, indeed, there are numerous occasions where both learners and their teacher laugh at the learners' attempts to master the language. In fact, the teacher sometimes explicitly remarks on aspects of their endeavours. The excerpt below is one example. In this instance, the group is practising the pronunciation of words which had previously caused them problems. As well as exemplifying the teacher's behaviour around inaccurate grammar or pronunciation, it throws light on why the teacher's teasing is taken in good grace and, indeed, appreciated:

EPISODE 58: WE'RE ON A ROLL

David:	((writes at the flipchart)) just say that word (2)
Juan:	figures =
David:	= fantastic fantastic (.) no problem ((continues to write)) (7) Marek (.)
Marek:	analysis =
David:	= perfect (.)
Marek:	@@[@@@
Juan:	[@@@
David:	((over the laughter) we're on a roll
Juan:	((punches the air))

David's evaluative contributions—"fantastic", "perfect"—could again be interpreted as sarcastic, given that the hyperbole within them hardly seems to be justified by the learners' simple accomplishment of repeating a couple of words. Indeed, the laughter from Marek, with which Juan soon joins in, shows an awareness that the teacher's remarks should not be taken at face value. I would argue that this reaction to David's

208 D. Hann

utterances recognises that, in fact, his words are an act of solidarity. He makes light of what the group is doing and, in the process, removes the face threat that such an exercise entails. It has been noted in the literature on play how teasing is as often a sign of bonding as it is of competition (Bongartz and Schneider 2003; Carter 2004; Holmes 2007; Norrick 1993; Straehle 1993). In this regard, the use of the first-person plural pronoun in the utterance "we're on a roll" is significant, suggesting that the group, including its teacher, are in the same boat together, despite the teacher having an evident advantage over the learners in his comparative mastery of the TL. This behaviour echoes the ways in which Juan makes fun of Marek's performance errors, but does in a way which foregrounds their collective shortcomings (e.g. EPISODE 43). The alignment of teacher with the learners is developed further in the next section.

8.4.4 The Teacher as Fellow Outsider

David allies himself with the group in another way. An illuminating incident occurs when Juan is again struggling with English pronunciation during a comprehension exercise. In it, he is asked to repeat what he hears in a recorded conversation:

EPISODE 59: TRY AND SAY THAT AFTER A PINT

Recording: *sorry (.) what exactly is she suggesting* (.)
David: ((*pauses the recording*)) so say it again what exactly? (2)
Juan: what exactly (.) what exactly (.) had she (.) suggested (.)
David: good (.) pronunciation is not easy there because you've got
s and sh [there
Juan: [no suggesting=
David: = what exactly is she suggesting (.)
Marek: what exactly is she suggesting =
David: = very good very clear (.) OK (.) what exactly =
Juan: what exactly is see suggested (.)
David: is she =

8 Humorous Play and Its Implications for Classroom Practice 209

Juan: = is she shuggested =
David: is she =
Marek: =@@[@@*
David: [@@* (.) you've got s and sh (.) it's not easy my god (.)
Juan: @@@@ ((*wipes mouth*))
David: try and say that after a pint it's not easy OK (.)
Juan: < @ no > @

The lack of inhibition that Marek and David have about laughing at Juan's struggles is evident. At the same time, David is careful to point to the difficulties in repeating the phrase. What is significant here is that he not only acknowledges the challenge—"it's not easy"—but he also adds a "my god" which seems to be a sort of public voicing of his inner thoughts, implying that he too finds it difficult to say the phrase accurately. This is an evident fiction but seems to be an attempt to demonstrate his appreciation of the difficulties the learners face. This is reinforced when he creates a scenario in which a native speaker could indeed conceivably struggle with saying the phrase, that is, after a drink.

What is happening here is that the teacher is attempting to position himself with the learners as someone who finds the target language challenging, as someone looking in on English rather than being immersed in it in his everyday existence. It has been noted in the literature that learners in an alien environment will often find common ground with their fellows by the very fact that they are "cultural outsiders" (Aston 1993: 239). David's attempt to portray himself as a fellow outsider is further promoted in another series of exchanges. He is explaining the word "euphemism" and, in order to do so, tells a story which triggers a related story from Marek that also features in EPISODE 29. Here, the prelude to Marek's story is included:

EPISODE 60: COMFORT STATION

David: when I went to the (.) first time I went to the States talking of
          euphemisms (.) I was looking for a toilet (1) in er I can't remember
          where (1) I really don't remember now (.) and I didn't know there
          was a sign in some parts of the States which says comfort station (1)

Juan:	comfort station? =
David:	= yeah comfort station and that's a toilet (.)
Juan:	((*shrugs shoulders*) @[@@*
David:	[I didn't know* I had no idea what it was but it's it's an example of euphemism (1) comfort [station*
Juan:	[@@* (2)
Marek:	in Poland you have (.) two marks (.)
David:	yeah yeah (5)
Marek:	((*draws a triangle and a circle in his notebook and shows the others*)) I always confuse (2)
David:	and that is for (.) toilet? (.)
Marek:	that is for woman and for for man (.) ((*points to the symbols*))
David:	oh really? (2)
Marek:	I didn't- I didn't- (.) I can't<@ I can't (.) remember what is what> =
All:	= @@@ =
Marek:	= <@ and I waited for… I waited* for someone who will> =
David:	= < @ OK > =
Marek:	= who will (.) <@ come in > =
All:	= @@@[@@*
David:	[serious Marek (.) serious* (3)
Juan:	((*leans across and draws a square in Marek's notebook*)) and this is for Barcelona supporters =
21 All:	= @@@@@@

David's story places him in an alien and disorientating culture by recounting his confusion when he first went to the USA. Marek immediately takes up the theme to explain his own confusion over the symbols for public toilets that he encounters when visiting Poland. There is plenty of research evidence that narrative, whether it be conversational anecdotes (e.g. Coates 2007; Eggins and Slade 1997) or fictional stories (e.g. Broner and Tarone 2001), attracts humour and play. It is also a means of assessing and confirming affiliations and shared viewpoints (e.g. Norrick 1997). Both David's and Marek's stories express the feeling of being at a loss in another country and culture, a sensation which is well documented (e.g. Block 2007: 21). So, David is placing himself in his learners' shoes, abroad in an unfamiliar environment.

It is also noteworthy here that both David and Marek tell stories that are self-denigrating rather than status-enhancing and, indeed, all three group members tell stories which involve embarrassment and social failure. At first glance, this may seem surprising, especially in a group which is newly formed and where social credentials need to be established. However, much as the learners (with the help of their teacher) laugh at their own performance errors, this process of making light of problems seems to be a way in which learners can actually enhance their statuses by showing that they can transcend them. The teacher here makes himself part of that transformational process.

Juan's reference to Barcelona supporters has previously been discussed as indicative of the incremental nature of play which is evident in much of the data in the preceding chapters. This incremental dimension to play is now turned to, especially with reference to the teacher's role in it.

8.4.5 The Teacher as Primer for Play

As previously discussed, one of the aspects of humour and play which is acknowledged in the literature but which is rarely investigated is the way in which it often builds over time as events and their associated language become more socially significant to a group on each occasion that they are evoked. In Chapter 7, we saw how two separate chains of humour are built up and sustained over the two days of the recorded training and revolve around two phrases—"OK" and "these things happen", with the former assuming totemic status within the group.

Looking at the moments where "OK" first comes to the fore is pertinent in terms of examining the teacher's role in play. The ubiquitous word "OK" first assumes special significance in the group when Juan and Marek are each required to make a simulated telephone call to a colleague in order to ask for help. We originally saw the way in which the phrase gained prominence in the feedback session. EPISODE 37 is reproduced below but with a few more lines of the exchanges included:

212   D. Hann

EPISODE 37: IT'S NOT MY PROBLEM

Recording: ((David's voice)) *I'm afraid he's not very well* (.)
David: ((*pauses recording*)) I'm afraid he's (1)
Marek: not very well (2)
Recording: ((Marek's voice)) *OK* (.)
David: <@ OK? (2) that's alright actually > (.) ((*turns to Juan*)) I'm
            afraid he's not very well (2)
Juan: ((*shrugs shoulders*)) <@ OK > =
David: = [OK*
Others: [@*@
David: I'm afraid he- =
Juan: = <@ it's not my problem (.) my problem is the figures >
All: ((*laughter builds*)) @@@ =
David: = he's not very well (.) OK =
Juan: ((*begins to cry with laughter at this point*))
David: = he died yesterday (.) [oh OK*
others: [@@*@@@@

As previously discussed, Marek's response in the simulation is clearly inadequate, something which Juan recognises by externalising the attitude which Marek's "OK" inadvertently represents through gesture (a shrug of his shoulders). He then follows this up with a voicing of that inappropriate attitude—"it's not my problem". As these exchanges develop, the group's laughter becomes more pronounced until Juan is reduced to tears.

The teacher's contributions towards the end of the extract are particularly significant. He juxtaposes the original news and the reaction to it in order to bring the latter's inadequacy into relief—"he died yesterday... oh OK". The utterance ratchets up Marek's seeming indifference by making the scenario far more serious. This sets a comedic precedent which Juan takes up on subsequent occasions during that day and on the following one. When he does so, he often mimics the pattern set up by David by both giving bad news and coupling it with the dismissive response of "OK". Indeed, on one of those occasions, Juan recreates the scenario David generates here where the sought-after interlocutor has died (EPISODE 39).

In these exchanges, David entextualises "OK". In other words, he instigates "...the process of rendering discourse extractable, of making a stretch of linguistic production into a unit—a text—that can be lifted out of its interactional setting" (Bauman and Briggs 1990: 73). As has already been seen, the teacher also begins a similar process with the phrase "these things happen" when he links it to his having to leave the training room (EPISODE 54). These phrases may have become part of an in-group repertoire without the teacher's intervention, but he appears to have a role in entextualising them, making them memorable and thus extractable for reuse in later contexts.

8.5   Conclusion

This chapter features only one small group recorded over two days, so it would be foolhardy to make any sweeping claims about the teacher's role in classroom play from the evidence of this group alone. However, it points to some interesting features which are worthy of further exploration and even suggests some tentative conclusions that can be drawn about the relationship between play and the teacher.

The evidence brings to light that much facilitation of play is a by-product of sound pedagogical practice in general. After all, any good teacher will scaffold the learners' communications and make moment-to-moment decisions about what to correct and what not to depending on the various linguistic, social and psychological priorities which prevail at any given moment. Furthermore, the ultimate aim in language teaching is to allow the learner to be the principal and author of their own words, not merely the language's animator, and the evidence demonstrates that humorous play is one avenue whereby learners take possession of the language they learn. Another aspect of sound pedagogical practice which can open up opportunities for play is the process of showing learners the relevance of the language they are being taught to their own lives and interests. This very process inevitably makes frameworks of interpretation more fluid as target lexis and grammar are taken from contexts found in a course book, comprehension exercise or role-play and their relevance shown to the learners' own lives. In fact, the teacher's evocation of particular frames is sometimes accomplished by assuming different roles, such as that of a police officer (EPISODE 26). Play often arises in this freedom of movement between roles and between frames. (It is interesting to note how "play" can also carry the meaning of freedom of movement.) In EPISODE 37's simulated call, for example, Juan assumes the role of callous interlocutor while David voices both sides of the conversation in one turn.

The ways in which play develops over time are one which a teacher needs to be aware of if they believe that play is something to be valued and encouraged within a group. A gradual accretion of shared language and the moments in which it arises can become the source of mutual enjoyment and fun. Of course, the accretion of shared language is the very stuff of any language classroom but what is crucial in terms of play is cultivating those moments which attract laughter and amusement.

The process of cultivating play throws up a surprising dimension to the teacher's role. On analysing the data, an aspect of my own behaviour as teacher was a revelation to me: the readiness with which I made fun of the students' performance errors, something which they also did themselves. This echoes a finding from Forman (2011) where the teacher makes fun of his students by framing their social behaviour as inappropriate. By its nature, this is a risky approach but, I would argue, can be a cathartic one for learners, transforming potentially face-threatening moments into resources for play and social bonding. The fact that the learners are able to laugh off their linguistic shortcomings is a way of transcending them. Such a process is not necessarily a comfortable one. Although Pomerantz and Bell (2011) persuasively argue that humour, primarily because of its deniability, is a "safe house" allowing learners to experiment with their identities, it can also have an edge, not just for its targets but also its instigators (indeed, these can be one and the same) precisely because of that same deniability.

One of the means by which the teacher seems able to preclude any offence on the learners' part is that he sometimes takes on the role of fellow outsider, occasionally parodying the very activities he asks the

8 Humorous Play and Its Implications for Classroom Practice 215

students to take part in, as well as commenting on the language itself as if it were foreign to him. Again, these findings chime with those from Forman (2011) and Van Dam and Bannink (2017).

The second way in which the teacher's behaviour helps to minimise the chance of learners taking offence is that he is not afraid to project himself anecdotally as someone vulnerable to social embarrassment. In this regard, the teacher needs to tread a fine line in order not to lose authority, but, as Van Dam and Bannink point out in discussing the teacher that features in their data, "[a]s a figure in the story the students may mildly mock her while respecting her in her institutional role" (2017: 272).

As stated above, it is important not to generalise too readily from this small case study. For example, it is worth considering whether a teacher would feel as comfortable teasing a student in a mixed gender group. Furthermore, in a more challenging learning environment, the extent to which a teacher can allow learners the same scope for play is open to question. In addition, play's ambiguous and potentially subversive nature means that differing cultural expectations of what sort of behaviour is appropriate in a classroom context need to be considered. However, the fact that groups featured in this book are multicultural in nature suggests that humorous play can have a place. In addition, it is important not to confuse the endorsement of play with a call for teachers to generate a classroom's fun and laughter, something which may be counter to the disposition of some (see the previous discussion in this chapter). What is important for teachers is that they are sensitive to the generation of humorous play by their students and reflect on ways in which this can be nurtured in appropriate and positive ways.

References

Aston, G. (1993). Notes on the interlanguage of comity. In G. Kasper & S. Blum-Kulka (Eds.), *Interlanguage pragmatics* (pp. 224–250). New York: Oxford University Press.

Bakhtin, M. M. (1981). *The dialogic imagination*. Austin: University of Texas Press.

Bakhtin, M. M. (1984). *Rabelais and his world.* Bloomington: Indiana University Press.

Bauman, R., & Briggs, C. L. (1990). Poetics and performance as critical perspectives on language. *Annual Review of Anthropology, 19,* 59–88.

Bell, N. D. (2005). Exploring L2 language play as an aid to SLL: A case study of humour in NS-NNS interaction. *Applied Linguistics, 26*(2), 192–218. https://doi.org/10.1093/applin/amh043.

Bell, N. D. (2009). Learning about and through humor in the second language classroom. *Language Teaching Research, 13*(3), 241–258. https://doi.org/10.1177/1362168809104697.

Bell, N. D., & Pomerantz, A. (2014). Reconsidering language teaching through a focus on humor. *EuroAmerican Journal of Applied Linguistics and Languages, 1*(1), 31–47.

Berwald, J. (1992). Teaching French language and culture by means of humor. *The French Review, 66,* 189–200.

Block, D. (2007). *Second language identities.* London: Continuum.

Bongartz, C., & Schneider, M. L. (2003). Linguistic development in social contexts: A study of two brothers learning German. *The Modern Language Journal, 87,* 13–37. https://doi.org/10.1111/1540-4781.00176.

Broner, M., & Tarone, E. (2001). Is it fun? Language play in a fifth-grade Spanish immersion classroom. *Canadian Modern Language Review, 58*(4), 493–525. https://doi.org/10.3138/cmlr.58.4.493.

Carter, R. (2004). *Language and creativity: The art of common talk.* Abingdon: Routledge.

Cekaite, A., & Aronsson, K. (2005). Language play, a collaborative resource in children's L2 learning. *Applied Linguistics, 26*(2), 169–191. https://doi.org/10.1093/applin/amh042.

Coates, J. (2007). Talk in a play frame: More on laughter and intimacy. *Journal of Pragmatics, 39*(1), 29–49. https://doi.org/10.1016/j.pragma.2006.05.003.

Deneire, M. (1995). Humor and foreign language teaching. *Humor—International Journal of Humor Research, 8*(3), 285–298.

Eggins, S., & Slade, D. (1997). *Analysing casual conversation.* London: Cassell.

Forman, R. (2011). Humorous language play in a Thai EFL classroom. *Applied Linguistics, 32*(5), 541–565. https://doi.org/10.1093/applin/amr022.

Goffman, E. (1981). *Forms of talk.* Oxford: Blackwell.

Holmes, J. (2000). Politeness, power and provocation: How humour functions in the workplace. *Discourse Studies, 2*(2), 159–185. https://doi.org/10.1177/1461445600002002002.

8 Humorous Play and Its Implications for Classroom Practice   217

Holmes, J. (2007). Making humour work: Creativity on the job. *Applied Linguistics, 28*(4), 518–537. https://doi.org/10.1093/applin/amm048.

Lantolf, J. (2000). Introducing sociocultural theory. In J. Lantolf (Ed.), *Sociocultural theory and second language learning* (pp. 1–26). Oxford: Oxford University Press.

Lehtimaja, I. (2012). Teacher-oriented address terms in students' approach turns. *Language and Education, 22,* 348–363. https://doi.org/10.1016/j.linged.2011.02.008.

Martin, R., & Kuiper, N. A. (2016). Three decades investigating humor and laughter: An interview with professor Rod Martin. *Europe's Journal of Psychology, 12*(3), 498–512. https://doi.org/10.5964/ejop.v12i3.1119.

Norrick, N. R. (1993). *Conversational joking: Humour in everyday talk.*

Norrick, N. R. (1997). Twice-told tales: Collaborative narration of familiar stories. *Language in Society, 26,* 199–220.

Pomerantz, A., & Bell, N. D. (2007). Learning to play, playing to learn: FL learners as multicompetent language users. *Applied Linguistics, 28*(4), 556–578. https://doi.org/10.1093/applin/amm044.

Pomerantz, A., & Bell, N. D. (2011). Humor as safe house in the foreign language classroom. *Modern Language Journal, 95,* 148–161.

Reddington, E., & Waring, H. Z. (2015). Understanding the sequential resources for doing humor in the language classroom. *Humor—International Journal of Humor Research, 28*(1), 1–23.

Schmitz, J. R. (2002). Humor as a pedagogical tool in foreign language and translation courses. *Humor—International Journal of Humor Research, 15*(1), 89–113. https://doi.org/10.1515/humr.2002.007.

Straehle, C. (1993). "Samuel?" "Yes, dear?" Teasing and conversational rapport. In D. Tannen (Ed.), *Framing in discourse* (pp. 210–230). New York: Oxford University Press.

Sullivan, P. (2000). Playfulness as mediation in communicative language teaching in a Vietnamese classroom. In J. P. Lantolf (Ed.), *Sociocultural theory and second language learning* (pp. 115–131). Oxford: Oxford University Press.

Tarone, E. (2000). Getting serious about language play: Language play, interlanguage variation and second language acquisition. In B. Swierzbin, F. Morris, M. E. Anderson, C. Klee, & E. Tarone (Eds.), *Second language acquisition: Selected proceedings of the 1999 second language research forum* (pp. 31–54). Somerville, MA: Cascadilla Press.

Tarone, E. (2002). Frequency effects, noticing, and creativity. *Studies in Second Language Acquisition, 24*(2), 287–296. https://doi.org/10.1017/S0272263102002139.

Van Dam, J., & Bannink, A. (2017). The first English (EFL) lesson: Initial settings or the emergence of a playful classroom culture. In N. Bell (Ed.), *Multiple perspectives on language play* (pp. 245–280). Berlin: Walter de Guyter.

9

Humorous Language Play: Lessons from the Second Language Classroom

This final chapter of the book brings together the overall research findings from this project, findings which have implications in terms of both further research and pedagogical practice. Like any research context, this one has its own specific features and limitations. Its limitations together with its modest scale mean that generalisations about its potential implications need to be somewhat circumspect. Nevertheless, it is in the caveats about generalisability that the potential avenues for further research lie and a number of these are suggested in the course of this chapter.

9.1 What the Findings Tell Us About the Nature of Play in the Language Classroom

Given the limitations that the language learners featured in this book have in terms of their mastery of English and given too the fact that they cannot assume shared cultural reference points, it might be surmised that their humorous language play is realised in rather different

© The Author(s) 2020 **219**
D. Hann, *Spontaneous Play in the Language Classroom*,
https://doi.org/10.1007/978-3-030-26304-1_9

220   D. Hann

ways than it is among L1 speakers with a common culture. Indeed, it is true to say that there is scant evidence of the manipulation of the semantic and phonological properties of the language that can be found in jokes and puns. However, the data indicates that, for the most part, the featured groups' play is not so different in form or effect from that found among native speakers. One such phenomenon is the playful emergent in-group reference point.

9.1.1 Putting Right a Research Oversight: Play's Part in Building a Classroom Community

The neglect of language's role as a means of cultivating relationships and forging a group identity in the SLA literature has already been noted, being seen as peripheral to the important business of acquiring the TL. This culture-building aspect of the learning experience has implicitly been regarded as something which is accomplished outside the classroom or as incidental to whatever activities are going on at any one time. As a result, the vital communicative work that learners carry out to this end and the role that humorous play has in the process have been an under-investigated area.

The reasons for this can readily be surmised. Firstly, integral to a research focus on the building of a classroom community is a longitudinal dimension. In this regard, it is noteworthy that, although Bakhtin's ideas about language's relationship to its social context are often cited in the linguistics field, the implications of viewing utterances as dialogical and heteroglossic (Bakhtin 1981) point towards the need to investigate them not only in relation to their immediate here-and-now context but also in relation to communication that has preceded them. This requirement, however, is rarely followed up in research, probably because it throws up logistical issues for the researcher around attempting to capture and plot the significant moments and exchanges which occur over time. Furthermore, an investigative focus on play has its own perceived constraints in the classroom setting. Its nature as "a temporary sphere of activity with a disposition all of its own" (Huizinga 1970: 26) means

9 Humorous Language Play: Lessons from the Second Language ... 221

that it can be seen to interrupt or, indeed, disrupt the classroom's official schedule. This disruptive tendency is often accompanied by subversion, as play's intent can be denied ("I was only joking"), allowing boundaries to be tested. It is easy to see why researchers focussing on the acquisition process may regard it as irrelevant or even obstructive to their aims. The paucity of research into the classroom as a social entity and specifically into the occurrences of humorous language play and their part in that process is one which the present investigation has sought to rectify and, in so doing, has shed light on the importance of play in the building of community.

The learners in this study have shown how language is playfully used to weave together a rich tapestry of humorous shared reference points. The opportunity to cultivate a bank of amusing in-group references lies to a great degree in the fact that the learners are forever recontextualising learnt language in surprising ways. A word or phrase associated with a shared experience is used in a new context to metonymically stand for that original experience. The speakers' wit lies in their ability to use language which is appropriate to the moment and, at the same time, to the evoked shared experience. To take a couple of examples, Antoine's ability to use language that is apt in the moment of a simulated negotiation while simultaneously evoking a grammar drill (EPISODE 10) and Juan's swift identification of the commonality between an anecdote about football and one about toilets (EPISODE 29) are not so different in terms of their wit to that of a speaker exploiting the semantic properties of a phrase to evoke opposing scripts (Raskin 1985: 111). It could be argued that the evocation of shared experiences through the recycling of language means that a lot of play witnessed in the data would make no sense to the outsider without explanation. But this can be as true of language play among native speakers as that among non-native speakers. As Baynham comments on the adult numeracy classes that he investigates:

> There are examples in the data of exchanges that clearly refer to on-going, in-group, joking, the full meaning of which it is hard for the analyst/outsider to gain access to. (1996: 194)

It is not unreasonable to assume that the locally emergent expression is actually more likely to outlive the conversation in which it first appears in non-native interaction than in its native-speaker equivalent because, in general, the linguistic repertoire of speakers in the former is narrower than that of speakers in the latter. This means that language learners are more reliant on a shallow pool of expressions to communicate their ideas. Moreover, as Bakhtin (1981: 276–277) points out, language is rooted in its contexts of use and, in many cases, the learners' expressions are strongly associated with the limited experiences that they share, whether drinking together, doing a language laboratory drill, simulating a phone call or saying something inappropriate in the TL. Yet this does not set them apart from L1 speakers. For the latter too, playful words and phrases accumulate meanings beyond their dictionary and conventionalised semantic definitions, carrying significance which reflects the social, professional and family circles of which they are a part and in which they operate. The humorous in-group allusion—I hesitate to call it an in-joke as it is not a ready-made concoction but is forged in the fluid give-and-take of spontaneous interaction—is a part of many different social networks and helps establish the distinctive communicative styles that they each develop. After all, language is never "out there" but can only be assimilated when it is owned by its speakers. It always takes on particular meanings among its community of users.

The phrases that the learners use show the birth of culture in that the first signs of the establishment of group myths can be discerned. This mythologising can, for example, take the form of the collaborative cultivation of a collective image of a group as hard-drinking (EPISODES 2 and 9). Interestingly, there are also a number of moments in the data where particular phrases are used to conjure up previous exchanges and yet these phrases are not actually used in the original interactions (EPISODES 37 and 39). Thus, they embody occurrences which are truly mythological in that they never actually happened as remembered. They become a subjective creation (McAdams 1993: 53) much as particular historical events become part of each nation's collective consciousness. Indeed, it could be argued that the ways in which L2 speakers mould the language to their own ends throw light on the ways in which language use develops in general and on the meanings it accumulates for particular social groups.

9.1.2 Limitations Can Be Strengths: Playing with What's Available

Despite the fact that the learners in the featured project are at the lower end of the proficiency spectrum, this clearly does not prevent them from playing in the TL. Indeed, they sometimes play in ways which one would associate with native-like wordplay. So, for instance, exploitation of the semantic ambiguities in language to evoke two different scripts can be witnessed in a couple of occurrences of HLP around the same phrase—"are you with me?"—by two different learners in different groups who play on the literal and more commonly used metaphorical meanings of the phrase (EPISODES 19 and 20). However, these are the only instances of punning in the data and it is noteworthy that both speakers play with the same phrase, suggesting that such linguistic dexterity is a challenge for learners at an early stage of acquiring the language. There is also evidence in the data of parallelism, a hallmark of creative speech that often features in humorous passages of everyday conversation, encompassing repetition (Tannen 2007: 48ff.) and what Carter (2004: 101–102) calls "pattern forming" and "pattern reforming". For example, in the case study data, Juan is seen to repeat stem phrases which he builds up and then subverts to dramatic effect (EPISODES 32 and 33). Imagery too can be found in Juan's description of certain common polite phrases in English as a form of "anaesthetic" (EPISODE 36). Yet, despite some evidence of learners being able to play in ways commonly regarded as witty, creative and humorous, an analysis that concentrated solely on such aspects would overlook the majority of occurrences of HLP through which the learners have fun.

Although native speakers' familiarity with their own language affords them certain advantages over the majority of non-native speakers, the latter's lack of such familiarity can, in some ways, allow them more opportunities for play. It can be argued that Juan's remarks about the anaesthetic qualities of certain English phrases (EPISODE 36) are evidence of a learner simultaneously having a critical distance from and taking pleasure in the language through his fresh perspective on its pragmatic norms. In this sense, the learner of a language has the potential to be more innovative with a TL than a seasoned native speaker, much as young children marvel and play with the properties of their mother tongue (e.g. Cook 2000). This fresh perspective is also evident in play around the phonological properties of English where the pleasure and amusement derived from uttering or attempting to utter particular phrases are not unlike the enjoyment that children take in playground chants and tongue twisters (e.g. EPISODES 30 and 31).

Apart from their fresh perspective on the TL, learners have another resource for play which is far less frequently available to native speakers: the errors they make in the language. Unsurprisingly, there are occasions where learners are made conscious of the fact that aspects of their language are regarded as erroneous by their teachers or, less frequently, by their fellow learners. Such moments are potentially face threatening. Yet the learners play with such moments, showing up the gap between what is said and what is meant by doing such things as pretending that their original utterances actually reflect their intentions. Thus, humour turns potential embarrassment into something celebratory and status enhancing. For instance, for Juan and Marek in the case study group, two of these errors become ongoing humorous reference points which they can depend on to generate laughter. Although there is a surprising lack of inhibition about laughing at one another's mistakes, the humour is communal and is actually a manifestation of solidarity. Indeed, on one occasion, Juan explicitly links the errors to their communal identity (EPISODE 43). So, humour becomes a necessary means of making light of the potential humiliation that lies in failure. Again, this is not so different to humorous play among L1 speakers. Glenn (2003: 117–121) notes how the butts of jokes can turn episodes in which they are laughed at into ones in which they laugh with their interlocutors. In my data, both teachers and learners laugh at the latter's performance shortcomings. Despite the inherent face threat in such reactions, what seems to prevent the learners from taking offence when others laugh at their errors or, indeed, actively play with those errors is that there is a mutual recognition, explicitly expressed in the case study group (e.g. EPISODE 43), and that they are in the same learning boat. Their playing with errors allows them to demonstrate that they can rise above their linguistic limitations and can laugh them off.

9 Humorous Language Play: Lessons from the Second Language ...   225

Another main resource for play is a common feature of the language classroom: the role-play. The data shows how learners are adept at transforming official play-as-rehearsal into unofficial play-as-fun. This means that learners are constantly flitting from the real classroom to the simulated role-play and back again. As witnessed in the data, this allows them to blend frames and do such things as die and come back to life, conjure up shared evenings in the pub, put their most junior members in charge of proceedings and operate in two simulated worlds at once. In short, learners bring into being Bakhtin's carnival world where the established order is suspended (Bakhtin 1984: 122–123). It is a world where boundaries can be tested because participants' statuses are themselves fuzzy and ambiguous, allowing speakers the fallback defence of saying that they are only joking or are merely in role. This blending of frames is not so different from that which can be found, for example, in comedy programmes on the radio and TV where different frames are brought together incongruously to humorous effect, such as when a panellist on a game show will, for comedic purposes, wittily link the current conversation with something said in a previous round (Sect. 2.4.3). In fact, to test how often this type of incongruous linking features in comedy, turn into a TV or radio show halfway through its broadcast and notice how much of the humour escapes you because it alludes to previous talk.

In sum, at first glance, the occurrences of HLP in the data may appear to be rather different from that to be found in native speaker play in that someone whose first language is English may find it unamusing on first hearing and, in some cases, puzzling. However, on closer inspection, it is, in fact, similar in kind to that found in everyday talk among native speakers. The puzzlement over instances of play is similar to that which people often feel when they first enter a new social group whose history and allusions they do not share. True, there is generally not the subtlety or nuanced allusions in the featured data that are sometimes found in the wit and banter of native speakers. Even so, irony, repetition, figurative language and the simultaneous evocation of different frames all feature in the play to be found in this data, so this is a matter of degree rather than kind. Also, the humorous play on errors in the recorded data echoes the sort of humorous play that

226   D. Hann

people use in order to cover for their (or others') acts which cause social embarrassment. Such humour triggered by social embarrassment is the stuff of TV comedies.

9.2   The Limitations of the Research: Avenues for Further Investigation

It has been stated from the outset that the research featured in this book is modest in scope. As such, its claims to generalisability are limited. The ethnographic dimension to my approach, by its nature, acknowledges the uniqueness of the context of its investigation. Even the seemingly restricted setting of the language classroom differs widely from institution to institution, country to country, teacher to teacher and even week to week. Classrooms differ greatly in terms of their physical layout, their size, the equipment they have, the conduct they sanction, what is taught and how it is taught. Indeed, every context is unique and every utterance contingent on its context. Actions (verbal and otherwise) in every classroom are infused with cultural meaning, as the data shows.

Even within my own research setting of only seventeen research participants (learners and teachers), there are clear differences in the play behaviour exhibited by each of them. Some learners play more than others: Juan, Viktor and Bilel tend to instigate episodes of HLP. In contrast, Marek rarely does so while Sandro and Takeshi only occasionally take part in such play, let alone prompt it. Also, although it is not systematically investigated in this study, there are clear differences in the collective playful behaviour of the different groups. The play in Group A is more aggressive in nature than any found in the other groups. For instance, Dieter is prepared to use it as a means of admonishing Antoine for his tardiness (EPISODE 7) while Mario's ribbing of Dieter for his talkative nature has an edge to it (EPISODE 13). At the other end of the spectrum, none of the HLP in the case study group could be described as anything other than good-natured. Furthermore, the

9 Humorous Language Play: Lessons from the Second Language ...

gender imbalance is significant. There are no female learners among the research participants and only one female teacher. Given that patterns of playful behaviour seem to be rather different in male and female groups, at least among native speakers of English (e.g. Coates 2007; Tannen 1991), this needs to be borne in mind when considering how generalisable the findings are.

However, despite the differing dynamics across the groups that feature in this research, the patterns and commonalities across them show that, although contexts are unique, this does not mean that we are unable to learn from them. After all, this process of generalising from the specific is what we undertake in learning to adapt to our world as we grow up. It is also the process we necessarily go through in adulthood whenever we move to a new environment, be that another job or another country.

In terms of further research, the inevitable uniqueness of my own investigative context suggests areas of further research which can bring to light instructive contrasts and commonalities in play behaviour across a range of circumstances and between a range of different speakers.

9.2.1 HLP and the Acquisition Process

Language acquisition was not the focus of my research project, and the observation timescales precluded any definitive claims to the role of HLP in acquiring new language. This therefore is an area which would benefit from further work. However, in saying this, I am well aware of the challenges of attempting to definitively identify language acquisition, given that it is a long-term and nonlinear process. These challenges are multiplied when investigating HLP's role in the process, something which, by its nature, is spontaneous. Thus, controlling for variables as a means to obtain specific findings on the acquisition of particular forms or lexis is self-defeating. Nevertheless, work on the relationship between play and acquisition is an endeavour which my own limited findings suggest would be worth pursuing.

My data shows how the learners, through play, take ownership of particular words and phrases which they have been taught.

228 D. Hann

In the SLA literature, there has been much discussion of the importance of concepts such as noticing (Tomlin and Villa 1994), consciousness (Schmidt 1990) and attention (Schmidt 1998) in learning. As discussed in Sect. 2.5.2, it could be posited that the heightened affective sense that seems to accompany play may help make particular items of language memorable for learners. It is not unreasonable to imagine that phrases such as "these things happen", "you missed the target" or "take one and pass them on" are now part of the active pool of language that some of the learners in this research have at their disposal. If so, these items may well have been remembered because of the humorous circumstances in which they were first encountered. This does not mean that the learners will not misapply them in future. This too is a natural phase in the process of acquiring a language, as seen in the overextension and under-extension of meanings that children give to words and phrases in their first language and, indeed, in the overextensions found in this study. The recontextualisation of language items during play may also eventually help them to become part of learners' active repertoire through repeated exposure (Tarone 2002). So, rather than being regarded as off task, further investigations may show how humorous language play is the opposite, an important strategic tool which many learners use to help them acquire their TL.

9.2.2 HLP and the Teacher's Role

The teacher is clearly a crucial figure in shaping what happens in the language classroom, and Chapter 8 has already discussed some of the roles the teacher takes up to allow and encourage HLP. The chapter focussed on David's interactive behaviour but, in fact, all three teachers in the project sanction play by creating and nurturing the conditions for it to flourish. For example, Ray allows play to develop through scaffolding (EPISODES 9 and 14) and joking (EPISODE 19), while Harriet joins in the appreciation of her students' wit (EPISODE 3). Much of the sanctioning of play has to be retrospective as it is instigated, for the most part, by the learners. When doing so, as noted previously, learners do not simply play at the times where the agenda allows it, but often

9 Humorous Language Play: Lessons from the Second Language ... 229

disrupt the business of the moment, be that a comprehension exercise or a revision session. The data shows that, even during simulations, the learners are likely to exploit the frames of interpretation open to them, creating the risk that the exercise will disintegrate as students go off task. In fact, within my data, this never happens, despite play sometimes leading to a temporary detour from the classroom agenda. Yet the chances of play having a detrimental effect on achieving the particular aims of a given activity are always present and the teacher needs to make continuous judgements about how much play to allow at the times where it occurs. In this data, there is no discernible evidence of teachers disallowing play, although the learners are sometimes brought back to the official agenda when the teacher deems it appropriate. Perhaps the reason for the teachers' relaxed attitude to play in the data is that they are never the personal target of any playful behaviour. When teachers are voiced through their utterances, this never seems to be done with personal or malicious intent. The voicing does not focus on any identifiable feature of an individual teacher's idiolect or mannerisms. Rather, it seems to send up particular aspects of institutional practices, such as the manic instruction to "repeat" (EPISODE 15). Classroom practices are also indirectly made fun of through the highlighting of the innate absurdity of simulated role-play (e.g. EPISODES 3 and 37). Again, the teachers featured let this subversive behaviour pass and, indeed, occasionally participate in it (EPISODE 37). As noted in the previous chapter, one of the few pieces of research to focus on the role of teachers in classroom play (Van Dam and Bannink 2017) also includes a moment where a teacher mocks the very activity she asks her students to participate in. The evidence points to the need for teachers to allow for and acknowledge the fact that certain routine activities in the language classroom are potentially laughable, especially when imagined beyond the four walls of the classroom itself. However, it is easy to imagine that the play evidenced in the relatively benign setting of a BizLang training room may not always keep its disruptive potential within officially acceptable bounds in other settings, and it is easy to imagine play being more challenging of authority in certain contexts. Other teachers in other settings can provide fruitful avenues of investigation in this regard.

Furthermore, the degrees to which the teacher overlooks errors (EPISODE 34), makes fun of those errors (EPISODE 22), aligns himself or herself to the students (EPISODE 59), is willing to reveal a more vulnerable side (EPISODE 60) or takes on other roles (EPISODE 26) are all potentially of interest in terms of investigating the teacher's relationship to play. One means of exploring further the effects of individual teacher behaviour on classroom play would be to see how the manifestations of playful behaviour in a particular group might be affected by their being taught by different teachers at different times (a not uncommon scenario).

9.2.3 HLP and Different Learner Profiles

Learner profiles may differ in a wide variety of ways, and I don't propose to identify them all here. However, the nature of my research context and my findings point to contrasting profiles which would be particularly interesting to investigate.

It has already been acknowledged that my research participants were, with the exception of Harriet, all male. Given that there are some generalisable characteristics of communicative style which tend to differentiate the talk of women and men (Fasold 1990: 89–118) and some of these differences can also apply to HLP (e.g. Coates 2007), this is an important factor to consider. Indeed, in my role as researcher, it struck me that particular manifestations of play, especially in Groups A and B, sometimes had an edge to them which might be described as particularly "male". This is something which could usefully be explored in a more systematic way (although generalisations in this regard must always be treated with circumspection). All-male, mixed and all-female groups could usefully be investigated. (The sex of their teachers would also be a factor.)

Another area of difference in learner profiles which is worthy of investigation is that between instrumental and integrative learners (Gardner and Lambert 1972). The learners in my research all had instrumental motivations. Furthermore, their interactions in the TL were predominantly with other L2 speakers. Therefore, they operated in

9 Humorous Language Play: Lessons from the Second Language ... 231

the world of ELF. From the perspective of investigating play, it is noteworthy that the HLP of integrative learners is usually regarded through the prism of the target culture (e.g. Bell 2005). In contrast to native-speaker talk, ELF is often promoted as having the potential to be a neutral, culture-free medium of communication (Seidlhofer 2011) In this regard, Seidlhofer says something very pertinent when describing the features of what she calls English as a native language:

> ENL is full of conventions and markers of in-group membership such as characteristic pronunciations, specialised vocabulary, idiomatic phraseology, and references and allusions to shared experience and the cultural background of particular native-speaker communities. (Seidlhofer 2011: 16)

Here, in the description of a variety of English which Seidlhofer actually contrasts with ELF are the very characteristics that can be found in the research. So, a phrase like "you miss the target" (EPISODE 14) carries a particular idiomatic meaning in the data—"you didn't stand your round"—which is unrecoverable without its context of use, one which evokes a shared experience of going to the pub together. It could be argued that such language is provisional in meaning and that its status is that of a work in progress, although, of course, this is true of all language acquisition and use: the linguistic behaviour witnessed in the data is a manifestation of language's dialogical, heteroglossic and incremental nature. The data reveals how words and phrases become part of the respective groups' collective identity. Thus, "these things happen", "take one and pass them on" and even the humble "OK" carry a social and symbolic significance that only holds between members of the particular groups in this study. This undermines or at least adds a caveat to Seidlhofer's (2011: 48) assertion that English (or even English-es) need not belong to a particular community. My data clearly indicates that every community that uses English inevitably develops its own variety of it, however ephemeral that variety might be, rapidly acquiring its own unique characteristics and meanings. In the light of this, looking at the commonalities and contrasts between the play of integrative and instrumental learners would be of interest.

232 D. Hann

Another factor with the potential to foreground how humorous play manifests itself and is shaped by its contexts of use is the one of culture. As discussed previously (Sect. 2.3), culture is not just determined by nation and, indeed, the findings in this research point to its fluidity. However, nationality remains an important factor in shaping people's outlooks and behaviours. In this regard, it is often said that humour does not travel well (Chiaro 1992: 5), although this observation is to some degree a reflection of a narrow definition of humorous play which sees it only in terms of wordplay. Nevertheless, nationality's influence on play is worthy of further exploration. The research that exists in this area points to significant relational differences in humorous play (Murata 2014). In my own research, it is difficult to draw even tentative conclusions about national HLP traits from the data: Takeshi does not tend to play while his compatriot Koji does; Sandro does not tend to play while his fellow Italian Michele does. Of course, looking for discernible patterns and traits in national humour becomes that much more complex when looking at interactions between nationality groups, especially when those interactions are in a language which is not the L1 of any of the participants. This is one of the aspects which I turn to in the next final section.

9.2.4 HLP Beyond the Classroom

From a research perspective, the classroom has the great advantage of being an enclosed space, allowing the researcher to capture most if not all that happens within its confines. However, it inevitably has its own particularities. For instance, it is a setting with its own hierarchical dynamic. The teacher has the ultimate authority to determine what happens within its four walls. Of course, different teachers will exercise their authority in different ways and to differing degrees. This is not to say that that authority cannot be undermined or disregarded. However, it could be argued that the moment when the teacher loses all authority becomes the time when the classroom ceases to be a functioning classroom. In the research findings from the project data, we have seen the ways in which learners can exercise their own power through play and how they

9 Humorous Language Play: Lessons from the Second Language ... 233

lay claim to being the principals and authors of the TL through that play. However, it needs to be conceded that L2 speakers are rarely mere animators of a language outside the classroom setting and that authority is rarely so clearly embodied in one figure as it is in the classroom. So, moving outside the classroom to look at L2 speakers' play is another potentially fertile area of investigation.

As noted previously, some interesting work has been undertaken in looking at L2 humour outside the classroom environment (Bell 2005; Schmidt 1983; Teutsch-Dwyer 2002). However, the focus has been on integrative speakers of the TL. Yet, participation in play by non-native speakers in multicultural and multinational environments such as those where commercial, political and academic transactions occur across the globe is an enormous and as yet untapped area for research. It is noteworthy that the participants who come to BizLang often comment that it is not necessarily the make-or-break presentation in English that they find most daunting but the socialising that precedes and proceeds it. To understand how humorous language play is used to forge relationships and project cultural identities, there needs to be longitudinal research into communication in the types of contexts in which my research participants might typically interact in the language, be that the video conference, the symposium, the dinner table or the board room. In this way, the extent to which localised in-group meanings establish themselves as resources for play, despite maybe only intermittent contact between interactants, can be investigated. Given that English's place as the world's lingua franca seems in little danger of being challenged for the foreseeable future (Seidlhofer 2011: 2), such research can throw light in microcosm on the importance of humorous language play in helping the world to broker deals, forge new commercial and economic ties and generally keep spinning.

9.3 Conclusion

When the idea for the research that features in this book first began to crystallise in my head, my main fear was that I would find myself trawling through hours of recorded classroom interactions without finding anything worthy of analysis. However, this fear was soon assuaged when I actually started to collect data. This echoes the experiences of Carter (2004) when he undertook his corpus analysis of humorous play among native speakers. What is surprising when investigating play is its ubiquity. This suggests that we are only fleetingly aware of its presence when navigating our everyday lives. Yet, as I hope my own findings help to show, humorous play is clearly a very important means of asserting our individual and collective identities, forging and maintaining our relationships, and generally facilitating our social interactions. This is why the impulse to play is such a strong one that many of us will attempt to indulge in it, whatever the linguistic and cultural barriers that face us. And, finally, as well as the social benefits that accrue through play, it needs to be remembered that we play because, for reasons which are not always easy to identify, it is pleasurable and fun.

References

Bakhtin, M. M. (1981). *The dialogic imagination*. Austin: University of Texas Press.

Bakhtin, M. M. (1984). *Rabelais and his world*. Bloomington: Indiana University Press.

Baynham, M. (1996). Humour as an interpersonal resource in adult numeracy classes. *Language and Education, 10*(2–3), 187–200. https://doi.org/10.1080/09500789608666708.

Bell, N. D. (2005). Exploring L2 language play as an aid to SLL: A case study of humour in NS-NNS interaction. *Applied Linguistics, 26*(2), 192–218. https://doi.org/10.1093/applin/amh043.

Carter, R. (2004). *Language and creativity: The art of common talk*. Abingdon: Routledge.

Chiaro, D. (1992). *The language of jokes: Analysing verbal play*. London: Routledge.

Coates, J. (2007). Talk in a play frame: More on laughter and intimacy. *Journal of Pragmatics, 39*(1), 29–49. https://doi.org/10.1016/j.pragma.2006.05.003.

Cook, G. (2000). *Language play, language learning*. Oxford: Oxford University Press.

9 Humorous Language Play: Lessons from the Second Language ...

Fasold, R. (1990). *Sociolinguistics of language*. Oxford: Basil Blackwell.

Gardner, R. C., & Lambert, W. E. (1972). *Attitudes and motivation in second language learning*. Rowley, MA: Newbury House.

Glenn, P. (2003). *Laughter in interaction*. Cambridge: Cambridge University Press.

Huizinga, J. (1970). *Homo Ludens*. London: Paladin.

McAdams, D. (1993). *Personal myths and the making of the self*. New York: William Morrow.

Murata, K. (2014). An empirical cross-cultural study of humour in business meetings in New Zealand and Japan. *Journal of Pragmatics, 60*, 251–265. https://doi.org/10.1016/j.pragma.2013.09.002.

Raskin, V. (1985). *Semantic mechanisms of humor*. Dordrecht, Holland: D. Reidel.

Schmidt, R. (1983). Interaction, acculturation, the acquisition of communicative competence. In N. Wolfson & E. Judd (Eds.), *Sociolinguistics and TESOL*. Rowley, MA: Newbury House.

Schmidt, R. (1990). The role of consciousness in second language learning. *Applied Linguistics, 11*, 129–158.

Schmidt, R. (1998). The centrality of attention in SLA. *University of Hawai'i Working Papers in ESL, 16*, 1–34.

Seidlhofer, B. (2011). *Understanding English as a Lingua Franca*. Oxford: Oxford University Press.

Tannen, D. (1991). *You just don't understand: Women and men in conversation*. London: Virago Press.

Tannen, D. (2007). *Talking voices: Repetition, dialogue, and imagery in conversational discourse* (2nd ed.). Cambridge: Cambridge University Press.

Tarone, E. (2002). Frequency effects, noticing, and creativity. *Studies in Second Language Acquisition, 24*(2), 287–296. https://doi.org/10.1017/S0272263102002139.

Teutsch-Dwyer, M. (2002). [Re]constructing masculinity in a new linguistic reality. In A. Pavlenko, A. Blackledge, I. Piller, & M. Teutsch-Dwyer (Eds.), *Multilingualism, second language acquisition and gender* (pp. 175–198). New York: Mouton de Gruyter.

Tomlin, R. S., & Villa, V. (1994). Attention in cognitive science and second language acquisition. *Studies in Second Language Acquisition, 16*, 183–203.

Van Dam, J., & Bannink, A. (2017). The first English (EFL) lesson: Initial settings or the emergence of a playful classroom culture. In N. Bell (Ed.), *Multiple perspectives on language play* (pp. 245–280). Berlin: Walter de Guyter.

Appendix

Transcription conventions:

rising intonation	?
pause (shorter than a second)	(.)
pause (a second or longer, timed to the nearest second)	(2)
starting point of an overlap	[
ending point of an overlap	*
turn-continuation or latching (no discernible gap between turns)	=
speaker's incomplete utterance	te-
paralinguistic and non-verbal activities	((*activity*))
laughter (each '@' representing one 'syllable' of laughter)	@@@
spoken while laughing	<@ text>
unintelligible speech; x marking approximate syllable number	(xxx)
assumed utterance	(text)
heard through speakers (recorded or on phone)	((speaker's name)) *text*

NB Capitals are used for the first person subject for proper nouns or to indicate the use of acronyms e.g. "IT department"

© The Editor(s) (if applicable) and The Author(s) 2020
D. Hann, *Spontaneous Play in the Language Classroom*,
https://doi.org/10.1007/978-3-030-26304-1

Bibliography

Adolphs, S., & Carter, R. (2007). Beyond the word. *European Journal of English Studies, 11*(2), 133–146. https://doi.org/10.1080/13825570701452698.

Appel, J. (2007). Language teaching in performance. *International Journal of Applied Linguistics, 17*(3), 277–293.

Armstrong, K. (2005). *A short history of myth*. Edinburgh: Canongate.

Aston, G. (1993). Notes on the interlanguage of comity. In G. Kasper & S. Blum-Kulka (Eds.), *Interlanguage pragmatics* (pp. 224–250). New York: Oxford University Press.

Atkinson, P., & Hammersley, M. (1998). Ethnography and participant observation. In N. K. Denzin & Y. S. Lincoln (Eds.), *Strategies of qualitative enquiry* (pp. 110–136). Thousand Oaks, CA: Sage.

Attardo, S. (1994). *Linguistic theories of humour*. Berlin: Mouton de Gruyter.

Attardo, S. (2000). Irony as relevant inappropriateness. *Journal of Pragmatics, 32*(6), 793–826. https://doi.org/10.1016/S0378-2166(99)00070-3.

Bakhtin, M. M. (1981). *The dialogic imagination*. Austin: University of Texas Press.

Bakhtin, M. M. (1984a). *Problems of Dostoevsky's poetics*. Minneapolis: University of Minnesota Press.

Bakhtin, M. M. (1984b). *Rabelais and his world*. Bloomington: Indiana University Press.

© The Editor(s) (if applicable) and The Author(s) 2020
D. Hann, *Spontaneous Play in the Language Classroom*,
https://doi.org/10.1007/978-3-030-26304-1

240   Bibliography

Bartlett, R. C. (1932). *Remembering: A study in experimental and social psychology.* Cambridge: Cambridge University Press.

Bateson, G. (1972). *Steps to an ecology of mind.* New York: Ballantine.

Bauman, R., & Briggs, C. L. (1990). Poetics and performance as critical perspectives on language. *Annual Review of Anthropology, 19,* 59–88.

Baynham, M. (1996). Humour as an interpersonal resource in adult numeracy classes. *Language and Education, 10*(2–3), 187–200. https://doi.org/10.1080/09500789608666708.

Beckoff, B., & Byers, J. A. (1998). *Animal play: Evolutionary, comparative and ecological perspectives.* Cambridge: Cambridge University Press.

Bell, N. D. (2005). Exploring L2 language play as an aid to SLL: A case study of humour in NS-NNS interaction. *Applied Linguistics, 26*(2), 192–218. https://doi.org/10.1093/applin/amh043.

Bell, N. D. (2007a). How native and non-native English speakers adapt to humor in intercultural interaction. *Humor, 20*(1), 27–48. https://doi.org/10.1515/HUMOR.2007.002.

Bell, N. D. (2007b). Humor comprehension: Lessons learned from cross-cultural communication. *Humor, 20*(4), 367–387. https://doi.org/10.1515/HUMOR.2007.018.

Bell, N. D. (2009). Learning about and through humor in the second language classroom. *Language Teaching Research, 13*(3), 241–258. https://doi.org/10.1177/1362168809104697.

Bell, N. D., & Pomerantz, A. (2014). Reconsidering language teaching through a focus on humor. *EuroAmerican Journal of Applied Linguistics and Languages, 1*(1), 31–47.

Bell, N. D., Skalicky, S., & Salsbury, T. (2014). Multicompetence in L2 language play: A longitudinal case study. *Language Learning, 64*(1), 72–102. https://doi.org/10.1111/lang.12030.

Belz, J. (2002). Second language play as representation of the multicompetent self in foreign language study. *Journal of Language, Identity and Education, 1*(1), 13–39.

Belz, J., & Reinhardt, J. (2004). Aspects of advanced foreign language proficiency: Internet-mediated German language play. *International Journal of Applied Linguistics, 14,* 324–362.

Berwald, J. (1992). Teaching French language and culture by means of humor. *The French Review, 66,* 189–200.

Block, D. (2007). *Second language identities.* London: Continuum.

Blommaert, J. (2010). *The sociolinguistics of globalization.* Cambridge: Cambridge University Press.

Bibliography   241

Bongartz, C., & Schneider, M. L. (2003). Linguistic development in social contexts: A study of two brothers learning German. *The Modern Language Journal, 87,* 13–37. https://doi.org/10.1111/1540-4781.00176.

Boxer, D., & Cortés-Conde, F. (1997). From bonding to biting: Conversational joking and identity display. *Journal of Pragmatics, 27,* 275–294. https://doi.org/10.1016/S0378-2166(96)00031-8.

Brkinjac, T. (2009). *Humour in English as a Lingua Franca.* Saarbrucken: VDM Verlag Dr. Muller.

Brock, A. (2017). Modelling the complexity of humour—Insights from linguistics. *Lingua, 197,* 5–15. https://doi.org/10.1016/j.lingua.2017.04.008.

Broner, M., & Tarone, E. (2001). Is it fun? Language play in a fifth-grade Spanish immersion classroom. *Canadian Modern Language Review, 58*(4), 493–525. https://doi.org/10.3138/cmlr.58.4.493.

Brown, G., & Yule, G. (1983). *Discourse analysis.* Cambridge: Cambridge University Press.

Brown, P., & Levinson, S. (1987). *Politeness.* Cambridge: Cambridge University Press.

Cameron, L. (2003). *Metaphor in educational discourse.* London: Continuum.

Carter, R. (1999). Common language: Corpus, creativity and cognition. *Language and Literature, 8*(3), 195–216. https://doi.org/10.1177/096394709900800301.

Carter, R. (2004). *Language and creativity: The art of common talk.* Abingdon: Routledge.

Cekaite, A., & Aronsson, K. (2005). Language play, a collaborative resource in children's L2 learning. *Applied Linguistics, 26*(2), 169–191. https://doi.org/10.1093/applin/amh042.

Chandler, D. (2002). *Semiotics: The basics.* London: Routledge. https://doi.org/10.1519/JSC.0b013e3181e7ff75.

Chiaro, D. (1992). *The language of jokes: Analysing verbal play.* London: Routledge.

Coates, J. (2007). Talk in a play frame: More on laughter and intimacy. *Journal of Pragmatics, 39*(1), 29–49. https://doi.org/10.1016/j.pragma.2006.05.003.

Cook, G. (1994). *Discourse and literature: The interplay of form and mind.* Oxford: Oxford University Press.

Cook, G. (1997). Language play, language learning. *ELT Journal, 51*(3), 224–231. https://doi.org/10.1093/elt/51.3.224.

Cook, G. (2000). *Language play, language learning.* Oxford: Oxford University Press.

242   Bibliography

Crystal, D. (1998). *Language play*. London: Penguin Books.

Crystal, D. (2003). *English as a global language*. Cambridge: Cambridge University Press.

DaSilva Iddings, A. C., & McCafferty, S. G. (2007). Carnival in a mainstream kindergarten classroom: A Bakhtinian analysis of second language learners' off-task behaviors. *Modern Language Journal, 91*(1), 31–44. https://doi.org/10.1111/j.1540-4781.2007.00508.x.

Davies, C. E. (2003). How English-learners joke with native speakers: An interactional sociolinguistic perspective on humor as collaborative discourse across cultures. *Journal of Pragmatics, 35*(9), 1361–1385. https://doi.org/10.1016/S0378-2166(02)00181-9.

Deneire, M. (1995). Humor and foreign language teaching. *Humor—International Journal of Humor Research, 8*(3), 285–298.

Du Bois, J. W. (1986). Self-evidence and ritual speech. In *Evidentiality* (pp. 313–336). Norwood, NJ: Ablex.

Du Bois, J. W., Schuetze-Coburn, S., Cumming, S., & Paolino, D. (1993). Outline of discourse transcription. In J. A. Edwards & M. D. Lampert (Eds.), *Talking data*. Hillsdale, NJ: Lawrence Erlbaum Associates.

Dynel, M. (2009). Beyond a joke: Types of conversational humour. *Linguistics and Language Compass, 3*(5), 1284–1299. https://doi.org/10.1111/j.1749-818X.2009.00152.x.

Eagleton, T. (1983). *Literary theory: An introduction*. Oxford: Basil Blackwell.

Eckert, P., & McConnell-Ginet, S. (1992). Think practically and look locally: Language and gender as community-based practice. *Annual Review of Anthropology, 21*(1), 461–490. https://doi.org/10.1146/annurev.anthro.21.1.461.

Eggins, S., & Slade, D. (1997). *Analysing casual conversation*. London: Cassell.

Eisenlohr, P. (2010). Materialities of entextualization: The domestication of sound reproduction in Mauritian Muslim devotional practices. *Journal of Linguistic Anthropology, 20*(2), 314–333. https://doi.org/10.1111/j.1548-1395.2010.01072.x.

Ellis, R. (1985). *Understanding second language acquisition*. Oxford: Oxford University Press.

Ely, R., & McCabe, A. (1994). The language of kindergarten children. *First Language, 14,* 19–35.

Fasold, R. (1990). *Sociolinguistics of language*. Oxford: Basil Blackwell.

Forman, R. (2011). Humorous language play in a Thai EFL classroom. *Applied Linguistics, 32*(5), 541–565. https://doi.org/10.1093/applin/amr022.

Bibliography 243

Gardner, R. C., & Lambert, W. E. (1972). *Attitudes and motivation in second language learning*. Rowley, MA: Newbury House.

Gibbs, R. W. (1999). Taking metaphor out of our heads and putting it into the cultural world. In R. W. Gibbs & G. Steen (Eds.), *Metaphor in cognitive linguistics*. Amsterdam: John Benjamins.

Glaser, B., & Strauss, A. (1967). *The discovery of grounded theory: Strategies for qualitative research*. Chicago: Aldine.

Glenn, P. (2003). *Laughter in interaction*. Cambridge: Cambridge University Press.

Goffman, E. (1959). *The presentation of self in everyday life*. London: Penguin Books.

Goffman, E. (1974). *Frame analysis*. Boston: Northeastern University Press.

Goffman, E. (1981). *Forms of talk*. Oxford: Blackwell.

Gordon, C. (2002). "I'm Mommy and you're Natalie": Role-reversal and embedded frames in mother-child discourse. *Language in Society, 31*(5), 679–720. https://doi.org/10.1017/S004740450231501X.

Gordon, C. (2008). A(p)parent play: Blending frames and reframing in family talk. *Language in Society, 37*(3), 319–349. https://doi.org/10.1017/S0047404508080536.

Gumperz, J. J. (1982). *Discourse strategies*. Cambridge: Cambridge University Press.

Hall, J. K. (1995). (Re)creating our worlds with words: A sociohistorical perspective of face-to-face interaction. *Applied Linguistics, 16*(2), 206–232. https://doi.org/10.1093/applin/16.2.206.

Hammersley, M. (1994). Introducing ethnography. In D. Graddol, J. Maybin, & B. Stierer (Eds.), *Researching language and literacy in social context* (pp. 1–17). Clevedon: Multilingual Matters.

Hammersley, M., & Atkinson, P. (2007). *Ethnography: Principles in practice* (3rd ed.). Abingdon: Routledge.

Harder, P. (1980). Discourse as self-expression—On the reduced personality of the second-language learner. *Applied Linguistics, 1,* 262–270.

Henig, R. M. (2008, February). Taking play seriously. *New York Times Magazine*. Retrieved from http://www.nytimes.com/2008/02/17/magazine/17play.html.

Holliday, A. (1999). Small cultures. *Applied Linguistics, 20*(2), 237–264.

Holmes, J. (2000). Politeness, power and provocation: How humour functions in the workplace. *Discourse Studies, 2*(2), 159–185. https://doi.org/10.1177/1461445600002002002.

244 Bibliography

Holmes, J. (2007). Making humour work: Creativity on the job. *Applied Linguistics, 28*(4), 518–537. https://doi.org/10.1093/applin/amm048.

Holmes, J., & Marra, M. (2006). Humor and leadership style. *Humor, 19*(2), 119–138. https://doi.org/10.1515/HUMOR.2006.006.

Hoyle, S. (1993). Participation frameworks in sportscasting play: Imaginary and literary footing. In D. Tannen (Ed.), *Framing in discourse* (pp. 114–145). Oxford: Oxford University Press.

Huizinga, J. (1970). *Homo Ludens.* London: Paladin.

Hymes, D. (1971). *On communicative competence.* Philadelphia: University of Pennsylvania Press.

Inkelas, S. (2006). J's rhymes: A longitudinal case study of language play. In J. Maybin & J. Swann (Eds.), *The art of English: Everyday creativity* (pp. 183–189). Basingstoke: Palgrave Macmillan.

Janesick, V. J. (1998). The dance of qualitative research design: Metaphor, methodolatry and method. In N. K. Denzin & Y. S. Lincoln (Eds.), *Strategies of qualitative enquiry* (pp. 35–55). Thousand Oaks, CA: Sage.

Jenkins, J. (2007). *English as a Lingua Franca: Attitude and identity.* Oxford: Oxford University Press.

Kanno, Y. (2003). Imagined communities, school visions and the education of bilingual students in Japan. *Journal of Language, Identity and Education, 2,* 285–300.

Kay, D. A., & Anglin, J. M. (1982). Overextension and underextension in the child's expressive and receptive speech. *Journal of Child Language, 9,* 83–98.

Kolb, D. (1984). *Experiential learning.* Englewood Cliffs, NJ: Prentice Hall.

Kolb, D., Rubin, I., & Olsland, J. M. (1991). *Organizational behavior: An experiential approach.* Englewood Cliffs, NJ: Prentice Hall.

Kotthoff, H. (2003). Responding to irony in different contexts: On cognition in conversation. *Journal of Pragmatics, 35*(9), 1387–1411. https://doi.org/10.1016/S0378-2166(02)00182-0.

Kramsch, C. (2006). From communicative competence to symbolic competence. *The Modern Language Journal, 90*(2), 249–252.

Krashen, S. D. (1982). *Principles and practice in second language acquisition.* Oxford: Pergamon.

Kristeva, J. (1980). *Desire in language: A semiotic approach to literature and art.* New York: Columbia University Press.

Kuczaj, S. A. (1983). *Crib speech and language play.* New York: Springer-Verlag.

Labov, W. (1972). *Language in the inner city: Studies in the Black English vernacular.* Philadelphia: University of Pennsylvania Press.

Bibliography   245

Lakoff, G., & Johnson, M. (1980). *Metaphors we live by*. Chicago: University of Chicago Press.

Lantolf, J. (1997). The function of language play in the acquisition of L2 Spanish. In W. R. Glass & A. T. Perez-Leroux (Eds.), *Contemporary perspectives on the acquisition of Spanish* (pp. 3–24). Somerville, MA: Cascadilla Press.

Lantolf, J. (2000). Introducing sociocultural theory. In J. Lantolf (Ed.), *Sociocultural theory and second language learning* (pp. 1–26). Oxford: Oxford University Press.

Lantolf, J. (2001). Introducing sociocultural theory. In *Sociocultural theory and second language learning* (pp. 1–26). Oxford: Oxford University Press.

Lave, J., & Wenger, E. (1991). *Situated learning: Legitimate peripheral participation*. Cambridge: Cambridge University Press.

Lehtimaja, I. (2012). Teacher-oriented address terms in students' approach turns. *Language and Education, 22,* 348–363. https://doi.org/10.1016/j.linged.2011.02.008.

Li, X. (2007). Souls in exile: Identities of bilingual writers. *Journal of Language, Identity and Education, 6,* 259–275.

Liang, X. (2006). Identity and language functions: High school Chinese immigrant students' code-switching dilemmas in ESL classrooms. *Journal of Language, Identity and Education, 5,* 143–167.

Linell, P. (1998). *Approaching dialogue: Talk, interaction and contexts in dialogical perspectives*. Amsterdam: John Benjamins.

Long, M. H., & Crookes, G. (1992). Three approaches to task-based syllabus design. *TESOL Quarterly, 26,* 27–56.

Martin, R., & Kuiper, N. A. (2016). Three decades investigating humor and laughter: An interview with professor Rod Martin. *Europe's Journal of Psychology, 12*(3), 498–512. https://doi.org/10.5964/ejop.v12i3.1119.

Maybin, J. (1994). Children's voices: Talk, knowledge and identity. In D. Graddol, J. Maybin, & B. Stierer (Eds.), *Researching language and literacy in social context* (pp. 131–150). Clevedon: Multilingual Matters.

Maybin, J. (2006). *Children's voices: Talk, knowledge and identity*. Basingstoke: Palgrave Macmillan.

McAdams, D. (1993). *Personal myths and the making of the self*. New York: William Morrow.

Meddings, L. (2006, January 20). Embrace the parsnip. *The Guardian*. Retrieved from https://www.theguardian.com/education/2006/jan/20/tefl4.

246 Bibliography

Morreall, J. (1987). *The philosophy of laughter and humour*. New York: State University of New York.

Murata, K. (2014). An empirical cross-cultural study of humour in business meetings in New Zealand and Japan. *Journal of Pragmatics, 60*, 251–265. https://doi.org/10.1016/j.pragma.2013.09.002.

Norrick, N. R. (1993). *Conversational joking: Humour in everyday talk*. Bloomington: Indiana University Press.

Norrick, N. R. (1997). Twice-told tales: Collaborative narration of familiar stories. *Language in Society, 26*, 199–220.

Norrick, N. R. (2007). Interdiscourse humor: Contrast, merging, accommodation. *Humor, 20*(4), 389–413. https://doi.org/10.1515/HUMOR. 2007.019.

North, S. (2007). "The voices, the voices": Creativity in online conversation. *Applied Linguistics, 28*(4), 538–555. https://doi.org/10.1093/applin/ amm042.

O'Halloran, K. (2006). The literary mind. In S. Goodman & K. O'Halloran (Eds.), *The art of English: Literary creativity* (pp. 364–389). Basingstoke: Palgrave Macmillan.

Pellegrino, V. (2005). *Study abroad and second language use: Constructing the self*. Cambridge: Cambridge University Press.

Pennycook, A. (2007). "The rotation gets thick. The constraints get thin": Creativity, recontextualization, and difference. *Applied Linguistics, 28*(4), 579–596. https://doi.org/10.1093/applin/amm043.

Petraki, E., & Pham Nguyen, H. H. (2016). Do Asian EFL teachers use humor in the classroom? A case study of Vietnamese EFL university teachers. *System, 61*. https://doi.org/10.1016/j.system.2016.08.002.

Pomerantz, A., & Bell, N. D. (2007). Learning to play, playing to learn: FL learners as multicompetent language users. *Applied Linguistics, 28*(4), 556–578. https://doi.org/10.1093/applin/amm044.

Pomerantz, A., & Bell, N. D. (2011). Humor as safe house in the foreign language classroom. *Modern Language Journal, 95*, 148–161.

Prodromou, L. (2007). Bumping into creative idiomaticity. *English Today, 23*(1), 14. https://doi.org/10.1017/S0266078407001046.

Rampton, B. (1999). Dichotomies, difference, and ritual in second language learning and teaching. *Applied Linguistics, 20*(3), 316–340. https://doi. org/10.1093/applin/20.3.316.

Rampton, B. (2006a). Language crossing. In J. Maybin & J. Swann (Eds.), *The art of English: Everyday creativity* (pp. 131–139). Basingstoke: Palgrave Macmillan.

Rampton, B. (2006b). *Language in late modernity: Interaction in an urban school*. Cambridge: Cambridge University Press.

Rampton, B. (2007). Neo-Hymesian linguistic ethnography. *Journal of Sociolinguistics, 11*(5), 584–607.

Raskin, V. (1985). *Semantic mechanisms of humor*. Dordrecht, Holland: D. Reidel.

Reddington, E., & Waring, H. Z. (2015). Understanding the sequential resources for doing humor in the language classroom. *Humor—International Journal of Humor Research, 28*(1), 1–23.

Richards, J. C., & Rodgers, T. S. (2001). *Approaches and methods in language teaching*. Cambridge: Cambridge University Press.

Rinvolucri, A. (1999). The UK, ELFese sub-culture and dialect. *Folio, 5*, 12–40.

Rogerson-Revell, P. (2007). Humour in business: A double-edged sword: A study of humour and style shifting in intercultural business meetings. *Journal of Pragmatics, 39*(1), 4–28. https://doi.org/10.1016/j.pragma.2006.09.005.

Sacks, H., Schegloff, E. A., & Jefferson, G. (1974). A simple systematics for the organization of turn-taking in conversation. *Language, 50, 696*–735.

Samuda, V., & Bygate, M. (2008). *Tasks in second language learning*. Basingstoke: Palgrave Macmillan.

Saussure, F. de. (1959). *Course in general linguistics*. London: Peter Owen.

Schmidt, R. (1983). Interaction, acculturation, the acquisition of communicative competence. In N. Wolfson & E. Judd (Eds.), *Sociolinguistics and TESOL*. Rowley, MA: Newbury House.

Schmidt, R. (1990). The role of consciousness in second language learning. *Applied Linguistics, 11*, 129–158.

Schmidt, R. (1998). The centrality of attention in SLA. *University of Hawai'i Working Papers in ESL, 16*, 1–34.

Schmitz, J. R. (2002). Humor as a pedagogical tool in foreign language and translation courses. *Humor—International Journal of Humor Research, 15*(1), 89–113. https://doi.org/10.1515/humr.2002.007.

Seargeant, P. (2012). English in the world today. In *English in the world: History, diversity, change* (pp. 5–35). Abingdon: Routledge.

Seedhouse, P. (2004). *The interactional architecture of the language classroom: A conversation analysis perspective*. Oxford: Blackwell.

Seidlhofer, B. (2011). *Understanding English as a Lingua Franca*. Oxford: Oxford University Press.

248 Bibliography

Sinclair, J., & Coulthard, M. (1975). *Towards an analysis of discourse*. Oxford: Oxford University Press.

Skehan, P. (1998). *A cognitive approach to language learning*. Oxford: Oxford University Press.

Straehle, C. (1993). "Samuel?" "Yes, dear?" Teasing and conversational rapport. In D. Tannen (Ed.), *Framing in discourse* (pp. 210–230). New York: Oxford University Press.

Street, B. (1993). Culture is a verb: Anthropological aspects of language and cultural process. In D. Graddol, L. Thompson, & M. Byram (Eds.), *Language and culture: British studies in applied linguistics, 7*. Clevedon: Multilingual Matters.

Sullivan, P. (2000). Playfulness as mediation in communicative language teaching in a Vietnamese classroom. In J. P. Lantolf (Ed.), *Sociocultural theory and second language learning* (pp. 115–131). Oxford: Oxford University Press.

Swann, J., & Maybin, J. (2007). Introduction: Language creativity in everyday contexts. *Applied Linguistics, 28*(4), 491–496. https://doi.org/10.1093/applin/amm047.

Symons, D. (1978). The question of function: Dominance and play. In E. O. Smith (Ed.), *Social play in primates* (pp. 193–230). New York: Academic Press.

Tannen, D. (1991). *You just don't understand: Women and men in conversation*. London: Virago Press.

Tannen, D. (2005). *Conversational style: Analyzing talk among friends*. Oxford: Oxford University Press.

Tannen, D. (2006). Intertextuality in interaction: Reframing family arguments in public and private. *Text and Talk, 26*(4–5), 597–617. https://doi.org/10.1515/TEXT.2006.024.

Tannen, D. (2007). *Talking voices: Repetition, dialogue, and imagery in conversational discourse* (2nd ed.). Cambridge: Cambridge University Press.

Tannen, D., & Wallat, C. (1993). Interactive frames and knowledge schemas in interaction: Examples from a medical examination/interview. In D. Tannen (Ed.), *Framing in discourse* (pp. 57–76). New York: Oxford University Press.

Tarone, E. (2000). Getting serious about language play: Language play, interlanguage variation and second language acquisition. In B. Swierzbin, F. Morris, M. E. Anderson, C. Klee, & E. Tarone (Eds.), *Second language acquisition: Selected proceedings of the 1999 second language research forum* (pp. 31–54). Somerville, MA: Cascadilla Press.

Bibliography **249**

Tarone, E. (2002). Frequency effects, noticing, and creativity. *Studies in Second Language Acquisition, 24*(2), 287–296. https://doi.org/10.1017/S0272263102002139.

Teutsch-Dwyer, M. (2002). [Re]constructing masculinity in a new linguistic reality. In A. Pavlenko, A. Blackledge, I. Piller, & M. Teutsch-Dwyer (Eds.), *Multingualism, second language acquisition and gender* (pp. 175–198). New York: Mouton de Gruyter.

Tomlin, R. S., & Villa, V. (1994). Attention in cognitive science and second language acquisition. *Studies in Second Language Acquisition, 16,* 183–203.

Toolan, M. (2006). Telling stories. In J. Maybin & J. Swann (Eds.), *The art of English: Everyday creativity* (pp. 54–102). Basingstoke: Palgrave Macmillan.

Trester, A. M. (2012). Framing entextualization in improv: Intertextuality as an interactional resource. *Language in Society, 41*(2), 237–258. https://doi.org/10.1017/S0047404512000061.

Van Dam, J., & Bannink, A. (2017). The first English (EFL) lesson: Initial settings or the emergence of a playful classroom culture. In N. Bell (Ed.), *Multiple perspectives on language play* (pp. 245–280). Berlin: Walter de Guyter.

van Lier, L. (1988). *The classroom and the language learner: Ethnography and second-language classroom research.* Harlow: Longman.

Van Praag, L., Stevens, P. A. J., & Van Houtte, M. (2017). How humor makes or breaks student–teacher relationships: A classroom ethnography in Belgium. *Teaching and Teacher Education, 66,* 393–401. https://doi.org/10.1016/j.tate.2017.05.008.

Victoria, M. (2011). *Building common ground in intercultural encounters: A study of classroom interaction in an employment preparation programme for Canadian immigrants.* The Open University.

Vygotsky, L. S. (1986). *Thought and language.* Cambridge, MA: MIT Press.

Widdowson, H. G. (1998). The theory and practice of critical discourse analysis. *Applied Linguistics, 19*(1), 136–151. https://doi.org/10.1093/applin/19.1.136.

Widdowson, H. G. (2004). *Text, context, pretext: Critical issues in discourse analysis.* Oxford: Blackwell.

Index

A

animator 88, 98, 119, 179, 180, 213, 233. *See also* author; principal

author 88, 98, 179, 181, 213, 233. *See also* animator; principal

B

Bakhtin, M. 28, 30, 54, 92, 102–104, 106, 109, 117, 125, 135, 143, 168, 194, 206, 220, 222, 225

Bell, N. 15, 24, 25, 33, 35, 40, 41, 51, 52, 65–68, 111, 128, 138, 192–194, 214, 231, 233

bilinguals 16, 17

Block, D. 15, 210

bulge, the 38, 39

C

carnival 37, 92, 134, 143, 149, 168, 206, 225

Carter, R. 4, 19, 22, 28, 33, 35, 36, 41, 53, 58, 65, 66, 94, 127, 130, 137, 143, 149, 151, 155, 158, 186, 208, 223, 234

children play 36, 58, 97

clustering of play 9, 22, 67, 86, 196

communicative competence 56

community of practice 13, 18, 19, 185, 186

contextualisation cues 25, 66, 67, 74, 91, 136, 194

Conversation Analysis (CA) 7, 49, 62

Cook, G. 4, 15, 20, 24, 32, 36, 39, 53, 58, 66, 80, 83, 84, 151–153, 186, 224

© The Editor(s) (if applicable) and The Author(s) 2020
D. Hann, *Spontaneous Play in the Language Classroom*,
https://doi.org/10.1007/978-3-030-26304-1

252 Index

D

decontextualisation 106, 107
dialogicality 30, 43, 103, 106, 123, 153, 194, 220, 231

E

Eckert, P. 18
emic perspective 66. *See also* etic perspective
English as a foreign language (EFL) 39, 133
English as a lingua franca (ELF) 6, 54, 137, 230, 231
entextualisation 105–107, 181
ethnography 49, 61, 62
etic perspective 66. *See also* emic perspective

F

face
    face threat 208
    negative face 31
    positive face 31, 162, 167
footing 39, 82, 86, 88, 92, 93, 98, 117, 122, 145, 168
frame(work of interpretation)
    lamination of frames 81, 84, 96, 134, 172
    play frame 21, 22, 24, 25, 33, 65–67, 79, 82, 92, 94, 101, 144, 145, 206
    primary frame 21, 81

G

Gardner, R. 16, 54, 230
Goffman, E. 7, 15, 21, 22, 31, 57, 59, 65, 66, 79–83, 86, 88,
96, 117, 134, 145, 172, 173, 179–181, 196
Gumperz, J. 25, 67, 82, 136, 144

H

heteroglossic 28, 103, 106, 220, 231
Holliday, M. 18
Holmes, J. 4, 22, 25, 35, 53, 65, 66, 86, 130, 133, 167, 186, 196, 208
Huizinga, J. 19, 21, 22, 27, 220
humour 3, 4, 6, 7, 10, 11, 16, 19, 20, 23–32, 34–36, 40, 41, 50, 65, 67, 68, 80, 83, 85, 86, 98, 101, 108, 109, 111, 112, 116, 118, 119, 125, 130, 133, 138, 141, 146, 149, 157, 161, 167–169, 171, 172, 179, 187, 193–196, 206, 210, 211, 214, 224, 226, 232, 233
humorous language play (HLP)
    ambiguity in HLP 31
    deniability of HLP 65
    incongruity of HLP 30
    incrementality of HLP 41
    subversion in HLP 221
hyperbole 94, 155, 207

I

identity
    group identity 42, 51, 130, 162, 173, 220
    individual identity 6, 16, 234
immigrants 16, 42
Initiation, Response, Feedback (IRF) 88, 121, 191
intertextuality 106, 107
irony 116, 118, 155, 158, 204, 225

Index   **253**

J

Johnson, M. 27
joking 20, 187, 221, 225, 228

K

keyed activities
  downkeyed activities 96
  rekeyed activities 102
  unkeyed activities 96
Kolb's Learning Cycle 56

L

Lakoff, G. 27
Lambert, W. 16, 54, 230
language drilling 5, 23, 57
laughter 3, 4, 25, 29, 34, 38, 66, 67,
  71, 74, 85, 86, 89–91, 93, 98,
  114–116, 118, 128, 133, 136,
  140, 141, 151, 165, 167, 172,
  174, 178, 183, 186, 207, 212,
  214, 215, 224, 237
Lave, J. 13, 18
learner
  instrumental learner 10, 17, 231
  integrative learner 230, 231
L1 speaker 3, 20, 24, 33, 55, 127,
  181, 220, 222, 224
L2 speaker 3, 24, 32–34, 36, 41, 50,
  54, 65, 104, 110, 111, 129,
  137, 179, 181, 222, 230, 233

M

McConnell-Ginet, S. 18
metaphor 27, 28, 155–157, 192
metonym 112
myth 9, 176, 177, 186, 222

N

native speaker. *See* L1 speaker
non-native speaker. *See* L2 speaker

O

observer's paradox 60, 63, 68, 135
off-task activities 6, 38
overextension 120, 123, 205, 228

P

pattern formation
  pattern forming 41, 155, 223
  pattern reforming 41, 155, 223
play
  play as fun 24
  play-as-rehearsal 5, 7, 57, 80–82,
    96, 97, 225. *See also* role-play
politeness 157
principal 88, 98, 119, 213, 233. *See
  also* animator; author
pun 127, 158, 220

R

Raskin, V. 25, 26, 33, 83, 84, 86,
  130, 221
recontextualisation 79, 105–109,
  112, 115, 121, 126, 130, 136,
  153, 178, 181, 228
reduced personality 34, 83, 129
reframing 105, 107, 108, 121, 175.
  See also frame
repetition of language 152, 192
ritual 9, 170, 183, 186
role-play 23, 24, 56–59, 63, 69,
  79–81, 83, 85, 86, 89, 90, 93,
  95–97, 101, 114, 118, 121,

134, 140, 162, 172, 173, 175, 177, 178, 186, 202, 203, 214, 225, 229

S

Saussure, F. de 26, 102, 103
schema 83–85, 101, 108. *See also* script
schema refreshment 84
script 26, 27, 83, 84. *See also* schema
second language acquisition (SLA) 4, 15, 16, 36, 38, 40–42, 54, 65, 81, 193, 220, 228
simulation 22, 24, 30, 38, 42, 82, 85, 86, 89, 93–96, 101, 116, 139, 163, 164, 166, 169, 172, 173, 175, 177, 178, 183, 196, 200, 203, 212, 229. *See also* role-play
small culture 18, 19
sociocultural theory 202
stylised intonation contour 170
symbolic competence 35

T

target language (TL) 6, 8, 11, 14, 15, 17, 22, 23, 27, 33, 34, 36–38, 43, 58, 65, 80, 84, 86, 109, 110, 113, 137, 140, 144, 151, 157, 185, 187, 194, 202, 208,

209, 220, 222–224, 228, 230, 233
task-based language learning and teaching 14, 81
teasing 24, 31, 35, 119, 121, 207, 208, 215
topicalisation 66, 89
topic management 62
turn-taking 62, 88

U

unofficial spaces 52

V

ventriloquating 37
voicing
  double-voicing 109, 164
  vari-directional double-voicing 109, 111, 117, 164
Vygotsky, L. 81

W

Wenger, E. 13, 18
wordplay 20, 23, 31–33, 36, 40, 43, 55, 108, 127–129, 136, 223, 232